It's OK! I'm from the *Daily Mail*

IT'S OK!
I'm from the
Daily Mail

TALES OF A FOREIGN CORRESPONDENT

Richard Shears

NEW
HOLLAND

First published in 2012 by
New Holland Publishers
London • Sydney • Cape Town • Auckland
www.newhollandpublishers.com • www.newholland.com.au

Garfield House 86–88 Edgware Road London W2 2EA United Kingdom
1/66 Gibbes Street Chatswood NSW 2067 Australia
Wembly Square First Floor Solan Street Gardens Cape Town 8000 South Africa
218 Lake Road Northcote Auckland New Zealand

A record of this book is available at the British Library and the National Library of Australia

ISBN: 9781742572093

Publisher: Fiona Schultz
Publishing manager: Lliane Clarke
Senior editor: Mary Trewby
Cover designer: Kimberley Pearce
Production manager: Olga Dementiev
Printer: Toppan Leefung Printing Limited

10 9 8 7 6 5 4 3 2 1

Follow New Holland Publishers on
Facebook: www.facebook.com/NewHollandPublishers

In memory of my friend and photographer Peter Carrette

Contents

1. The First-ever North Korean International Amateur Golf Tournament   11
2. An Unmarried Mum in a Council House in Torquay   24
3. The Jumbo Jet, a Pair of Boots and a Broken Pen   38
4. A Royal Assassination Attempt   52
5. Then They Kissed. *Click* Went My Camera   59
6. Revolution in Paradise   67
7. Princess Margaret Patted the Sofa and Said, 'Come and Sit Beside Me'   78
8. A Missing Baby and a Dingo in the Desert   86
9. Some Like It Jungle   102
10. Love on a Desert Island   111
11. The Schoolboy 'Spy'   125
12. The Sinking of the *Rainbow Warrior*   132
13. A Thorny Time for Colleen   144
14. Confessions of a Temporary Royal Paparazzo   152
15. Never Play Golf with an Ape   157
16. 'The Groom's Eloped with the Best Man!'   164
17. The High-Class Escort with Friends in High Places   177
18. Captain Mark Phillips and the New Zealand Love Child   189
19. Lord Maxwell and the Israeli Arms Dealer   199
20. 'I've Found Them! They're All Alive!'   212
21. 'He Wants to Put You in Jail, He Says You Are a Spy'   230
22. A Senseless Death in the Jungle   243
23. The Peter Falconio Mystery   252
24. The Missionary and the Cloned Dog   270
25. Taming the Tiger   279

Acknowledgements

I have to thank all those on the *Daily Mail* who sent me off to the world's diverse places on assignments that broadened my personal horizons. It's impossible to name them all but I have mentioned a few in the book.

I must also say a big thank you to my wife, Isobelle, who has endured my sudden departures without question and put up with me when I returned.

CHAPTER 1

The First-ever North Korean International Amateur Golf Tournament

Somewhere between Sinuiju and Pyongyang I banged my head. I banged my head because the train pulled up with a screech of wheels and shot me into the doorway between the carriages. I'd been told to prepare for incidents like this: the diesel train was ancient, prone to breakdowns and the track was unstable, prone to collapse.

'It won't happen, everything will be OK,' said Mr Oh at the start of the journey. 'We are very efficient in North Korea.'

I looked out of a window. A couple of policemen who had jumped from the train were looking under my carriage. If the track had come unhinged it was going to be a bloody long wait.

'Jesus Christ,' said the Finn who was sitting at a window on the opposite side. 'Did you see that? They've just picked up an ARM. Didn't you see it? What can you see on your side?'

'I can't see anything except some cops looking underneath. What do you mean, they've picked up an arm?'

'It's gone now. I think they've carried it onto the train.'

'What kind of an arm?'

'A whole arm. Jesus Christ. From the shoulder down and dripping with blood.'

The policemen on my side were still looking underneath the carriage. Presumably for the owner of the arm.

'They've got her,' said the Finn. 'I just saw them carrying her in.'

'A woman without an arm?'

'It was horrible. They carried her in and somebody picked up her bag and carried that in as well.'

I didn't see any of this because it had all happened on the Finn's side of the train.

'How old is she?'

'About 30ish. Youngish kind of woman. Like a kind of peasant.'

'Well I haven't seen anything on my side. Just two cops having a look underneath.'

'They've put her in the carriage behind us. She looked in a bad way.'

A woman without an arm … that was the understatement of the day.

'You sure about this? I didn't see anything. Just the two policemen. But now they've gone.'

I stepped into the gap between the carriages to investigate the car behind. One of the policemen I'd seen outside was back on board. He put his hand up so I went back to my seat.

'What did you see?' asked the Finn.

'Nothing, I was stopped.'

'Well, there's definitely a woman back there without an arm.'

Or an arm that wasn't attached. I still wondered if he'd made it all up. There just wasn't any panic anywhere. And he'd been hitting the local liquor in the restaurant car for the past couple of hours.

We reached a station an hour later. No, said Mr Oh, we weren't allowed out to stretch our legs. So I sat on the Finn's side of the carriage and looked out the window. Brown-uniformed soldiers wearing backpacks scurried to and fro. I could hear a woman singing a patriotic song through loudspeakers. There was a big portrait of the late Great Leader, Kim Il Sung, on the front of a ten-storey building just outside the station. Then again, his image was everywhere, reminding the populace that big brother was either watching over them or, more to the point, watching them.

'There it is again!' said the Finn. 'There's the arm!'

The policemen were carrying something about three feet (30 centimetres) long wrapped in a piece of cloth.

'You reckon that's the arm?'

'Yes, that's the arm. It's the same length. Can't you see the blood, there—there on the cloth?'

It could have been blood. Then again it could have been a grease stain, and the object could have been a long railway spanner wrapped in cloth so the policemen wouldn't stain their uniforms. But I went with the Finn: policemen wouldn't be carrying three-feet long spanners around. And why were four other men running towards the back of the train with a stretcher?

'Did a woman get run over by the train, Mr Oh?'

'No, no, no, no, no, no, no.'

Being an official government guide—although minder was closer to the truth— it was his job to ensure that I, and the group I was travelling with, saw nothing that would show North Korea in a bad light. Deny everything. Unless it was good—and then agree to it all.

It was April 2011. I'd got into North Korea because I was a world-famous golfer. Better clarify that. I'd made it into the pages of London's *Daily Mail* playing golf with two orang-utans (fully dressed in sports clothes and brandishing their own made-to-measure clubs) in Malaysia; hitting a ball around the most dangerous course on the planet, in Kabul, where unexploded ordnance lay in the bunkers and abandoned howitzer guns lined the fairways; and teeing off on Mars (well, the outback of Australia, actually, where the landscape north of Coober Pedy was likened to the Martian landscape—as captured by the NASA robot, which was rolled out there before it crashed into a rock).

Early in 2011 I heard about the first-ever amateur golf tournament to be staged in the secret country of North Korea. The idea had been suggested by a Scottish golfer because he thought that, well, it was a good idea. North Korea. Who had ever played in an international golf tournament in North Korea? Nobody. But what hope did I have of getting a visa? None. Journalists, writers, photographers— call us what you like—are spurned by Pyongyang. At the time of my visit, the then leader—'Dear Leader'—Kim Jong Il was mightily peed off with stories in the western press about the country's nuclear programme, its aggression towards South Korea, mass starvation, burgeoning prison camps filled with political dissidents and a population of 22 million suffering under a brutal iron fist.

Scores of journalists pretending to be carpenters, teachers, bankers—you name it—applied to Dylan Harris, who was arranging the tournament from his British travel agency. He soon caught them out. A few taps on the keyboard and Google revealed their true identities. I went the 'up front' way, explained who I was and said that I simply wanted to add to my unusual golf resume. 'They've accepted you,' Dylan informed me weeks later, an announcement that took some time to absorb. I could bring my own clubs or hire them at the Pyongyang Golf Club. It was hard to imagine a golf course even existed in North Korea, given the reports that the country was dry and brown and nothing grew there, particularly grass, but I'd soon find out. I decided to hire clubs, surprised to learn that they were manufactured by the enemy, South Korea.

There were 20 of us of varying handicaps—from the UK, Australia, Germany, Finland, South Africa, Poland, Luxemburg and France—and we made our way to Dandong, the eastern Chinese city that is the only point of entry into North Korea, by plane and train. I opted for the train from Beijing—a 14-hour journey in a top bunk, which meant stepping on the heads and sprawling arms of three bodies beneath me to have a pee in the night.

I had a glimpse of life in North Korea before entering the country. At Dandong I had time for a boat trip on the border river, the Yalu, because the train to Pyongyang did not leave until the following day. We crossed the invisible line into North Korea in the centre of the waterway so we could observe activity on the North's wharf. Through my long camera lens I saw soldiers watching over bonfires, fishermen unloading their catch and, in one memorable vignette, two laughing old men squatting on the dockside cormorant fishing, using their trained birds to catch that night's supper, the birds swallowing the fish and then regurgitating them into the men's baskets. What was that, I suddenly thought? Two old men laughing? Did people laugh in North Korea? Not according to all the reports I'd read of misery, starvation and brutal soldiers on every street corner ready to lay a baton into those who dared to show they were enjoying themselves. This jolly scene was in stark contrast to the evil reputation of the Democratic People's Republic of Korea.

I and my fellow golfers had to board a bus and join a queue of lorries to cross the Sino-Korean Friendship Bridge that spans the Yalu River. Items that could not be taken into North Korea were our long lenses, our mobile phones and our laptops. 'Shit, how am I going to manage without my iPhone?' bemoaned one of the group. Oh, that was me, but others said the same thing about their BlackBerries, Samsungs and Nokias. The North didn't want us bringing anything in that would allow the populace glimpses of the fine life we were all enjoying in the West. Nor did they want us carrying phones that would allow us to communicate with dissidents within the country—which was all a load of nonsense really because our SIMs wouldn't work there and we wouldn't be able to buy local ones because an order (which we were to hear many times) would be given: 'It is not allowed.'

It didn't take long to realize how isolated the North is. During the inspection of our bags at the frontier a senior customs officer, in his brown uniform and high-peaked hat, wandered over to an Australian golfer and stared at his state-of-the-art golf bag with its crush-proof cover for a full minute.

'What is this?' he asked, patting the top.

I wasn't surprised at the question. The bag looked like it could have contained a bazooka.

'It's a golf bag … for carrying my clubs around.'

'Show me your clubs.'

The Australian unhooked a clasp and peeled back the top. The officer took the covers off the drivers and ran his hand over them, nodding appreciatively. Other customs men were revealing their lack of knowledge of the game that is played just about everywhere in the outside world, opening packs of golf balls (we'd been asked to bring our own because of a severe shortage in the country) and tossing them from one hand to the other and examining the titles of novels and guide books some of us were carrying.

Why were these guys so paranoid? Well, we all know about North Korea, don't we—or rather, what we've all heard and read about the world's most secretive country. The Americans, the Brits, the Germans, the … well I won't go on … all insisted Kim Jong Il's scientists were working on nuclear weapons and might well have built them and aimed them towards nations they don't like in the West—and the South for that matter, because Seoul would undoubtedly be the first target.

Then there were the reports of slave labour camps, filling rapidly with dissidents. As the customs people went through my bag, I was not to know that within a few days Amnesty International would release a report and satellite photos claiming to show the prison camps were expanding. The report was enhanced by comments from a former camp intern who had escaped to South Korea and claimed that prisoners were so hungry they were forced to hunt for rats to eat. Maybe I'd find something out for myself. Maybe. Maybe not.

Remembering those reports about 'nuclear missile technology'—whatever that meant, whether it was diagrams, computer programmes or physical weapons parts—I took a close look at the trucks that were passing across the Friendship Bridge to and from China. They were leaving the North Korean border empty while those returning were so overloaded with sacks of what appeared to be rice that they were almost toppling over sideways. Maybe those stories were right and people were going hungry in the Stalinist state. Or maybe the rice sacks were a blind and in reality were full of nuclear technology, which, according to experts who claim to be in the know, were being sent to Pyongyang from Iran, using China as a go-between. The missile parts and documents were carried by air through China, it was claimed, but I couldn't help wondering who would suspect trucks carrying food from Dandong. Was 'technology' being smuggled into North Korea on these trucks too? There was no way of checking because, while at first glance there did not appear to be any security cameras in the customs hall, a more discreet glance around my surroundings revealed they were everywhere. I suspected that if I tried to point my point-and-shoot Samsung WB650 at any of the trucks I'd be sent packing back into China.

We were driven a short distance from the border post to a hotel in the frontier city of Sinuiju. I thought I was immune to culture shock, having worked in some grim places around the world, but I was stunned by the view through the bus window. There wasn't a car in sight. The wide, straight boulevards were filled with people on bicycles, like China of 30 years ago. They were smartly dressed even on their bikes, the men in dark suits, the women in modern clothing—pants and skirts and colourful jackets. We were ushered into a large hotel, with a cavernous marble-floored foyer, where smiling waitresses in red-and-white uniforms served us lunch of fish, chicken and meat—a veritable feast in a country that was said to be bereft of everything. But then, it could have been a show, just for us. Later, as we waited at the hotel entrance for the bus to pull up, we watched the bikes roll past. There was no sound, no car horns, no engines, just the swish of bicycle tyres. Sinuiju was a silent city. We were desperate to pull out cameras but our minders were vigilant, watching for such a move. 'No pictures, no pictures' was a cry we were to hear often.

Interrupted by the accident with the woman with the missing arm and the occasional unexpected grinding to a halt for other unidentified reasons, we made the slow six-hour train journey to Pyongyang, playing poker in the restaurant car for about ten minutes before we were ordered by an officious man in a smart suit to put the cards away—not allowed. We stared out of the windows at miles of brown land and not a tree in sight, the landscape broken here and there by small villages of slate-roofed houses.

Under a grey sky, groups of people worked in the fields using hand tools, and here and there were small toy-like red and blue tractors. There were children among the workers and, surprisingly, soldiers too, their jackets stripped off, sleeves rolled up as they bent over furrows and dug away with hoes. This was the region where, according to all the reports, there had been mass starvation. From the train window we saw no living skeletons. People were rosy-cheeked and many were laughing.

Was it all a show: were they 'plants', ordered into the fields to put on an appearance of happiness for the group of western golfers who would be passing by on the train? I concluded that such happy scenes would be far too difficult to organize across a vast area. But what were these people living on? Nothing was growing, not even a weed.

'Excuse me, Mr Ho, what do people eat?'

Mr Ho and his colleague Mr Ha were a diverse couple—a kind of good cop, bad cop combo. Mr Ha was dressed in a very smart charcoal grey suit, his hair neatly cropped, a fresh boy-like face with a permanent grin. Mr Ho wore a long Gestapo-style leather coat, his hair a mess, a cigarette dangling constantly from turned-down lips. Got to say it, though, I liked him because he seemed to be so, well, 'ordinary', whereas Mr Ha, fine fellow that he was too, tended to be more formal.

'What?'

'I was asking, Mr Ho, what people eat. I can't see anything growing.'

'They've just come out of winter. Of course there's nothing growing,' he said dismissively. Gee, he could turn on a scowl.

'But what do they eat during winter?'

'Last summer's crop. What do you think they eat? They give it to the government and the government spreads it out to everybody.'

That was it. Impossible to find out what they grew, how much, how it was distributed. I managed to grab a few pictures out of the window before I heard a swish of leather beside me and Mr Ho was there, settling in for a fake snooze. With one eye open.

When 20 golfers find themselves travelling on a slow train with nothing much to do they order another beer. Long before the train pulled into Pyongyang station the bar had been drunk dry. Local stuff, wasn't too bad, 3.5 strength. The station was bustling, inside and on the main courtyard outside, even though it was now nine o'clock at night. Sinuiju had given us the clues: nobody had a car—it was either walk, ride a bike or use public transport. I was to learn that trains were often late, resulting in large crowds building up at the stations.

The Yanggakdo Hotel, where we were to be domiciled for the next five days, towers for 47 floors over an island in the middle of the Taedong River, which divides Pyongyang. It seemed that every light was on in the hotel, in contrast to the city where all the tall modern buildings were in darkness. The lobby was huge, a throwback to a Stalinist era, although the hotel was opened in 1995. Over dinner—much the same chicken, fish, meat and rice as in Sinuiju—served as the restaurant rotated slowly over the darkened city, it was made clear to us that there could be no escape into the great metropolis—the bridge over the river was controlled by armed guards. The only places we would be allowed to see would be those we were taken to.

I made my way to the basement to have a game of ten-pin bowling—what, ten-pin bowling? Yes, that and snooker and table tennis, all for the benefit of the few westerners who visited each year. On the way I learned that the first-ever North Korean international amateur golf tournament would not be running over three or four days, but for just one game only.

'But what about the rest of the time, Mr Ha? Are we going to be stuck in this hotel for four days?'

'Oh no, we have some enjoyable visits for you. You will see places of great memory.'

And off we went at eight o'clock in the morning on our magical mystery tour, Mr Ha standing at the front of the bus with a microphone. We swept over the guarded bridge and drove through streets bereft of vehicular traffic but with footpaths crowded with people hurrying to work in offices. They did all kinds of things in offices, we were told, but no specifics were given. There was no sign of poverty, no misery on faces—in fact, there was no real emotion on any face, pretty much like in any western city as people made their way to work.

I'd had a chance to find out a little about my fellow golfers, all of whom, I'd learned, were not so much interested in playing in a golf tournament but were interested in this particular event because of the location. Were they all writers and photographers who had managed to sneak through the net, pretending to be teachers, bankers, IT experts and so on? It transpired they really were who they said they were, except for one. I couldn't help noticing the Frenchman who joined us, complete with his own clubs and who turned out to be a very good player.

I'd worked with enough press photographers over the years to pick a stance, a movement, the way they worked with their gear, the angles they looked for, and so on, to mark him from day one. He constantly talked about his teaching work but I wasn't fooled. When it was all over the truth emerged when his photos appeared on a news agency's website, along with other pictures he'd taken around the world. These people!

On the way to Mount Myohyang—the so-called Mysterious Fragrant Mountain, 100 miles (160 kilometres) north-east of the capital and which is something of a tourist centre for Chinese visitors—we were led into a vast exhibition hall. We were instructed to pull woollen covers over our shoes and follow a female guide, in a flowing traditional dress, into a kind of Madame Tussauds waxworks where a solitary figure greeted us: a very lifelike image of Great Leader Kim Il Sung, standing in a grey suit amidst a garden of plastic flowers. We stepped reverently towards him, for we had been ordered by Mr Ha to show the greatest of respect, just as the local people did to the Dear Leader wherever his statue stood or his portrait smiled down from buildings throughout the country.

'You will please stand in a line in front of Great Leader Kim Il Sung,' said Mr Ha.

Which we did, as soft music played. 'Now do as the guide does,' whispered Mr Ha, and when the woman in the blue dress solemnly bowed her head towards the Great Leader we did the same, although I could have sworn I heard a muffled chuckle coming from one of my companions. And don't say that was me. Please. Because I'd like to go back one day and try their nightclubs—all the guide books assured me that they do exist. Oh yeah? So far we hadn't even seen a shop, even though we had driven through the main streets of the capital.

OK, folks, onto the exhibition halls. Glass cases filled with gifts for Dear Leader Kim Jong Il filled walls in room after room: silver and gold trinkets, paintings, chests, stuffed bears' heads from the former Soviet Union and Romania, a painting from Cambodia of a broom sweeping US troops out of Asia, a plaque with an image of London Bridge from a group calling itself the Britain-Korea Friendship Committee and, what I thought was the most astonishing of all, a stuffed baby crocodile perched upright holding a tray of wooden goblets from Nicaragua.

One of the enduring stories to emerge from North Korea centred around Kim Jong Il's supposed private train, which was said to have its own station and its own track leading into Beijing, which he visited from time to time to receive medical treatment and to drop in on the Chinese hierarchy. Well, Mr Ha, or you Mr Ho, is that true?

'Let me show you something,' said Mr Ha, ignoring the question, before leading our group to two railway carriages occupying pride of place within the exhibition hall. How on earth did they get there? The only entrance to this particular area was along a very long corridor, far too narrow for two train carriages. The only logical conclusion was that the exhibition room was built around them. One of the carriages was donated by Chinese leader Mao Zedong, the other by Stalin. The Chinese car is bullet-proof, although neither of the guides would explain why. Perhaps there was some truth in the rumour that there had been assassination attempts on father and son at various times—what about that Mr Ho? He smirked and marched us on to a floral display. All right. Excuse me, Miss Ann, what do you know about any assassination attempts on Great Leader or Dear Leader?

'I do not understand your question, come hurry, we are getting left behind.' There you go.

Miss Ann was actually a very nice woman. She was in her mid-20s, at a guess, and was dressed in a padded fawn-coloured jacket, her hair pulled back and tucked in with a floral brooch and just a touch of make-up. If anything, she seemed rather shy, but astonished us all when she jumped up at the front of the bus and gave us all a propaganda talk about the imperialist aggressor that was the United States.

We were taken to Buddhist monasteries to demonstrate that religions were tolerated, and we were led into bookshops in the middle of nowhere where we could buy stamps and postcards and where the only English-language publications were on political topics and propaganda aimed against the United States. 'America as the Empire of Terrorism' was everywhere.

It was more than a mere hint of the closeted world we had entered.

Once again I had golf to thank for placing me in unusual circumstances. I love the game, even though I'm not all that good (playing off 18). But it's the challenge and the circumstances I've often found myself in that prompt me to carry a bag of clubs in my car or, if I'm overseas, to keep a glove and a handful of tees in my overnight bag. I didn't even tell Dylan, the travel agent, this as I outlined my repertoire to him, but I've even rubbed shoulders with Tiger Woods, sort of—although I suspect if Tiger can get without swinging distance of me he might try a few practice shots. But more of that later.

Meanwhile back in North Korea Mr Ho was bending away from the wind, lighting up another cigarette in his cupped hands. Where are we going today then, Mr Ho? The DMZ? Wow!

The demilitarized zone, dividing North and South Korea and stretching some 160 miles (250 kilometres) from side to side and 2½ miles (4 kilometres) wide, was established in the Armistice Agreement in 1953 at the end of the Korean War. A thin line marks the exact middle of the DMZ. You wouldn't want to try walking from North to South across the DMZ—you'd be gunned down by soldiers hidden in camouflaged pill boxes and blown up by mines. As it is, North Korean soldiers stare aggressively through their binoculars at South Korean troops, who are supported by Americans, which, of course adds to North Korea's hatred of the US.

We were driven past vast concrete blockades and coils of razor wire to a large building that served as an observation headquarters, with a view across the demarcation line into South Korea to a similar building. A tall South Korean soldier in a green uniform paced up and down staring aggressively towards us.

'They put the biggest soldiers they can find on duty for intimidation purposes,' said Mr Ho. 'They don't frighten me,' he added, even though he is not the tallest of men.

As I absorbed this fascinating moment I saw a group of western men, about 30 of them, step out of the South Korean building and walk to within 45 metres (50 yards) of the demarcation line.

'This is very unusual,' declared Mr Ha. 'Whenever I have come here I have never seen another group on the other side like this. Now you people from the West can look across at some other people from the West.'

The small point-and-shoot camera I'd been allowed to bring into North Korea had a 15-times zoom lens, which allowed a good close up of the westerners on the other side. With their shaven heads and the way they reacted to commands from a uniformed US officer, there was no doubt they were American servicemen, brought up to the border from Seoul to stare across the border, perhaps, at masses of North Korean soldiers and starving peasants slaving away in the fields. Instead, they saw me and my fellow golfers who were by now waving and smilingly cheekily at them. They lowered their heads and did not smile or wave back. I wonder what they told their colleagues back in Seoul, or wherever they were based.

We were taken to a magic show where Ri Thai Gum, dubbed the David Copperfield of North Korea, made a tram disappear from under a cloth cover, people levitate and elephants vanish, then the magician himself disappeared only to reappear in a real-live helicopter that hovered over the stage, its rotors coming frighteningly close to some of the arena's supports. I couldn't help imagining the worst … NORTH KOREAN MAGICIAN DECAPITATES 500 PEOPLE IN ONE SECOND! And I wouldn't have been around to write the headline.

Despite numerous requests, our minders refused to take us to any shops or nightclubs. Not even Mr Ho could be made to budge on that one. Even so, as the bus carried us from one monument to another and yet another towering statue of Great Leader, I was able to get a sketchy impression of daily life. Definitely no cars for the populace and towering blocks of flats, which, according to Miss Ann—who surprisingly tucked her arm into mine one morning to ask if I liked her country—are provided free to married couples. All their medical treatment is free too, and although western medicine is used in conjunction with traditional herbal medicines, it is the Korean that is far more effective at preventing disease, she said. I wondered for a moment if Miss Ann was a shareholder in the ginseng business, such was her enthusiasm for it, but that was a silly notion.

Mr Ha mentioned that Miss Ann was an expert table tennis player. As I had once played for Devon I thought it was worth, half-jokingly, challenging her to a game in the hotel. To my surprise, she accepted, with the agreement of Mr Ha and Mr Ho. Watched by several of the other golfers who were enjoying the local beer, I faced her across the table. She did one of those funny Asian serves where she threw the ball a mile into the air and then gave it a little chop which sent it curving in all directions onto my side of the table. Devon v North Korea. Final result: North Korea 6, Devon 0. Enough said about that.

'I offer you all my best hopes when you play golf tomorrow,' she said, which might or might not have been a comment about my sporting abilities. Fortified by a breakfast of pickled cabbage, sautéed pork, rice and green tea, we were driven the 20 miles (30 kilometres) or so to the Pyongyang Golf Club, the headquarters of which was a rather bleak building set in spectacular surroundings: a lake and rolling tree-covered hills. We were introduced to a couple of club officials, who gave us what seemed to me a genuinely warm welcome. Then those of us who hadn't brought our own clubs were led to our numbered sets, beside each of which stood a young female caddy in a blue-and-white uniform. My bag was number four, my caddy a rosy-cheeked Miss Nim. She didn't appear to speak a word of English and it would have been unfair of me to expect her to.

Over the previous four days I'd tried to work out the strengths or otherwise of the other golfers as I attempted to estimate my chances in the tournament. The danger man was a 25-year-old Finn, Olli, who had been the Finnish national youth champion, or something just as frightening, and who had a handicap of just one. There were no less than three other Finns, two of whom appeared to be in good shape, while the third had a migraine. One down, maybe. The others were keeping their skills to themselves.

Olli and a German, Chris, were among the first to tee off. As soon as Olli hit, I knew I was dead. His ball sailed out of sight, curving as if by remote control around the dog-leg right. Chris scared the life out of me too. He didn't even use a tee—just dropped a ball onto the grass, took out a two-iron, the second hardest of all clubs, and hammered his drive straight down the middle to set himself up for a perfect shot to the green.

As I stepped onto the tee, the wind came up. Excuses. You bet. Leaves were torn from the trees and then came the rain. But I managed to hit a fair shot down the middle. After that it was downhill all the way around the course, which was extremely tight with out-of-bound markers everywhere. Miss Nim did her best to encourage me, picking out clubs that she thought I should use and clapping politely even when I missed easy putts. I'm sure those South Korean clubs they'd provided me with were doctored, just so I could curse Seoul. All I'm going to say is that I didn't win and I didn't lose. But I raise my hat to Miss Nim, who did not clap with the other caddies when Olli, yes Olli, was awarded the winner's cup at a small ceremony in the clubhouse. It might have been because she was holding a glass of orange juice in one hand and a sandwich in the other. I like to think she had prepared herself for the moment to ease my pain.

Despite all the reports about people living under an iron fist and a brutal regime—of which I had seen no evidence—I liked North Korea. Perhaps I'll go back one day, if they'll let me in, and I'll take on that golf course again and also try to win back some self-esteem on the table tennis table against Miss Ann.

Before I left I had one very important story to check out: Kim Jong Il's famous 11 holes in one. That, a discreet check among officials at the Pyongyong Golf Club revealed, was nothing more than an urban myth. Not that anyone was prepared to say so publicly. And now that he is gone I wonder if his son and successor, Kim Jong Un, will inherit his father's golf bag and head for the first tee one day. It will be a hard act to follow in more ways than one.

Chapter 2

An Unmarried Mum
in a Council House in Torquay

I've worked for the *Daily Mail* and its sibling, the defunct *Daily Sketch*, longer than anyone. I'm not saying that's a claim to fame or otherwise—it's just the way it is.

I wasn't exactly a cub reporter when I started because the British nationals didn't have 'cubs'. You came up through the suburbs back then in the 1960s and you carved a niche for yourself, and if you didn't show you were up to the job you were out on your ear. There were a few close shaves in the early days. Fair enough. Call them teething troubles, finding my way through the tough, competitive world of Fleet Street.

Since then, in the more than 40 years that I've been working for the company that owns the *Mail*—first as a staffer in London and New York and then as an Australian-based correspondent—the most extraordinary stories have come my way. No politics, very little sport, but more murders, mysteries and mayhem than you can poke a stick at. And there were wars, con men, the royals, celebrities, killers, victims, babies, medical breakthroughs, disappearances and reappearances, miraculous survivals, animals and so many assignments that were just darned good fun. I trudged through a desert looking for a model on a camel and I sweated through the rainforests of Indonesia hunting for a real live hobbit. At sea I was the first newspaper journalist to watch the incredible rescue of yachtsman Tony Bullimore, who had been given up for dead after his yacht capsized in the Southern Ocean in January 1997, and I was there to welcome down from a Borneo mountain-top a team of British soldiers who had been long given up for dead too.

Along the way, of course, I've seen and experienced many changes in the newspaper world that has been so much a part of my life. I was there in the editorial office (oh heck, I think now as I look at those alarming sideburns in a historic photo) as the entire staff listened to the *Daily Sketch*'s deputy editor Louis Kirby announce on 10 May 1971 that that would be the final production night for Britain's oldest tabloid. The next day's paper would be the last. We would all receive envelopes. If there was a pink slip inside it was goodbye and thanks for your services. If there was a white slip it meant, 'Welcome to the *Daily Mail*' (which was just up the road) 'and we'll see you in the office in the morning.'

The *Mail*, under editor Sir David English (who had earlier headed the *Daily Sketch*), had switched from a broadsheet format to what he described as a 'compact'. It leaned towards the ladies and the Right and to this day, when newspapers around the world struggle against free social journalism, the *Mail*, under current editor Paul Dacre, continues to hold a steady circulation of more than two million sales daily, while its online editions—*Mail Online*—goes from strength to strength and is the world's second-most-read internet edition.

The *Mail*'s demands on its reporting staff are extreme. Always have been. But the results keep it ahead of the game. It's true that reporters are only as good as their last story so you keep on your toes. I've learned to work under the belief that even though I'm pretty sure there's no-one from an opposition paper following the same story, they are out there somewhere—shadows who are going to destroy me—and I've got to pull out all the stops. I work against ghosts and tell myself never to be complacent, although there have been times when I've let my guard down. Once, while chasing a story in Malaysia about a British woman who had died on a climbing trip, I helped out a reporter from an opposition newspaper. The reporter couldn't drive so I offered a lift in my car and drove her around all day, suggesting who we should visit and so on. Little did I know that she was working secretly with a colleague who had tucked the family away in a hotel and was working on an exclusive interview. I, the dumb chauffeur, didn't find out about it until it was far too late. Oh yes, dirty tricks have abounded in the profession over the years. But I have noticed a change in recent times: the fierce competitiveness seems to have dropped away, at least among reporters, and they tend to share their stories as if seeking a comfort zone.

It's said you make your own luck and I've found that to be true. But there have been many occasions when good fortune has touched me in the most unexpected ways. Serendipity: the occurrence and development of events by chance in a happy and beneficial way … a happy coincidence … good fortune.

◆

Perhaps it all started with me and the pram. Wait, let's go back a little further. There's my mother lying in a hospital in Exeter, Devon, at the end of the war. She's giving birth to a kid who's going to be a problem for her. That was me. My father, whoever he was, had skipped. Hence the problem. Winnie came from a cloistered suburb in the seaside town of Torquay and an unmarried mother was destined to be the gossip of the neighbourhood. She gritted her teeth and moved us in with her Aunt Gertrude, who lived in a grey concrete-rendered council house perched half-way up a hill. Aunt Gertrude had a son, Cyril, then aged about 24, who worked in a photo-processing factory. Together we were one peculiar family.

OK, here's my first serendipity experience. Winnie had parked me in the pram outside the house while she went back inside for her purse. Perhaps she had forgotten to put the brake on or it freed itself—whatever the reason the pram began rolling down the hill. At the bottom of the hill was a T-junction of another hill coming from the right. And coming down that hill was a number 31 bus. The pram and the bus were on a guaranteed collision course. The pram was destined to be squashed flat, with me in it. But in the last few seconds a man stepped from his house at the bottom of the hill, saw the runaway pram and grabbed it. The bus hurtled by.

What had placed that man there at that very moment? A coincidence, yes. But was there something more to it? I'll never know and it wasn't until years later that I learned the story—along with a revelation that my luck hadn't ended there. Our destinies are shaped from our early years, I have no doubt about that.

At the time the welfare authorities were 'rounding up' women who had 'strayed' and given birth to illegitimate children. Mother and child would be separated and, chances are, I would have ended up like others in the care of a church or a children's home. Winnie was having nothing of it. With me wrapped in a blanket, she caught a train to what was then far-away Essex, where she settled into a women's shelter. Within weeks, the authorities had tracked her down, but as they came in through the front door Winnie made her escape through a rear window with me under her arm. She hurried back to Torquay where I was hidden in Gertrude and Cyril's council house again.

There was a parachute in a cupboard which, at the age of three, I tried running with one day in the hope of making it billow. I did, but it pulled me backwards and ripped half the skin off my knees. Like the mysteries of my background, I never found out where the parachute had come from. But I suspect an airman's link was there somewhere—my mystery father.

One day, when I was about four years old, a florid rolly-polly figure of a man turned up at the door, a small wooden trunk beside him. He was dressed in a navy blue woollen polo-neck sweater and a sea captain's hat. Uncle Charlie had returned from the merchant navy and he took up residence in one of the three upstairs bedrooms. So now the house was occupied by me, my mother, my mother's Aunt Gertrude, Gertrude's son Cyril and Uncle Charlie.

From a wooden trunk Uncle Charlie produced an old seaman's brass telescope, which he gave me. I would look at the stars with it, although I found it difficult to keep the instrument trained on them with my still small hands. Also from the trunk he brought out a commode decorated with blue Chinese patterns. He placed it carefully under the bed to use during the night. He called it his 'poe'.

Uncle Charlie had more than one use for his chamber pot. He despatched me each morning to the local pub, the John Bull, with the poe, which I had to hand over to the barman. The poe was duly filled with cider, which I then carried back to the house, a five-minute walk away, cider slopping over the sides. During the evening Uncle Charlie would sit in his room and consume the contents of the poe, dipping a cracked cup into it until it was empty, and then he would pull it out from under the bed during the night when nature called.

The time came when Winnie decided to make something of her life. She was an attractive, dark-haired woman with bright blue eyes (which I didn't inherit). Still in her late 20s, she had a lot of living to do. Believing I was in safe hands with 70-year-old Gertrude, 20-something Cyril and Uncle Charlie, she made her way to Bristol where she married a lorry driver called Jack.

She came back to visit me from time to time. Although, from the age of seven, I was now attending primary school, I had to remain out of sight while at home as much as possible. Kids from all around the country were being shipped off to Australia and she didn't want that to happen to me. This confined me to the back garden where I made a den in an air raid shelter, a corrugated iron structure which was overgrown with grass and weeds. I was an Indian, a cowboy, Batman, Superman. I made my own fun there while the other kids in the neighbourhood were playing hop-scotch or rolling marbles in the gutter out in the street. I made myself a bow and arrow and was enjoying being an Indian so much that one evening when Aunt Gertrude called me in for dinner—potatoes and meat, again—something made me turn and unleash the arrow at her. The blunt point struck her in the chest, sending her reeling backwards into the scullery where her legs struck a low wooden barrier and she keeled over into the coal cellar. From my horrified position on top of the air raid shelter, I saw two legs, encased in cotton breeches, kicking in the air. Funny how you have these visions of childhood.

Aunt Gertrude emerged, blackened, and I was ordered to the bedroom. Uncle Charlie filled the house with a seaman's roar of laughter when he heard about it and chuckled for weeks to follow. That was until I went into his room one morning and found him sprawled on his bed in his pink-striped pyjamas, the purple veins that had covered his face like a map of the world now as blue as the seven seas he had sailed across. Uncle Charlie had enjoyed his last poe of cider—and he hadn't even got around to any recycling that night.

After the funeral, Aunt Gertrude made immediate claim to the poe. For as long as I could remember she had suffered a very bad ankle ulcer, a hideous weeping hole that she would bathe, using carbolic soap, in a small tin bath we kept in the scullery. But the poe was perfect, its brim happily accommodating Aunt Gertrude's unhealthy foot. She could be found once in the morning and once at night sitting on the end of her iron bed with her foot dunked in the soapy water.

But life and death being what it was, her destiny came a year after Uncle Charlie's. I found her lying on her bed, although the scene was rather more dramatic because her foot was still in the poe and she was sprawled back on the bed, frothing at the mouth. A few hours after she had been taken off to hospital, Cyril returned from the phone box down the road and said, 'Your aunt's gone to heaven. Now it's just you and me.'

I was eight, Cyril 27. I recall a dark-haired woman in his life much earlier, helping him wash the dishes at the stone kitchen sink, but she faded from the scene. While Cyril was still mourning his mother, my own mother arrived from Bristol with two young daughters—my half-sisters Susan and Linda—in tow to check on my welfare. An arrangement was made for Cyril to become my legal guardian, although how the authorities were persuaded to agree to this with no woman in residence, I don't know. Winnie was back on the train with her daughters as soon as everything was arranged.

Cyril worked at a photo processor's but it went out of business and he was out of work. He spent weeks going to the labour exchange but there just weren't any jobs around. He was provided with some subsistence, but poverty descended. They were dark days. My clothes came from jumble sales. I wore a pair of girl's shoes with a buckle strap across the top of the foot to primary school, much to the mirth of my classmates.

Our dinner was frequently a newspaper cone of threepenny-worth of 'scribbles', the loose bubbles of crispy fat that were left over at the local fish-and-chip shop. As a change of menu we would sit down to a meal of bread pieces dropped into a bowl of Oxo cubes and hot water. There just wasn't enough money to go around, and if the council had found out how we were living there's no doubt the welfare authorities would have grabbed me. But Cyril did a brilliant job persuading everyone in the neighbourhood that things were fine—and that my mother was always there and any absence was due to her caring for a distant relative. In a way this was true because her husband, who had taken to the bottle, was forever lying drunk in Bristol, his lungs exhaling black smoke from his five packs of fags a day even when he was unconscious.

Eventually the council decided that a larger family needed our house and Cyril and I were despatched to a housing estate that consisted entirely of pre-fabricated buildings put up during the war. Some were made of aluminium, others asbestos. Asbestos! They're tearing it out of ceilings these days to stop any more people dying, but back in the early 1950s people were encased in it. Fortunately Cyril and I were housed in the aluminium variety, with two small bedrooms, a lounge, kitchen and bathroom, all assembled in a day or two.

Tall and slim with thinning brown hair, Cyril was a very caring man. It was only later that I came to realize the personal sacrifices he'd made to ensure that no misfortune befell me. There is no doubt that the course of my career would have been different had I been taken away by the authorities. Without doubt I would have ended up in a children's home or been sent to Australia.

Cyril, who I referred to as my uncle, although in reality he was a cousin, found another photographic job, which he would cycle off to on a bike someone had donated. But one day in the dead of winter when I was in my early teens, I returned home from my secondary modern school and found him hunched miserably over our heating source—a Valor paraffin heater—with his arm in a sling. He'd come off his bike on the ice and broken his arm and fractured his collar bone. No more work for him. No more income again, apart from a few pounds he was given at the labour exchange.

But Cyril was resourceful. Despite his incapacitated state he got hold of some three-ply wood, borrowed a fretsaw from a neighbour and cut out a pile of shields, about the size of a hand. He used some of our dinner money to buy stick-on transfers, an artist's paintbrush, and two small tins of black paint and varnish. The finished product was a souvenir shield emblazoned with a butterfly or a bird transfer, with the words 'Paignton Zoo' underneath. He had no arrangement to make these for the zoo. It was a gamble. He set off by bus for Paignton, eight miles (13 kilometres) away, the shields wrapped up in newspaper—and returned triumphant! The zoo had taken all 20 of his samples and asked him for more. He didn't make much money, but he'd started a small cottage industry. Our standard of living improved a hundred per cent. He bought a packet of tea, butter, jam, tins of baked beans and sardines. We ate like kings.

After school I hung around with a group of other kids in the neighbourhood, playing football in the street or clambering around a disused quarry where we'd crack open rocks with hammers looking for fossils. We found quite a few, mostly of bugs with scaly backs. One day I was given a pair of shiny rollerskates by one of the boys. He also presented skates to two others. He explained his father had come into some money and had given him some so he could buy presents for his friends. The early-teen girls began wearing colourful necklaces and bracelets, one boy ran around firing a starting pistol at everyone and another surveyed the neighbourhood through a shiny new pair of binoculars. Our friend had a very generous father. But within a week the police came around and retrieved everything from us. Our benefactor was never seen again. We learned that he'd found his widowed father's life savings under the bed and had decided to splurge out on his friends. The boy disappeared from the neighbourhood and none of us thought to wonder at the time why we weren't arrested for being in possession of the proceeds of crime!

Cyril found a diversion from life in the prefab, where we'd read in the evenings or listen to the radio—we both enjoyed the comedy shows, *My Word*, *The Clitheroe Kid*, *Beyond Our Ken*—when he began attending the local Baptist church. He dragged me along and I learned to play table tennis in the church hall and gasped as I watched

Cyril being baptized, walking down the steps between the opened-up floorboards beside the pulpit and being dunked by the Reverend David Abernethie.

We still couldn't afford school lunch money, and an arrangement was made for me to have lunch at the home of an elderly couple who belonged to the Baptist church. The old lady had a kind heart but no culinary skills. The potatoes were boiled for only a few minutes so they were as hard as bullets, and the cabbage was cooked to a sloppy mash. She stood over me each day encouraging me to 'eat it all up—it will put some weight on you.'

During the school holidays I worked as a delivery boy at the Maypole Grocery Store in Torquay's main street. They gave me a white apron and an old bicycle with sit-up-and-beg handlebars. It had an iron carrier over the front wheel on which I would stack as many boxes of food that I could safely carry.

Like Rome, Torquay is built on seven hills, which meant that delivering the groceries was very hard work. But returning to the store was a joy—downhill all the way! One day I hurtled down Market Street, peddling as hard as I could at the top of the hill to begin the hairy descent. The heavy iron crate, now facing downwards, assisted in the build-up of speed. About half-way down the hill I noticed a blind man at the kerb slowly raising his white stick. I still remember thinking at the time: 'If he steps out, there's going to be trouble.' I was almost level with him, but the brakes proved to be totally ineffective, and he still hadn't moved. The bike had no bell and I didn't think of shouting a warning. But I was certain I'd avoided a terrible accident—until the moment when he shoved the white stick forward, like a fencer with a sabre. It went right through the bike's front wheel spokes. I became aware of pieces of white stick flying all around me as I hurtled through the air. All the wind was knocked from me as I hit the ground. My elbows and knees were scraped raw, blood poured from my nose, my white apron was stained red. I turned around to see the blind man lying on his back on the pavement, half a stick beside him, the rest in pieces on the road. He survived, I survived. I got away with a severe warning from the Maypole boss after witnesses had explained to the police that 'while the young man was going rather fast, the poor blind man didn't see him coming.' I suspect my employer had let me off the hook to some extent because the police had come down heavily on him for providing me with a bicycle without a bell.

It was time for fate to step in for the better.

◆

I had had no thoughts of what I 'wanted to do' when I left school. But I was well aware that even if I was clever enough to pass the required exams I wouldn't go on to university. Cyril's income was hardly supporting us and I would have to go out to work as soon as I was of age. The only future I saw was as a worker in an engineering factory—I had been fairly successful in basic metalwork classes, pounding iron into pokers and candle holders, although I realized my shortcomings when serious maths were required to build a small jet engine. I was totally baffled by the qualifications required.

Another boy in my class asked if I'd seen the British Rail film. It was doing the rounds and there was a competition associated with it. Students who watched the film, which was about the joys of travelling around the country by rail, were invited to write an essay about on the subject and the winner would receive two tickets to travel by train anywhere they liked around the British Isles.

I watched the film, wrote a very flowery essay—and won first prize. But the tickets were wasted. Cyril couldn't leave his new job at a photographic processor's and when I wrote to my mother explaining that I could come to visit her in Bristol, there was no reply. Fate, though, was playing a role. Or had I made my own luck? Or, well, who knows …

If I'd taken the train trip I would not have been called into the headmaster's office and been told that an apprenticeship for a 'cub reporter' had come up at the local newspaper. The position was open for 24 hours—and the headmaster had taken it upon himself to arrange an interview for me as a result of my winning the essay competition.

The following morning I sat nervously in the office of the editor, George Matthews, nodding vaguely as he told me that I must have been considering a career as a writer. I told him that I would really love to be a reporter. It wasn't that at all, of course. It was a job on offer and I was ready to grab it. The editor said he'd let me know if he was prepared to take me on.

Cyrilwas delighted that the chance of a job had come up because there wasn't a lot of work to be found in Torquay in the late 1950s. The town depended largely on its tourist industry and when winter came the queues of the unemployed grew.

A week later I was called back to the *Herald Express* office and told that I'd got the job. 'And for heaven's sake,' said Mr Matthews, 'please wear long trousers.'

It was true—at the age of 15, I was still in schoolboy shorts because we couldn't afford long trousers. But I was nearly as tall as Cyril so he gave me his Sunday best to wear for my first day at the *Herald Express*. The turn-ups dragged a little but, hey, at least you couldn't see my knees.

I started at the bottom. I was given the task of filling up paste pots, ensuring that the senior reporters had enough slips of copy paper to roll into their typewriters, that the subeditor's pencils were kept sharpened and I was on hand to answer every phone on the long reporters' table. I was clumsy, making all kinds of mistakes, and was constantly being scolded by the chief reporter, whom I only ever knew as Mr R.J.D. Smith.

But the day came when I was given my first assignment—a court case. It was a complicated affair, with a coal delivery man being charged under the *Weights and Measures Act* with short-changing his customers. The courtroom was filled with chatter about hundredweights and scales and hidden profits. As I struggled to write the story later, pecking away at a Underwood typewriter and trying to read my scrawled longhand notes, one of the senior reporters, looking over my shoulder, collected each page, containing a paragraph at a time, and smiled wickedly. He said, 'very good, very good,' before screwing them up and tossing them into the rubbish bin. Then he said: 'If I asked you to sum up the case in one sentence, what would you tell me?'

'Well,' I stuttered, 'this man was fined 50 quid for cheating his customers when he delivered coal to them.'

'Then those are the main points of your intro. Keep it short, write the first thing that comes into your head, give us his name, then describe the case.'

The reporter, who had the unforgettable name of Neville Tortoishell, became a good friend. His was sound advice that generally worked for many of the news stories I wrote in following years.

My 'beat', eventually, was the whole of Torbay, covering the seaside towns of Torquay, Paignton and Brixham. I wrote about dog shows, funerals, parish council meetings, amateur dramatic shows and I sped from job to job on my Lambretta motor scooter, purchased on hire purchase from my £10 a week salary. But I often seemed to be luckier than the other reporters by being in the right place at the right time. When police swooped on a burglar breaking through the roof of a shop in the main street late one night, I was the only witness and had my first 'scoop'. I was there when a drowning woman was saved, and was on board when a passenger ferry became stranded in thick fog and was almost run over by a cargo vessel.

Perhaps it was because I put myself out and about that I was there for the stories when they broke. It certainly has held true for some of the remarkable tales that I came to cover in time: always go to them, never try to do it by phone. When the internet came along, I fought, and still fight, against being a lazy 'online fact gatherer'.

One of my pals was Malcolm Ross—Rossy—a reporter who had grown up in the Dartmoor town of Tavistock. He was tall and lanky like myself with a wicked—and juvenile—sense of humour. Reporters always have the opportunity to remain out of the office, on the basis that stories were taking longer than expected to pull together, even if they weren't. That gave Rossy and me the chance to go out hunting for more characters for our 'Curiosity Album', a scrapbook of photographs of people who tended to stand out in a crowd.

We would take candid photos and I would develop them in my bathroom before sticking them in the album. Oh, it was cruel but, hey, it was funny. There was The Face, a woman who had an exceptionally long face—I mean seriously long—who was always hanging around Woolworths; there was the inevitable bag lady; the Spider Man, who wore a long black cloak, had a club foot and shuffled through the back lanes of Torquay; and there was the water-wings man, a strange character who could be seen walking around the harbour with deflated water wings under the arms of his immaculate suit. I never did find out what happened to our collection of curiosities.

I worked hard at my typing speed, covering my hands with a cloth and working out where the keys were from a diagram at my side. I went to night school—once—to learn shorthand but the giggles from the rest of the class, all girls, led to me teaching myself. I sent away to the US for a book called *How to Write 240 Words a Minute in Pitman's Shorthand*, written by Maurice Kligman, a US Supreme Court reporter. It was full of wonderful outlines for such phrases as 'what did you say to him and what did he say to you?' and 'will you tell the judge and jury …' which is all very well if you're in court but the speed-phrases were absolutely useless for a parish council meeting discussing the village sewage system.

Rossy's brother was into repairing old cars and one day Rossy turned up at the *Herald Express* office in a metallic blue Austin Healey 100, a 1955 sports car. We'd go roaring around the streets of Torquay in it, sometimes with the hood down and the windscreen removed, just for the hell of it. We took it to Dartmoor in the dead of winter and practised handbrake turns on the ice on the narrow roads, until

Rossy—or perhaps it was me—lost control and we hit a farm gate and smashed in the headlamps.

Rossy moved into one-room lodgings in a boarding house not far from my own one-room flat, but while I had a fabulous view of the harbour, he looked out onto a brick wall. And he admitted that he was very, very, worried about the strange man who lived in the room next door, an artist who painted under the name of 'Nance'. Nance could often be seen dressed in women's clothes, which was obviously why Rossy was uneasy. But what sent Rossy rushing from the building, never to return, was the snipping sound that woke him one night. Flicking on the bedside lamp, he watched in a mixture of astonishment and horror at a pair of scissors that were protruding through the wafer-thin wall and cutting a circle just above his head. Then the circle was punched inwards onto Rossy's bed and Nance's face, made up with mascara and lipstick, peered through.

'Hellllllo-o-o-o-o-o-o-o,' said Nance.

It took Rossy all of one minute to grab a bag and get out of there for good.

Such were the diversions from a job that I took very seriously because I was becoming aware that there were broader pastures in journalism. Aside from Rossy, my colleagues on the *Herald Express* had families, steady girlfriends and/or mortgages, which dampened any ambitions to move on to larger newspapers

◆

At the age of 21 I was roaring along the highway to Birmingham in a vehicle that was a rare sight on British roads in the mid-1960s—a Messerschmitt bubble car, circa 1958. It had two wheels in the front, one at the rear, was powered by an engine that could propel it along at 56 miles (90 kilometres) per hour, and had a gear change 'stick' located in the side panelling. I had bought it for £25 from Neville Tortoishell, who assured me it was a 'good runner'.

My destination was the *Birmingham Post and Mail*, which had offered me a job in their Redditch office, near Stratford-on-Avon.

I was lucky to arrive. The shape of the 'Schmitt was not too far removed from that of a coffin, which I almost ended up in after trying to overtake a convoy of trucks in the dead of night and feeling the engine cut out, just as another convoy headed towards me. There was no way out but at the last moment the engine restarted and I scraped through.

'If I can get away with that,' I thought, 'I can get away with anything'.

Is there such an entity as 'fate'? Or are such seemingly impossible escapes from disaster just damn good luck?

The 'Schmitt served me well on my rounds for the *Birmingham Post and Mail*, where I covered pretty much the same kind of jobs I had undertaken on the *Herald Express*. Most of the people I met on my regular calls to mayors, police officers and clubs always knew when I was approaching by the sound of the noisy motor. But the vehicle continued to win many admiring glances. Sadly, its life came to an end in much the same way as a real Messerschmitt plane. Returning from a meal in Stratford-on-Avon with the local barmaid from Redditch, the car burst into flames. I swerved into a field, hitting the side of the vehicle on a post and smashing the release lock on the Perspex lid. We were trapped in a blazing Messerschmitt! With one final desperate heave, I managed to get the roof open and the barmaid ran off screaming into the night.

Soon it was time to move on. At the age of 23, I headed down the M1 in a far more salubrious vehicle, although it still had only three wheels—a Reliant Supervan, which had a fibreglass body, one wheel in the front, two behind and a proper gearstick. Like the 'Schmitt, I was able to drive it on just a motorcycle licence.

In October 1966, I'd driven down the motorway in the Reliant to cover one of the biggest stories of the decade: the collapse of a huge slag heap onto the small town of Aberfan, in Wales, smothering a school and killing 116 children and 28 adults. They were horror scenes. The one that still stands out in my mind is the moment when Sergeant Vic Jones carried one of the surviving children from the rubble. As the full impact of the disaster became clear, the authorities closed the disaster area off. I just managed to get inside the security circle and was able to report on the desperate search for survivors.

◆

It was time, though, for the 'big time' in London. I was going to apply for a job as a holiday relief on the *Daily Sketch*. Each year, they gave three months' work to four casual reporters while staff journalists took their holidays. At the end of that time there was a chance that one or two of the casuals would be kept on as staff. The *Daily Sketch* was the smallest of the national papers but it was the gateway into the

'Mecca' of the newspaper business. I'd sounded out one of the journalists working there a few weeks earlier. No point in writing a letter to the powers that be, I was told. You turn up and take your chances.

I rather apprehensively approached the deputy news editor, Alan Sollaway, a soft-featured man in his 30s, sleeves rolled up as he read someone's copy on one of the slips of paper I was so familiar with. I told him I'd driven down from Birmingham to look for a job as a holiday relief. I'd covered this story, I'd covered that story. Hardly had I finished when he began shaking his head. Sorry, all the relief jobs had gone. Come back next year.

Dejectedly, I walked through the sea of clacking typewriters, senior reporters all smoking as they bashed out their stories. Someone was grabbing a coat and rushing out. I didn't smoke but this was the world I wanted to be a part of. This was the big time. Aberfan had been a baptism of fire for a young reporter, but then it had been back to the old routine of council meetings and car crashes. I was faced with driving back to the old rounds again.

But as I walked through the lobby of the *Sketch*'s Carmelite House, overlooking the River Thames, a young woman came running down the stairs behind me. She was calling my name. Come back. Mr Solloway wants to see you again. My heart gave a leap.

Alan was grinning as I approached the News Desk.

'You're in luck—as you were walking out one of the holiday reliefs called in to say he's not going to be available. You're here—you can take his place.'

A couple of minutes later and I would have been gone, walking back to the car, driving back to Birmingham. Fate had stepped in again.

And that's when it all really began.

CHAPTER 3

The Jumbo Jet, a Pair of Boots
and a Broken Pen

My three months as a holiday relief at the *Daily Sketch*—during which news editor John Womersley described me as his 'sausage machine' because I was happy to take on anything he threw at me—resulted in a full-time staff job. John was to be tragically killed years later when he was hit by a train in France, joining a list of colleagues I had enjoyed working with and who had died in unusual circumstances: Iain Walker, a friend from the *Mail on Sunday* who plunged to his death over a cliff on a skiing holiday, and Nigel Benson, a great Scottish reporter who checked himself into an upstairs room at a pub across the road from the *Sketch* and drank himself to death.

The *Sketch*'s foreign editor Brian Freemantle—later to become a best-selling author with his fictional hero Charlie Muffin—despatched me on my first foreign assignment: as a passenger on the inaugural commercial flight of a Pan Am Boeing 747 jumbo jet that was due to fly from New York to London on 21 January 1970.

'Fly over to New York, get on the plane and write about the trip,' Brian instructed. 'Nice simple job to break you in to foreign reporting.'

David English, who was to become the most powerful editor in Fleet Street with his hard-working, sleeves-up approach to the job, called me into his office a few hours before I was due to fly to the US.

'I've ordered a pen, a very special fountain pen, to be picked up by our bureau in New York and I'd also like you to bring back a pair of specially ordered boots for my wife,' he told me as I sat rather nervously across the desk in front of the great man. 'The boots are very important—they're the last in a line and I must emphasize the care that must be taken with them.'

I collected the pen and the boots in New York and several hours later was attending a cocktail party at Kennedy Airport to 'launch' the flight that would be taking me and 323 other passengers across the Atlantic to London. The pen was in my inside jacket pocket and the boots, in a plastic bag, were being guarded by an airline official as I clinked my champagne glass with the other passengers. Then it was all aboard for the historic flight. The engines started up, the aircraft taxied into position and as it began to pick up speed along the runway everyone cheered. And then they all shrieked as the big jet came to a shuddering stop, throwing everyone forward. There was no explanation from the crew but we knew we were turning around and heading back to the terminal. This was a story! The world's first scheduled passenger flight of a jumbo jet and the plane didn't even get off the runway.

I had to get off and file a story for the last edition of the paper but the crew insisted that everyone remain in their seats. I begged, I pleaded, but heads shook. No-one was allowed off. Then by a stroke of luck it was decided that the passengers could go back into the terminal because there had been a 'technical hitch' which might take 'some time' to fix.

This being my first foreign job, I had no idea how to make a reverse charge call to London. I'd changed my US dollars back into pounds and couldn't even feed a payphone. In desperation I turned to the disembarking passengers and shouted: 'Does anyone know how I can make a reverse charge call to London?'

'You mean a collect call?' someone asked, before advising me to call the White Plains operator. Minutes later I was dictating a story to the *Daily Mail* about the take-off party that had gone so terribly wrong. It just made the last edition of the paper. Then I joined the others, continuing the champagne reception that we thought had ended earlier. Eventually a replacement jumbo took off more than six hours late at 1.30 in the morning—the problem had been an overheating number four engine. By then many of us had consumed a fair amount of alcohol. I'd sent my story, it was going in the paper and I had no need to refuse another glass. But my jubilation at having a scoop on my first foreign assignment popped like a champagne bubble on arrival in London.

The editor's wife's boots! Where were they? Were they still in the airport lounge in New York? Had I taken them back on board? Were they in the aircraft's overhead locker? Had I taken them with me when I rushed to the phone and were they waiting for me to come back and collect them? I had no idea. My last memory was seeing them on the floor beside one of the airline staffers in the lounge as we toasted the imminent departure of the jumbo. My panicky request to Pan Am officials to check the locker over the seat I'd vacated came back with the answer I feared: 'The locker's empty.'

Later that day, nursing the mother and father of a hangover, I stood fearfully in David English's office. I listened to his congratulations on my getting the story over so quickly. Then, leaning back in his chair, he said:

'So, do you have the boots and my pen?'

I could hear the tremble in my voice as I explained that the boots had been temporarily mislaid—but that I was on to it and that I had no doubt that the airline would deliver them to me, er, shortly.

'Well, I hope so,' said the editor, his smile replaced by a thunderous expression. 'My wife has been looking forward to them.'

'But,' I added, hoping to lighten his mood, 'I do have your fountain pen.'

I handed him the pen case, bound in beautiful black leather. He placed it on his desk and opened it. I had never observed the phenomenon of blood draining from a face, but now it was happening right before my eyes. David English turned the pen case around and slid it across the desk towards me. He would have seen the same whitening of my own face as I stared down at the pen. Or rather, the two fractured halves, with a dark stain of spilled ink decorating the silk lining of the case, like blood that had seeped from a murder victim.

I couldn't explain it. I couldn't even find words to fumble out an excuse. There just wasn't one. This was the end of my career as a foreign reporter, surely. Wrong, I suddenly thought. It was the end of my career, full stop.

But the editor, who I found out as I got to know him turned out to be not only the toughest but among the fairest of newspaper men in Britain, sat back in his chair, spread his hands helplessly and said: 'This is a double disaster. But your quick thinking in filing the story has cancelled it out. But please, go and find those boots.' He then put his own boot in as he added: 'As for the pen, I'll make do with a biro in the meantime.'

I kept up the pressure on Pan Am throughout the following week. But the boots had disappeared and it was eventually agreed that the airline would refund their cost. I was still convinced that the episode would put an end to any other foreign travel. But a few months later Brian Freemantle told me that he and the editor had decided to send me on a new overseas assignment. To Biafra in west Africa. So this was my delayed punishment, I thought.

◆

The breakaway Nigerian state had been at civil war with the central government for three years from 1967 until 1970. My role was to tour the ruins of the state, if I could get in there, and report on the aftermath of the conflict. I was warned that great care was needed because former guerillas with a hunger for murder were at large.

Photographer Norman Potter and I managed to get travel permits to enter Biafra, by then known as the Eastern States. We employed a driver, Ojo, who insisted his 12-year-old son accompany us. Ojo was an enormous, sweaty man, whose girth suggested that, while many Biafrans were starving, he had no trouble enjoying life in the Nigerian capital, Lagos.

In Ojo's rusty black Morris Minor, we passed through bomb-smashed towns and bullet-riddled villages, sleeping and eating wherever we could find a semblance of accommodation. One evening, while trying to sleep on the springs of a bed that had no mattress—oh, and did I mention that there was no roof for the room?—a figure appeared at the doorless doorway. A naked woman, illuminated by the moonlight.

'Me want eight pounds.'

'What's that?' I asked, trying to sit up straight on the springs.

'Me want eight pounds.'

'Eight quid! What do you want eight quid for?' Then I realized what this was all about.

'Thanks for dropping by,' I said, 'but I'm going back to sleep now.'

'Your friend give me eight pounds. Now you give me eight pounds.'

It took some persuasion to get her to leave. (*News of the World* journalists exposing ladies of the night in those days always claimed to have made their excuses and left before things went too far.) Finally, she slipped away into the shadows. In the morning Norman told me that he'd found a tin hut masquerading as a bar in the dark and dangerous-looking alleyways nearby, and had picked up what he described as a 'jungle bunny'. He thought he was doing me a favour by passing her onto me.

'You're a dope,' he said. 'You could have charged her against expenses. Put her down as petrol or food.'

Was this, then, the life of a foreign correspondent? Enjoy your 'extras' and claim them back in expenses from the paper? I was to find out that, unlike the care that had to be taken in claiming expenses back on a regional newspaper like the dear old *Herald Express* in Torquay, exaggerating expenditure was rife throughout the national newspaper industry. One journalist, who shall remain anonymous, had extensions added to his house and an in-ground swimming pool built, all from the profits of his expenses. But my training in claiming expenses at the *Herald Express* was so ingrained that I have never been able to follow that route,. There have even been occasions when my charges have been queried—because they were too low!

We were in what would have been central Biafra when the car troubles began. Ojo, who had already shown his true colours by getting his son to do all the necessary chores, cursed as the tired old Morris came to a stop on a slippery incline in the middle of the jungle. Although his young son had proved his efficiency in driving the car, when it came to having to push the car up the slope it was Ojo who insisted on sitting behind the wheel while his son, Norman and I pushed the car up the hill, our clothes soaked with perspiration.

We eventually got it going and for the rest of the day the car would run along the flat, but like a recalcitrant horse refused to climb each hill. Out we would get and push while tubby Ojo relaxed behind the wheel.

At dusk we were several miles from the next town when the car decided that even a straight stretch of road was too much for it. It refused to start and the three of us who were doing the pushing were too exhausted to carry on. So Norman and I slumped down on the tattered back seats in the cramped rear while Ojo and his son prepared for the night in the front.

Ojo wound up the windows and pressed down the door locks.

'Hey, open up!' cried Norman. 'We'll die of heat in here.'

'Not good open,' said Ojo. 'Mosquitoes and …'

'Don't worry about them,' Norman interrupted. 'It's too hot.'

'… bandits.'

Mosquitoes we could understand. Bandits we had not anticipated, although we suddenly remembered earlier warnings about homeless soldiers.

In broken English Ojo explained that at night rag-tag bands of former Biafran freedom fighters were stopping cars, robbing the occupants and sometimes killing them. That was in the towns. Out in the bush they didn't bother to ask questions.

Fat lot of good a closed window was going to make if any of those desperadoes found us—as they suddenly did at about three o'clock in the morning. Their faces, hardly visible in the moonlight penetrating the tree canopy, were at the side windows. So were their guns. Ojo broke into terrified stuttering as he wound down his window while Norman and I tried to control our bodily functions. Their gestures told us to get out. They began screaming orders at us and pointing towards the trees.

'We dead, we dead!' cried Ojo.

It was only the thought of a couple of decomposing westerners lying under a pile of leaves in the jungle that forced desperate words from my lips as I turned to the quivering Ojo.

'Tell them we have come here to find them because we want to take their picture and write their story about their struggle. We have come a long way, all the way from England, to find them and make them famous. They will be heroes. Tell them to stand over by the trees with their guns and my friend will take a nice picture of them.'

Incredibly, the guerillas did as they were asked, posing in their tattered camouflage uniforms with their guns as Norman fired off half a dozen pictures with his Nikon, the flash illuminating the surrounding forest. And their smiles. I can still see their white teeth in my mind's eye. We told them we would send the photos to London and everybody would admire them. We thanked them for posing, they thanked us for taking the pictures. Then they melted back into the jungle as silently as they had arrived. I couldn't believe our good fortune.

But we all spent a nervous night. At dawn Ojo turned the ignition key and the engine, cool and rested, burst into life. On the outskirts of the town we had tried to reach the night before, I finally found words to raise the incident with Norman—we'd been left speechless by the terrifying event and hadn't wished to jinx our luck by talking about it the during the remainder of the sleepless night.

'At least we've got some good pictures to send back to the paper,' I said.

'Yeah, sure,' said Norman. 'I wasn't even loaded up.'

By that he meant he didn't have a film in his camera. He'd unloaded his Tri-X film when the car had died for the night. Not anticipating any photo opportunities during the night, as you don't in the middle of a Biafran jungle, he'd planned to prepare his equipment at first light.

So, no photo of a band of ruthless killers.

But we were still alive to tell the tale. Once again, I found myself thinking: 'If I can get away with that, I can get away with anything!'

We managed to get through to Brian on the Foreign Desk by telex, having found a machine in a factory that was a subsidiary of a western company, and relayed our escape. Such incidents were all part of the job, Brian telexed back— I could even hear his indifference—and without any pictures our experience could go straight on the spike, a reference to any potential story being canned. Brian wanted to know if we could accede to the editor's request and find a picture and story that summed up the desperate plight of the forgotten people of the civil war. We'd gleaned some good human interest stories, but we both agreed there was nothing that really stood out as the story of the war's aftermath.

But in a village near the war-ravaged city of Benin, about 150 miles (250 kilometres) east of Lagos, we found it. An old man was sitting under an umbrella on a parched patch of land. The shade covered his emaciated body and a tiny green tomato hanging from a withering vine attached to a stick. Through Ojo, he told how his two sons had been executed on the orders of Biafra's military commander, Chukwuemeka Odumegwu Ojukwu, for refusing to fight government troops, his wife had succumbed to a recurrence of malaria and his neighbours were dying of starvation all around him. He had been ill after drinking bad water in a well, but he had been able to get bread when a woman from a neighbouring village brought it around. It was the tomato, though, that would give him nourishment, he said. He was watching it, encouraging its growth every day, waiting for the time it would be ripe enough to pick and then he would eat it with the bread.

As Norman took his pictures, I wondered whether he would live long enough to see the day when the tomato had ripened. It emphasized that while we in the West might complain about this or that hardship, nothing could compare with the plight of this poor man.

His story also epitomized the cruelty of war. The editor thought so too, for the picture ran as a spread in the *Daily Sketch*. Saved again—the pen and the boots had, it seemed, become a distant memory if the welcoming grin on the editor's face was anything to go by on my return to London.

But within a few months, there were many sad faces on the editorial floor when the *Sketch* closed.

♦

I spent the next four years on the *Daily Mail*. I threw myself at whatever job came my way, whether it was a criminal trial at the Old Bailey or a train crash in Surrey. I worked night shifts on the News Desk, dealing with the usual band of 'nutters' who decided after an evening in the pub that they wanted someone to talk to. But I was happy to deal with anything.

I was in Londonderry, Northern Ireland, for the aftermath of the Bloody Sunday massacre when 13 unarmed civil rights demonstrators were shot dead by British paratroopers on 30 January 1972. Along with scores of journalists, photographers and TV crews, I crowded into the City Hotel, which was to be blown up two years later, and slept on the floor because no more rooms were available. I spent much of the night talking to two of the great war photographers of Fleet Street, Don McCullen of the *Sunday Times Magazine* and Terry Fincher of the *Daily Express*. On the second night a reporter from the Press Association said he was going for a stroll around the darkened streets because he was bored. I said I'd go with him.

Everything was eerily quiet as we wandered around, but the tension in the air was almost tangible. I had no idea what I was doing there. Then I thought I saw something glint in the shadows of a shop doorway and walked over to have a look. Suddenly I was staring at the whites of the eyes of a camouflaged soldier and something very hard—the muzzle of his rifle—was pushing upright into my ribs.

'Oh!' I exclaimed.

And he said, 'Piss off you stupid fucker or I'll have your balls.'

I conveyed this information as calmly as I could to the man from the Press Association and then we ran like rabbits with buckshot chasing us back to the hotel. Jesus, said the man from PA, we could have been shot. Your call, I reminded him. But you came with me, he said. Call it a draw in absolute lunacy.

On a second visit I had to leave Northern Ireland in a hurry with award-winning photographer Monty Fresco, on the orders of a delighted editor, after we had got an exclusive interview in a council house with IRA leader Joe Cahill. The story ran as a centre-page spread in the *Daily Mail*. On my arrival back in London I found two gentlemen from Scotland Yard's Special Branch waiting for me in the office. They wanted to know exactly where the interview had been held. The truth was I didn't know—Monty and I had been blindfolded when we were taken to the house.

◆

I enjoyed the unexpected, not knowing when I got out of bed each morning where I would be sleeping that night. It all depended on what was happening in the world, or rather in Britain, because the *Mail* had its own network of foreign-based reporters and a New York office manned by staff writers—as did the other national papers. In addition there were numerous trusted 'stringers', reporters who had jobs with newspapers in cities around the world but who could be called upon to write stories for the *Mail* or make inquiries on the paper's behalf. As well as the stringers, foreign-based news agencies earned their living by keeping up a constant run of stories to the British nationals. Finally, there were non-staff: full-time correspondents who were paid retainers to work just for the *Mail* and who were ready to travel anywhere at a moment's notice at the paper's behest.

I've often been asked whether I had a mentor as I was coming up through the ranks. But Fleet Street didn't work like that. At least not in human terms. The paper itself was my mentor. I learned what it wanted because the people running the desks—foreign, news, features, pictures or sport—were pros: company men, perhaps, but pros all the same. If you didn't think like they thought and turned in a story that didn't answer all the questions that the editor of the day was likely to ask, you'd soon know about it. There were many occasions when I felt I had got it right and the foreign editor or the news editor I was dealing with had got it wrong. It was always a grand feeling to see an original story published word for word and the rewritten version, demanded by an editor, ending up on the spike. Of course, it happened the other way around, too, and they were right and I was wrong.

I wanted the best for the paper because it had given me all the chances that I'd dreamed of and it was up to me to return the favour. It was an attitude that has remained with me, despite the down times which befall most reporters when things don't run as they would wish.

But just like at the *Herald Express*, I began to get itchy feet. I'd moved from Torquay to Birmingham, Birmingham to London, but foreign climes were now beckoning. Should I take a chance, pack in my job and just go travelling, writing for the *Mail* as a freelance and earning a living that way? Did I have enough faith in myself to do that? As I was mulling over the idea, fate stepped in again and made the decision for me.

I was given my next overseas assignment, the dream of everyone working in Fleet Street: a posting to the *Daily Mail*'s New York bureau.

There, in January of 1972, in the *Daily News* Building on 42nd Street, I joined veteran journalist Dermot Purgavie, learning the routine from him as we walked a couple of blocks to the famous Costello's Bar, the haunt of such legends as the Australian knock-about *New York Post* journalist Steve Dunleavy. A biting wind roared through the streets but I didn't notice. This was New York, a city that wrapped itself around you, thrilled you by allowing you into its heart. I was a real foreign correspondent!

The agreement was that Dermot would continue writing his chatty New York column. My role would be to cover news stories, those breaking not only in the US but in surrounding countries. I found an apartment in a brownstone building on First Avenue, not far from the UN Building. Unlike the often cold and gloomy flats that I'd rented in London, this one was overheated to the extreme and the only relief I found was to open the window to the elements even in the dead of winter. I had my photograph taken for an official police press pass, which was in the shape of a green shield. For the picture, I wore a shirt with a deep collar and a tie with a huge Windsor knot. I wanted to look like all the other American reporters I'd seen in the *Daily News* Building. When I look at that formal police picture now I can't help thinking, 'What a wanker'.

They were exciting times. Mafia wars were raging, with the nephew of mobster boss Carlo Gambino being kidnapped and executed by rival hoods. Manny Gambino's body was found in a sitting position in a New Jersey dump, sparking more violence. I felt like I was walking through a movie set as I talked to real live gangsters in seedy bars—particularly when one asked, 'Are you wired?' It was a silly question, because they allowed me to write down what they were saying in any case. They always seemed happy to talk to a British reporter and then it was a question of sorting out fact from fiction. I took some silly risks—obviously not learning a thing from my scare in Londonderry—walking home late at night through dark, deserted streets (getting mugged only once, by an old man who asked for ten cents to make up a train fare) and dancing in a Harlem night club, the only white face there.

I'd been in New York for only a few weeks before I had to fly to Yellowknife, in Canada's North-west Territory, to follow up on reports that a British pilot had become the world's first known modern-day cannibal, forced to eat the flesh of a dead British nurse after his mercy-flight aircraft had crashed in the snowy wastelands.

It was an extraordinary story because Martin Hartwell's rescue on 8 December 1972 came literally 15 days before the discovery of survivors of the Andes plane crash. While 16 Andes survivors were eating their fellow passengers to stay alive, Hartwell was boiling up the flesh of the nurse in a tin of frozen snow. It was incredible that tales of cannibalism should emerge from two plane crashes at the same time.

The Andes crash has been well-documented and a film was made about it, but Hartwell's experiences have faded into history. And although the Andes survivors had others they could talk to during their ordeal, Hartwell was completely alone in a frozen landscape, helpless with two fractured ankles, following the death of his three passengers.

I sat by his hospital bed and he recalled how he had set off in a Beechcraft 18 plane on 8 November from Cambridge Bay, north of the Arctic Circle, on a medical mercy mission, carrying a 14-year-old Eskimo boy who was suffering from appendicitis, an Eskimo woman with labour complications and 27-year-old British nurse Judy Hill, who by coincidence came from my own home county of Devon and who, I believe, was living at home in Kingsbridge when I was doing my rounds for the *Herald Express*.

Hartwell's plane crashed 200 miles (320 kilometres) north of Yellowknife and, despite a widespread search by Canadian aircraft after a faint SOS signal was picked up, the wreckage could not be found. The Eskimo woman and Hill were killed and Hartwell had broken both his legs and was helpless.

Pale and gaunt with a greying beard, he reached out from his hospital bed to clutch my arm, as if he still wanted to feel a living human at his side. He told how the young Eskimo boy failed in his bid to walk to a frozen lake to try to catch fish and then laid down beside the wrecked plane and died. Alone and starving, able only to drag himself around on his broken legs, Hartwell cut flesh from Miss Hills' buttocks and boiled it up in a tin over a fire he had lit with matches he found in the plane. He was rescued ten days later.

◆

I could not imagine that such an extraordinary story would fade so quickly, but then the Andes survivors were found. And then came another dramatic incident which made me forget all about Hartwell. Within a month I was on a plane to New Orleans. A Black Power sniper had gone on the rampage, gunning down everyone in sight and the death toll was steadily rising—seven, eight, nine ...

The 23-year-old, Mark Essex, had entered the Howard Johnson Hotel via a fire escape, telling three black employees not to be scared because he was there to shoot only white people. Essex had already left a trail of death on his way to the hotel, and now gunned down a doctor and his wife in cold blood before using lighter fuel to start a fire in the doctor's room. Then he went on a rampage through the building, his .44-magnum carbine blazing. Two police officers who rushed to the hotel were shot dead. Everyone he saw, as long as they weren't black, was gunned down. Then he made his way to the roof and used a small concrete building as a sniper post as darkness fell. It seemed clear that Essex was not prepared to surrender.

I jumped into a cab at New Orleans airport and asked to be taken to the Howard Johnson Hotel. The cabbie turned to me in amazement, obviously questioning my sanity. Did I know what was going on there? Didn't I read the papers, hear the news? Besides, he said, the police had blocked off all the streets and everyone who could get away from there was fleeing. That was OK, I said. I asked him to get me as close as he could. He dropped me off in a deserted street and pointed: 'It's down that way—but it's quite a walk. And good luck, pal.'

I started walking. I didn't see another soul. I could hear gunshots in the distance but couldn't place the exact location. Half an hour or so later, emerging from a side street I was standing right in front of the Howard Johnson. Looking back, I saw police barriers blocking off all the main roads about 300 feet (100 metres) away. The road that I was in had not been blocked off. I found out later that the police had not dared to get that close to the hotel because it was in the sniper's sights.

'Get down, get down!' a voice boomed through a loudspeaker. 'Get out of there!'

Police officers were waving, gesturing to me to get down low and to run. A wave of panic struck me and I saw that the nearest shelter was actually the hotel lobby. I dashed across an open area and virtually threw myself onto the lobby floor. There was no-one in sight—and I realized the sniper could emerge from a lift or come running down the stairs at any second. I had to hide.

What was most curious though—and I remember the feeling to this day—was that despite placing myself in a life-threatening situation I was acutely aware that I was a reporter on a job and I could get away with things that 'ordinary' people couldn't. That feeling did not make me bullet-proof but in a flash of absurd reasoning I imagined my friends in the *Daily Mail* editorial department urging me on because nothing bad could happen to a working journalist. Of course it was nonsense to think that, but that belief swept over me as I crawled along the lobby floor.

Then, in one of the most bizarre scenes I can remember, a grey-haired head began to rise up from behind the reception desk.

'Hello,' said the elderly lady, whose face had now appeared. 'Have you come to get me out?'

I ran behind the desk and crouched down with her. She told me she was one of the receptionists. I explained who I was.

'Are you crazy?' she said. 'Even the police can't get in without getting shot.'

'Believe me,' I told her. 'I didn't expect to be here. It's just that the hotel loomed up in front of me.'

The police had phoned her to stay hidden behind the desk. That was the day before and this was day two. But she had managed to sneak off to the toilet before returning to her hideout behind the desk where she had access by phone to the outside world. She had her knitting there too, she said, and held up a half-completed child's top. She'd mentioned a phone. Of course! So she got on with her knitting and sharpshooters in a police helicopter pumped round after round into the rooftop concrete bunker where Essex may have been still hiding. And I dictated a story to the *Mail*'s New York office from the heart of what was the biggest story in America. Scores of journalists trapped behind police lines refused to believe that I'd got into the hotel until they interviewed the receptionist later. She told them about a 'mad Englishman' who had hidden behind the desk with her.

Police eventually recovered Mark Essex's body from the roof. He'd been hit with more than 200 bullets fired from the helicopter. But his own toll was nine dead and 13 wounded.

◆

At the end of my posting I drove an Oldsmobile across the United States under a scheme that gave people the opportunity of seeing the country as they delivered vehicles to their owners. Fuel and accommodation were at the driver's expense and you were allowed eight days from east coast to west before handing the vehicle over. I drove mostly along Route 66, but zigzagged across large areas of the country, taking in, first, Intercourse, Pennsylvania (wow, had to go there—boring), then back up to Chicago, Oklahoma, the Grand Canyon, through Native American villages and Boot Hill.

The car's owner was a multimillionaire proprietor of a vast orange orchard on the outskirts of Tucson, Arizona. He was standing smiling at the entrance of his enormous house, silver hair just visible under the wide brims of his Stetson, as I drove up the long white-gravelled driveway and presented him with his shiny car. I'd had it thoroughly cleaned at a nearby wash place, where $200 was neatly lifted from the glove box, which was my own stupid fault for leaving it there.

'Yuv done a grand job, son,' he said after inspecting the vehicle inside and out. 'Just hold on there. I got something for yuh.'

Ah ha—a tip. Might help to make up for the deeds of the rotten thief in the car wash. Five minutes later he came back out and handed me an orange.

'Picked it fresh m'self,' he said. 'Enjoy it, son. And thanks again for bringing my little baby back to me.'

Then he retreated, closed the enormous double doors and left me standing on the porch staring down at the orange in my open palms.

CHAPTER FOUR

A Royal Assassination Attempt

I was having a chat to the Queen when she came out to Australia, where I now live, a few years ago. Protocol forbids me from relaying her exact words as we stood in a reception room at the Stamford Hotel in Brisbane but the conversation revolved around what I ventured to say was the declining standard of airline food.

'On domestic flights, we used to get a cooked lunch in economy and now it's a cardboard box with a biscuit inside, or a sandwich if you're lucky,' I told Her Majesty.

A little later I was flying back to Sydney, sitting beside an elderly couple, as our lunch was served. There you go: cardboard box and a biscuit.

'Is this all we get?' the man asked his wife.

'It certainly is,' I said, butting into their lives. 'I was only telling the Queen this morning how airline food is going downhill and you should have seen the look on her face.'

The old gent stared at me as he edged closer to his wife. I thought I heard him whisper the word 'nutcase' to her, but I could have been mistaken.

Although I'm not a royal correspondent—heaven forbid—I've covered numerous royal tours when the Queen and the Duke and their offspring and relatives have travelled to Australia and south-east Asia. The Duke has always been good for a story, mainly because of his comments. On Her Majesty's and His Royal Highness's 2006 trip to Singapore, I overheard him ask his ageing wife to remind him how often she had been to the island republic. She came about every

15 years, she said, to which he rather indelicately responded, 'Well, this will be the last time then, won't it?'

And I won't forget their visit to Cairns, in northern Queensland, when they watched an Aboriginal stage show. When the Duke went backstage later to meet the bare-chested male performers, who were adorned in traditional face paint and carrying various weapons of war, he asked one of them, 'Do you still throw spears at one another?' It caused outrage and tribal leaders demanded an apology.

◆

Yes, the royals. Always worth a good story—and I was thrown in at the deep end, if you like, after I'd returned to the London office of the *Mail* following my stint in New York. After the excitement of America, I was back in a familiar routine, sitting on the reporters' table, doing the occasional night shift and wishing 'something would happen'.

Then came a call to say there had been a shooting of some kind in the Mall. The tipster had no details—just that there had been a shooting and there were a lot of police milling around a big black car half-way along the Mall near Buckingham Palace. A shooting in London was hardly the stuff of a national newspaper by then—readers had moved on from the days of the East End gangs, including the notorious Krays—but the reference to a 'big black car' made the tip worth checking out. Perhaps someone 'important' was involved.

I grabbed a cab in Fleet Street and asked the driver to take me to the Mall.

'Can't go that way, mate,' he said. 'The police have closed it off. Something going on up there.'

I asked him to drive as close as he could, with memories of the sniper in New Orleans coming back. We headed towards Trafalgar Square. Police road-blocks—that was going to be my next problem. Leaving the taxi and hurrying to the start of the Mall, I saw a group of police on the far side of the road with one officer redirecting traffic. He didn't see me slip past in the shadows. Ahead, I could see the flashing blue lights of police cars. I was able to approach by keeping close to the trees lining the Mall—and got close enough to snatch pieces of conversation.

'They're back at the palace … bit shaken, but they're OK … yes, we got him … James and the others … don't know their condition … No, Anne's fine … And Mark …'

The palace? Anne? Mark? Surely not Princess Anne and her new husband Captain Mark Phillips? I took a closer look at the car, parked at an angle facing the kerb. It was a black limousine, just like one of the fleet the royals used. A white car was parked a short distance ahead of it on the same angle. I hung around long enough to pick up more information about the incident, but still didn't know if 'Anne' was Princess Anne. A detective approached and asked who I was. Was I a witness? Not as such, I told him, but took a gamble and asked him if Princess Anne was all right.

'She's fine,' he said and then told me to leave if I wasn't a material witness. It was time to reveal my identity. *Daily Mail* reporter. His face nearly exploded and I thought at first he was going to arrest me. I made good my escape.

I'd gleaned enough. The detective had confirmed that Princess Anne, then aged 23, had been in a royal limousine that had been fired at. As for the rest of the story, I had to try to make sense of it. It was close to the last edition deadline. I ran back down the Mall thinking, phone, phone, I need a phone. It was March 1974, long before the introduction of mobile phones. I remembered there were a bank of phones in the Trafalgar Square underground.

Reporters were always encouraged to have enough change to make a phone call in case they found themselves on an urgent story—and this incident proved the wisdom of that advice. I had to take a chance on the story. Someone had fired shots at the limousine carrying Princess Anne and Captain Phillips, her husband of four months. That meant it was an assassination attempt, so that was the story I dictated. It made the last edition of the paper. But I spent an uneasy night wondering if I'd gone too far. What if the detective who had said 'she's fine' had considered I was some kind of nosy passerby asking about Princess Anne, when the Anne in the car was simply an employee at the palace? What if the whole thing had been a police exercise, training for a real assassination attempt? Or a movie set?

There are times when journalists have all the parts of a story but the final version cannot be confirmed. And a deadline is looming. It's then a question of using logic and taking a chance that that logic is right. It's rather like doing maths with words: if a reporter has fact A and fact B, then logically it should equal fact C. In theory. But there's also a rule that is firmly implanted in every young reporter from day one: never, ever assume.

But there was another rule: never sit on a story long enough for the competition to catch up. On this occasion, standing breathlessly at a phone booth in an underground railway station, I'd broken the 'don't assume' rule and made an assessment of an incident without any official confirmation of what had really happened. Buckingham Palace was making no comment at the time. I imagined the worst: a big apology to the Palace and to the princess being printed in the next day's issue, complaints to the Press Council, lawyers and a very serious internal investigation at the *Mail* into how I could have possibly mistaken a film set, or something like that, for an assassination attempt.

But within 24 hours police had confirmed my hastily thrown-together story, and added details it had been impossible to establish on the night. As the princess and her husband were driving back from seeing a documentary film about horsemanship, a white car had overtaken their limousine, forcing it to the curb. A gunman had jumped out and sprayed the limousine with six shots in an attempt to kidnap Princess Anne. Her personal bodyguard, Inspector James Beaton—the 'James' I'd heard someone refer to—and the chauffeur had been the most seriously injured in an exchange of bullets. The gunman had been caught and a ransom note addressed to the Queen had been found in his car.

The gunman, Ian Ball, later admitted attempted murder and attempted kidnapping. He was sent to jail for an indefinite period under the Mental Health Act. The last word on the incident was left to the princess, describing how Ball tried to get her to leave the limousine.

'It was all so infuriating,' she said. 'I kept saying I didn't want to get out of the car—and I wasn't going to get out. I nearly lost my temper with him. But I knew if I did, I'd hit him and he'd shoot me.'

◆

It was the last big story I was to cover in London. A few months later, in June 1974, I arranged with the *Daily Mail* to take leave and use all the months of holidays I was owed. My plan was to visit Australia. The hard way. By road. I just wanted a challenge.

London was a fabulous city to work in. There were stories aplenty, whether it was covering a big case at the Old Bailey or hunting down Soviet spies who were still active in and around the city in the wind-down of the Cold War. When I wasn't working I'd be down at the riverside pub in Chiswick with my old mate from Torquay, Rossy, who had come to London to work on the *Hounslow Chronicle* and had taken out a lease on a damp ground-floor flat with me. The two of us would go on driving trips to Europe in my Volkswagen Beetle. But other holidays, before and after the posting to the US, were often spent with a reporter on the *Mail*, Dougie Thompson. Again in my Beetle, we'd head for Greece or Turkey, with half the holiday spent on the road and the other half wondering if we had enough money between us to buy fuel to get back to London.

On one mad occasion, during a drunken discussion in an Indian restaurant in King Street, Hammersmith, a group of us were arguing whether the curries in London were as good as the ones you could buy in the street in India. The argument ended with Dougie and I committing ourselves to drive to Pakistan (which was closer than India), buy a takeaway curry, drive non-stop with it back to London, have it heated up in our favourite curry restaurant and then compare it with a similar London-cooked dish. After four days of hard driving, somewhere in the south of Turkey we decided that Pakistan was too far. We didn't have any documentation to take the VW through Iran and Afghanistan and decided to sit on a beach instead. It was a wise decision because we also ran out of money. Once we budgeted for petrol, all we had to barter with for a bottle of ouzo was a pair of scissors. Our bodies suitably fuelled, we drove back to London and admitted our failure. But it was fun and such long adventures on the road were never a daunting challenge for me.

I even set off to Russia on a three-week break in Volkswagen's first attempt at a water-cooled car, a K-70, heading to Moscow, then north to St Petersburg/ Leningrad and then south to Georgia. I came to question the wisdom of my choice of vehicle when the water pump failed. The Russians couldn't fix it, so I had to drive until the engine reached a dangerously high temperature, wait for it to cool down, before travelling on for the next few miles. Eventually the Poles managed to make me a leather gasket from someone's boot, which got me to Berlin, where the vehicle was repaired.

No more long-distance travelling for me for a while, I thought, But within weeks the wanderlust spirit was revived. There was so much more of the world I wanted to see—which is why I chose Australia as the next adventure.

◆

With the water pipes thrown out of the back of the Ford Transit plumber's van I'd bought for £400, I set out across the continent and central Asia. The van was blue and the number plate was BLU so I affectionately called it … Blue. Those were the grand days when relatively safe travel was possible through Iran, Afghanistan and Pakistan and convoys of 'van people' would set out from Europe, following the hippie trail to Nepal. I'd been warned that there were thieves to be found along every mile through central Asia and that wheels were a prime target. So I fitted locking wheel nuts on the van's wheels—it turned out to be a sound investment. What I hadn't planned for was the theft in Turkey of the windscreen wipers and the wing mirrors. Driving along wet muddy roads behind another vehicle without wipers would have been perilous. And as the van was a right-hand drive and traffic through Asia travelled on the right side of the road, a left-hand mirror was vital. Fortunately I was able to find replacements—no less than four times on the journey.

In Isfahan, in the south of Iran, my travels across Asia—and through life—could have come to a violent end. I'd driven into the grounds of a hotel, a popular and safe rest-stop for van people, and was sitting in the back of Blue eating a breakfast of fruit, which had been washed in a germ-cleansing solution of potassium permanganate—I'd seen too many white-faced dysentery-stricken travellers to ignore this ritual—when a stranger approached.

'I couldn't help noticing that your springs are very dry,' he said, with a faint accent I couldn't place. 'If you don't mind me saying, you should get them greased.' He asked which way I was going and when I said east he made a show of looking under the van at the springs and said, 'If you don't grease them, you'll break them. There are some bad roads.'

We struck up a conversation and then the stranger, who had dark curly hair and looked Asian, invited me to join him for tea in the small guest house he was staying in. Thinking nothing of it, I made my way into a dingy whitewashed building, where my new-found 'friend' had a room at the back. There was a low single bed, a small table with a washbasin on it, a sink, another table and two chairs. On the floor was a portable stove, which the man, who introduced himself as Charles, used to boil water for tea. He asked me if I smoked, pulling out a packet of weed. No thanks.

We chatted for an hour or so about our travels. I told him about my plans and he told me about his—which were to continuing travelling back and forth along the 'hippie highway'. He told me he knew the roads through Asia well and had a great system of buying and selling vans as travellers up- or down-graded their vehicles. Then he asked if I was hungry as he had prepared some food for himself, which was in the resthouse kitchen. I declined.

Charles hung around the hotel grounds for a couple of days, inviting me for tea and a meal, but by now I was feeling as though he was getting too close and backed off.

I learned later that the man who had introduced himself as Charles was Hatchand Bhaonani Gurumukh Charles Sobhraj, aged 30, and a killer on the prowl. He was to end up in jails in India, Thailand and Nepal with at least 12 murders linked to his name. Looking at his photo later and comparing his modus operandi with the approach he had made to me left no doubt about the identity of my hippie highway 'friend'. I should have been suspicious right away about his story of buying and selling vehicles, because a *carnet de passage*—basically an import-export document—made it impossible for travellers to sell their vans in any country apart from Nepal.

Sobhraj's prey were mostly travellers on the hippie trail. He'd invite them for tea, a meal and a smoke, drug them, kill them, burn their bodies, steal their passports and their identities and continue on, zigzagging back and forth through central Asia, changing his appearance to fit the passport photos and using money and the vans he stole from his victims to move on to his next port of call. He lurked in hotel grounds and preyed on the unsuspecting in the incense aroma atmosphere of tea houses in Kabul's famous hippie Mecca, Chicken Street.

Sobhraj's exact movements during late 1974 and 1975 when I was on the road are unclear. But investigators have established he was travelling through Asia in the months spanning those years, and they are also certain that the 12 deaths linked to his name are not the true total—they believe there are many more. Sobhraj is currently serving life behind bars in Nepal for the 1975 murder of Connie Jo Bronzich, an American backpacker who was slashed to death and her body burned.

I sold Blue in Nepal for the same price I'd paid for it—£400—in London. It was bought by a village who intended turning it into a mini-bus. Thirty-four years later, I returned to Kathmandu to write about the visit of actress Joanna Lumley who had been invited there as a 'goddess' so she could be thanked for working tirelessly for poverty-stricken Gurkhas who had fought for the British.

As I travelled around Kathmandu with Miss Lumley—a charming lady—I kept my eyes peeled for a Ford Transit and thought what a wonderful reunion it would be if I could find my faithful old van. But it was not to be. One day, perhaps.

CHAPTER 5

Then They Kissed. *Click* Went My Camera

I travelled on by plane to Bangkok, train to Singapore and then ship to Perth in Western Australia. My first impressions were that Perth with its rising skyscrapers and green traffic signs was more like a US city than anything British, despite many UK migrants making their home there. The family cars—Fords and Holdens mostly—added to the impression, for they were bigger than most of the vehicles you would find in Britain.

I arrived in Melbourne in early January 1975 and found myself a temporary flat until I was ready to return to London. I called Brian Freemantle on the *Mail*'s Foreign Desk to say if there was anything he wanted me to do while I was in Melbourne to let me know.

'Anything I want you to do! Bloody hell, if only you'd arrived a couple of weeks ago. I've had to send a reporter out from London because of Stonehouse. You didn't call in. Why didn't you call in?'

I'd committed the fatal mistake of not keeping in touch with the office, but then again, I weakly tried to assure myself later, I was on extended leave.

'What … who …?'

It was a huge story and I wasn't in the right place at the right time. John Stonehouse, a British cabinet minister, was lingering in a Melbourne jail after being arrested for entering Australia illegally. Those were the basic facts. The story behind his arrest was dramatic in the extreme, the stuff of novels: Stonehouse had tried the old 'fake death' trick.

A BBC comedy series about a man called Reggie Perrin, who fakes his death in Spain, was a big hit in the 1970s. Make-believe or real, mysteries surrounding the missing are always intriguing.

John Stonehouse had been postmaster-general in Harold Wilson's government, an arrogant man who considered himself to be God's gift to women. He had ambitions to become prime minister and while he worked away at his political career he also worked away at young women in the Labour Party, including his secretary, Sheila Buckley. There was talk that he had even set her up in his Westminster flat while his wife, Barbara, unaware of the affair, continued to play the devoted cabinet minister's wife.

Determined to make himself a million pounds within seven years, he set up a number of businesses and also established an investment bank for Bangladesh citizens. But things began to go wrong and the more he borrowed to stay afloat, the deeper he sank into a financial mire. He began raiding his companies and even took money from the Bangladesh Children's Fund. Inspired by Frederick Forsyth's *The Day of the Jackal*, he applied for two false passports in the names of dead men as part of an audacious plan to fake his death and set up a new life with Miss Buckley on the far side of the world, in New Zealand. He didn't care who he hurt or used as he set about planning his future.

Eventually he was ready to set himself up with two new identities—as Joseph Markham and Donald Mildoon. And, having asset-stripped his companies, he had no less than £2 million in cash. He chose Miami Beach as the place he would 'die'. After one unsuccessful attempt, he was ready to go through with the plot again. This time he carried the plan through, leaving two piles of clothing in different parts of the beach. He made a show of stripping off down to his swimming trunks in front of a group of people, then swam along the beach to come ashore near the second set of clothes. Then, after changing his hairstyle and appearance to fit that with the photo in his fake passport, he flew out of the US to South America.

As expected, the alarm was raised about his abandoned clothes. Stonehouse's wife and children were told that he was believed drowned. Miami police admitted they were puzzled. Invariably, the body of anyone who drowned would be washed ashore within a couple of days. Perhaps, they suggested, he had been robbed and murdered by the Mafia. The FBI were called in and agents even ripped up the floor of a carpark looking for his body. Then came suggestions that he must have been torn to pieces by sharks. As wild rumours flew about on both sides of the

Atlantic, Stonehouse's political colleagues suggested that he had been spying for the Russians, had been spirited out of Britain and given a new identity in the Soviet Union, like other British spies.

But Stonehouse was far away on a stop-over in Hawaii, wearing his new appearance with spectacles and his hair parted in the middle. Eventually he flew on to Australia, landing in Melbourne. Using one of his false names, he began pouring cash into Melbourne banks. But the best-laid plans can fall apart because of an oversight, a silly mistake—or sheer bad luck, as was the case of the Canoe Man and that photograph in Panama. For Stonehouse, it was just bad luck and a remarkable coincidence.

When he began depositing his stolen funds, Melbourne banks were on a fraud alert which had nothing to do with him. But he was snared in the net. Using one of his two fake identities, he went into the ANZ bank and withdrew a large sum of money he had on deposit there. Then he went up the road and deposited it at the Bank of New Zealand using the other identity. The police were alerted and Stonehouse was placed under observation. But he still managed to leave the country temporarily, travelling around the world. In Denmark, he met up with Sheila Buckley, who had agreed to remain in London until the shock of his 'death' had passed and she could quietly leave her job and join him in New Zealand.

On his return to Australia, police surveillance cameras were trained on him, not because they suspected he was Stonehouse but for an equally dramatic reason: they believed the tall Englishman with a double identity was runaway peer Lord Lucan, who was wanted for questioning after his children's nanny was clubbed to death in the darkness of his London home. She had been killed on 7 November 1974, just a few weeks before Stonehouse was put under observation.

Stonehouse was arrested on suspected passport fraud, fingerprinted and his photo and prints were sent to Scotland Yard. The Yard was stunned. Melbourne police had arrested the 'dead' MP John Stonehouse! He played his 'excuse card', telling detectives that he had gone through an elaborate process to hide his identity because he was being blackmailed in the UK and his life was in danger.

Barbara Stonehouse, overjoyed that her husband was alive, flew to Australia, where he had been granted bail on a charge of entering the country illegally under a false passport. British police, who had begun digging into his financial affairs, wanted him sent back to the UK, but Stonehouse was determined to vigorously fight any attempts by Scotland Yard to have him extradited.

Stonehouse and his wife bunkered down at a secret address while the British journalists who had flown out to Australia to cover the sensational story returned to the UK.

That was about the time I arrived in Australia, unhappy at learning I had missed all the fun by just a few weeks. But there was much more to come. The *Daily Mail* told me to stay where I was and continue working on the ongoing Stonehouse saga until, well, until it reached some conclusion.

The first task was to find out where Stonehouse and his wife were staying—but the police weren't saying anything about that. I assumed, however, that because he was on bail he would have to report to the police on a regular basis. Just where and when was the question. If he had been given permission to report to the police station nearest to his mystery address, it would have been virtually impossible to find him. But I guessed that Melbourne's main police station would be his check-in point.

From 7am until dusk I hung around the entrance, as discreetly as possible, watching for the suave Englishman. Long surveillance for a single person is never easy. There are toilet breaks—and the nearest one was in the court building across the street—and a need to grab a sandwich or a cup of coffee every so often. Even if this was the right police station, I could not be sure I was watching the entrance he would use. And would he be arriving by cab, on foot, or in a rental car driven by his wife? It meant watching every vehicle that arrived, and carefully checking everyone who entered the police station in case Stonehouse had made himself look different or was wearing a hat or dressing in a jacket with a collar turned up. And to add to the identification problems, I had never seen Stonehouse in the flesh, only photographs.

And then one day there he was. Casually dressed, he was unmistakable as he strolled along the street at ten o'clock in the morning, walking from a nearby police carpark. He was in the police station long enough to sign a 'check in' register and then he headed back to the carpark. My own vehicle was some distance away so I couldn't follow him. But I saw he was driving an old white Valiant with a yellow number plate, not the white of Victorian plates, indicating it had been registered in the neighbouring state of New South Wales. Was Stonehouse living over the state border?

The second time around I was ready. I parked close to the carpark the following day at the same time and, sure enough, there was that Valiant. It took three 'follows'—losing him on the first two attempts—before I found out where he was living. Following people for the sake of a story might be frowned upon but I felt no guilt about keeping tabs on Stonehouse. He had stolen the identities of two of his constituents, duping their widows, stolen from investors and robbed a children's charity. He had hurt a lot of people and if there were more lies to be uncovered, I wanted to expose them.

He was living in a townhouse at the end of a narrow driveway that allowed access to other properties in the row. But it was impossible for me to park there without blocking the drive. There was only one option—and that was to stake out the entrance to the driveway from the main road. It was not an easy task because if he came out and drove in the direction opposite to the way I was facing I would lose him. It took several weeks before I found out that the blonde woman I had seen in the car with him was his wife. They drove to the local shops and did nothing out of the ordinary.

One day I saw a dark-haired woman in the passenger seat. She definitely wasn't Barbara Stonehouse. I managed to get a fuzzy picture of her as they passed my parked car and sent it to the *Daily Mail*, asking if they knew who she was. What I had suspected was confirmed: it was Stonehouse's secretary, Sheila Buckley, who had 'replaced' Barbara as his companion. Mrs Stonehouse had returned to the UK, perhaps learning of his relationship with Miss Buckley.

Stonehouse appeared in court from time to time, for by now the British authorities had begun extradition proceedings. One of his tactics was to try to get the Australian media onside. He called press conferences to speak of his love of Australian people and tell of the treacherous British government which had built up a false case against him. He refused to have any British newspaper representatives present, having identified me, along with a couple of others, as UK journalists.

'Any relationship between me and Miss Buckley is purely the imagination of the British press,' he declared angrily one day. There was, he insisted, no plan to steal money and set up a new life with Sheila on the far side of the world. It was outrageous and libellous to suggest it.

I continued to watch the townhouse and the police station, where Stonehouse was still required to check in each day, wondering what I could expect to gain by it. Now and again I changed rental cars in the hope of throwing off suspicion that I was following him around. He went to extraordinary lengths to ensure he did not have a tail, dashing through traffic lights just as they turned red, doing two or three complete circuits of a roundabout, stopping around a blind corner. He lost me several times with these tactics, so changing my car occasionally was essential.

By chance, I woke early one morning and decided to go to the police station earlier than usual. I parked near the police station at eight o'clock, at least an hour earlier than Stonehouse had ever checked in, and was surprised to see him arrive, hurrying up the steps. When he drove out of the carpark I saw that he had a passenger—Sheila Buckley, the woman he insisted was just his secretary who was helping him with his business affairs and was staying with him to save money.

I managed to stay with him as he headed away from Melbourne. This was new. He was going north-east, onto the Hume Highway which leads to Sydney, 540 miles (870 kilometres) away. I couldn't believe my good fortune in waking early.

I had to drop right back, keeping three or four cars, and sometimes more, between us. Then he turned onto a minor road—and so began five hours of tense driving. For me. With just my Ford and his Valiant on long stretches of road, at times I had to wait until he disappeared around a distant corner or brow of a hill before I could accelerate and get him into my sights again. Even then, I had to edge around each bend, in case he had parked.

In the movies no-one seems to run out of petrol when following another vehicle. But my petrol gauge was getting desperately low. Eventually, from a distance, I saw him pull into a filling station, the first one I'd seen for miles. But I couldn't follow him in. I had to wait until he emerged and continued on his way before I could speed up to the petrol station, beg the attendant to fill the tank urgently because of an 'emergency', then speed on after the Valiant.

I was convinced he hadn't picked my car, but back on the road I lost him. I sped along for 30 miles (50 kilometres) or so, but there was no sign of him. I assumed he'd turned off—but which side road had he taken? I consulted a map and saw that the only feature in the area was Mount Buffalo, in winter a ski resort, but, as this was late summer, a bushwalker's paradise.

With no other option, I turned back and joined the Mount Buffalo road, winding up through the tree-lined mountain route. I was feeling glum at having put in so much work and then losing the two of them. At the top was a hotel, known as the Mount Buffalo Chalet, a historic building which opened in 1910 and which offered spectacular views across the Victorian Alps and the surrounding valleys. And there in the carpark was a white Valiant with the yellow New South Wales number plate! Had John Stonehouse and Sheila Buckley gone to the chalet for tea or to stay for a night or two? I parked as far from their vehicle as possible and tentatively stepped out into the carpark. If he saw me … well, I didn't care to imagine.

But I need not have worried.

The MP and Miss Buckley were standing at Bent's Lookout, staring out across the fabulous landscape. With a mid-range lens on my camera, I moved carefully to a large rock that was within a few yards of the couple. He put his arm around her. She put hers around his waist.

Then they kissed. Passionately. Click, click went my camera.

The following day the *Daily Mail* ran the picture of the couple kissing on the mountain-top as a centre-page spread. The heading across the top of the photo was straight from Stonehouse's lips: 'Any relationship between me and Miss Buckley is purely the imagination of the British press.'

Of course, it totally destroyed his claims that there was no romance and only served as evidence that they planned to live together on the far side of the world.

Stonehouse lost his fight for extradition.

The *Daily Mail* asked me to get on the plane with him when he and Sheila Buckley were extradited back to Britain. He sat, handcuffed, beside Superintendent Ken Etheridge of Scotland Yard who had flown out to Melbourne to fetch him. Miss Buckley sat behind them with a policewoman. A photo of them on the plane would be sensational—and the sooner, the better.

I worked out a plan with a Melbourne photographer. The chances of it working were pretty low, but it was worth a try. I was going to take the picture as soon as I boarded and then beg to be allowed off the plane for a few seconds so I could pass the film to one of the ground staff—and ask for it to be given to the photographer, who would be waiting on the other side of the immigration area.

I was able to take one shot of the disgraced couple before Superintendent Etheridge raised his hand. Enough. I rewound the film, put it in a small canister and asked the chief purser if I could just slip off the plane for a second. Certainly not. But he asked me to give him the film.

Later on the flight he said he had given the canister to one of the ground crew. Of course, it wouldn't happen these days of tight security. But did the film get to the photographer? And did he send the picture to the *Mail*? I found out when the plane touched down in London. There it was on the *Mail*'s front page. But the rotter had also sent it to the opposition *Daily Mirror*. Sometimes that was just the way things went.

CHAPTER 6

Revolution in Paradise

'The workings of a great newspaper,' said Lord Copper, feeling at last thoroughly Rotarian, 'are of a complexity which the public seldom appreciates. The citizen little realizes the vast machinery put into motion for him in exchange for his morning penny … We shall have our naval, military, and air experts, our squad of photographers, our colour reporters, covering the war from every angle and on every front.'

Scoop by Evelyn Waugh (1938)

I couldn't settle in London once Stonehouse had been delivered into the hands of the British justice system, which eventually saw him being jailed for seven years for fraud. I found myself sitting at the same reporter's table, the same chair, looking across to the same News Desk crew. When I went to the pub across the road, the Harrow, and climbed the stairs to the upstairs bar, there were the same subs and News Desk staff standing in the same positions, the same pints at their elbow.

I found myself repeating 'been there, done that' as stories began to take on a similarity. The characters changed and obviously the circumstances were different, but I could not shake off the feeling that I'd covered the same assignments before. In fact, I was beginning to think it was all getting a bit too easy. Complacency was creeping in—and that was dangerous. That was when mistakes were made.

I felt I had reached a plateau. I was bored and restless. Perhaps it was my imagination but I believed several of my colleagues were experiencing the same moods—it was a case of 'let's bash this story out and go for a beer'.

You could walk into any pub in and around Fleet Street in the mid-1970s—the Harrow, the White Swan (also known as the 'Mucky Duck'), the King and Keys, the Old Bell, the Punch Tavern—and it would be thick with journalists, all on call should a story break, but I couldn't help the feeling that the job was playing second fiddle to booze and fags.

Rupert Murdoch had won control of the *News of the World* group in 1969 and there were rumours that he was not going to stop there. There was talk of a change in the air. But it would not be until 1986 that he moved his newspaper empire to the London Docklands, resulting in a clash with the print unions: instead of using hot metal for his printing processes, his pages were reproduced electronically, resulting in the old school printers losing their jobs. But in the mid-1970s that revolution was still a long way off. None of us foresaw the biggest change of all that was to come three decades later when the internet killed jobs—and in many cases imaginations—put newspapers online and changed the whole mechanics of news gathering.

I had loved my time in Australia during the 'Stonehouse era'. I'd made a number of journalist friends in Melbourne. While some maintained part-time relationships with London newspapers as stringers, they all had steady jobs and could only fit in requests from Fleet Street if they weren't caught up with local commitments. On the other hand, I would be free to work around the clock for the *Daily Mail*.

So I reached an agreement with David English—personally. When I explained that foreign fields were calling, he said he wished I would consider staying on (perhaps he was just being kind), but eventually gave me his blessing to head off to the other side of the world. I would be paid a retainer to work only for the *Mail*. It was a gamble, the success of which depended not so much on my enthusiasm for the new venture but on 'what happened'. No stories, no pay. The retainer was generous but it would have to be enhanced by story payments.

◆

I flew back to Australia in early 1977 and began a new life that would take me to some of the most astonishing parts of the planet, filled with wonder, danger and madness.

Curiously, London followed me. The Queen and the Duke of Edinburgh visited Australia in March that year and many of the reporters and photographers I knew in London flew out as part of what was known as the 'royal rat pack'. The *Mail* asked me to pick up the royal tour and cover it—and in doing so saved themselves the cost of flying a reporter across the world.

In my new position as the *Mail*'s Australian and south-east Asian correspondent (I'd managed to persuade Sir David to enlarge my 'patch' beyond the Australian continent), I read all the local papers, watched every TV news bulletin and kept my ear to the radio, watching and listening for breaking news stories. I'd write them up on a 100-year-old portable Corona typewriter that I'd picked up for fun in an antique shop for $80, then dictate the story to a copy typist—also known as a telephone reporter—in the London office. Compared with today's email speed, it was a slow process: dictating a feature could take an hour or more. Thankfully, it was no problem to make a reverse-charge call or quickly call the switchboard and ask to be called back.

I found myself a bachelor pad in Port Melbourne, what was then a working-class suburb of the Victorian capital and is now a trendy spot with luxury apartments fronting Port Phillip Bay. The real estate agent was in a shop directly below the one-room flat. On several occasions I just phoned down to say the rent was on its way—and one of the staff would run out onto the footpath to collect the envelope containing that week's payment that I tossed down from my window.

In early 1980 reports began emerging that a tribal chief had taken over an island in the north of the New Hebrides, a group of Melanesian islands in the western Pacific now known as Vanuatu, as the central government, in Port Vila, was preparing for independence. The sketchy reports would hardly have raised a flicker of interest on British newspaper news desks had it not been for the fact that the New Hebrides were administered by Britain and France in what was known as a 'condominium'—but, as I was to soon find out, 'pandemonium' would have been a better description. What followed was to be life-changing experience for me.

The *Daily Mail* put me on standby to fly to the northern island of Espiritu Santo where the rebel chief, Jimmy Stevens, was standing defiantly against the might of the two European powers and declaring that Santo would not be part of the new national structure when independence came the following August. There were rumours that a shadowy American figure, who wanted to set up a fantastic resort for rich tourists on Santo, was behind Jimmy's rebellion. Jimmy might have thought that this, at last, was the time when anyone who followed the local 'cargo cult' dating from World War II—which believed that American soldiers would return to the Pacific bearing gifts—would see their dreams turn to reality.

Soon after arriving at the tiny airport in Port Vila, I went to the museum to find out something about this tiny Pacific nation that had caught the eye of media organizations around the world—although at that stage it seemed I was the only journalist who had actually flown in to find out what was going on. The museum curator, Kirk Huffman, a British anthropologist, spent hours giving me what he said was only a glimpse of the Y-shaped island chain's incredible history.

Santo, lying some 300 miles (480 kilometres) to the north of Port Vila, had been discovered by the eccentric Portuguese navigator, Pedro Fernández de Quirós, who had been commissioned by the king of Spain to sail to the Solomon Islands. On 21 December 1605, de Quirós set out from Peru with three ships carrying six Franciscan priests, four monks, and 300 soldiers and sailors. They completely missed the Solomons but several weeks later they sighted a land so great that it could not possibly be an island. Rowing ashore, as a group of islanders peered out from the palm trees, de Quirós proudly announced that he had discovered a great southern continent. He named it La Tierra Austral del Espiritu Santo, or 'the Southern Land of the Holy Ghost'. He was not standing on the Australian continent but a beach beside what is now known as Big Bay on Espirtu Santo.

Sickness from eating poisonous fish, malaria and general boredom prompted the 'discoverers' to head home to Spain. Next came the explorers, including Captain Cook who named all the islands around Santo as the New Hebrides because they reminded him of Scotland, and traders from around the world. Ignorant of the fact that Captain Cook had claimed the New Hebrides island chain for Britain, a fleet of vessels with French crews arrived in 1848 and raised the tricolor. Scores of French migrants arrived and a fierce diplomatic row broke out between London and Paris. In the end they decided the two nations would run the place side by side.

Consequently, some people spoke French, others English. The original inhabitants adopted Bislama, a common pidgin English that allowed people with 115 traditional languages to converse with one another. There was also a picture language that seemed to combine a bit of English and pidgin, resulting in a brassiere being described as 'basket blong titty'. I learned that if you listened carefully, or looked at the written words long enough, you could work it out. A toothbrush was 'broom blong tut' (brush belonging to tooth), a helicopter was 'Mixmaster blong Jesus Christ'. My favourite was the description of a piano, for which there were two versions. 'One big fella bokis, ee got tut blong him way black, way white, you killum now him sing sing out': a big box with black-and-white teeth and when you hit him it sings. The other was even more descriptive and probably invented by an islander who had no idea what was meant by a musical instrument and found it easier to describe a punch up between a white man and black man: 'Boxis where men 'e fight 'im white more black feller something along face blong 'im, belly blong 'im, 'm e talktalk too much 'e tell 'im out good feller talk.'

The modern-day condominium, Kirk Huffman explained, had two police forces and two jails. Foreign visitors who ran foul of the law could elect to be tried either by the French or British system. Most preferred the French because the gendarmes served wine with meals. The Union Jack flew on one hill, the tricolor on another. The official French Resident lived on a hill above Port Vila, the British High Commissioner lived on an island in the harbour. They kept a wary eye on one another as the indigenous government prepared for independence in August 1980.

As we drank tea I pulled out a telex I'd received from London and asked Kirk if he knew anything about its contents. He laughed at the terminology. 'And you think pidjin English is strange—this is just as crazy. Is this how journalists talk to one another?' The telex from the *Mail*'s Foreign Desk read: CANST CONFIRM URGENTEST PRINCE PHILIP LAUDED AS GOD BY JUNGLE TRIBE STOP

'Oh yes, it's true,' said Kirk. 'The Duke of Edinburgh came here years ago with the Queen and when they saw him in his white uniform standing on the deck of the royal yacht, they thought he was the Messiah returned. He is still worshipped by the tribes on Tanna,' an island lying to the south.

I made a point to check it out, but the priority, the *Mail* told me, was to get an interview with Jimmy Stevens, who they saw as an evil Tonton Macoute figure, the equal of the Haitian paramilitary force of the 1960s who terrorized government opponents.

I flew to Luganville, the Santo capital. The plane bounced along the crude gravel runway between oil drums marking its edges. A battered red Toyota taxi was waiting at the shed that served as a terminal. I've always wanted to say to a taxi driver, 'Take me to the war'—but it didn't apply here because there was no war, just a feeling I had that something bad was in the air.

That instinct grew as we drove through the wide main street, built by American forces during the Pacific war against the Japanese. The place was deserted. Shop fronts were boarded up. There wasn't a soul in sight. Then I saw the cars. Many had their windows smashed, the bodywork dented. I asked the driver what had happened.

'Jimmy's men,' he replied. 'Smashem up good.'

'That's not good,' I said. I hadn't told him yet where I wanted to go because I needed to get the feel of the town, talk to a few people. That obviously wasn't on, so I asked the driver to take me to Jimmy Stevens. At first he refused but eventually, doubling his fare, he set off along narrow roads and jungle tracks to Jimmy's headquarters. The driver's English proved to be good and he told how Jimmy's men had sent his Big Bad Boys into town to terrorize everyone who had not thrown their support behind him in his quest to make Santo independent. Hundreds of people had fled into the jungle or had taken small boats to other islands. Santo's force of 30 policemen were heavily outnumbered and gave up the fight. The government's minister for natural resources found his plane blockaded by truncheon-wielding vigilantes and he had to make his escape by ship.

An English-style farm gate marked the end of the one-hour taxi ride. I climbed from the cab and walked towards five thick-set men wielding clubs and machetes.

'Morning,' I called cheerfully. 'Jimmy at home?'

I explained who I was. They shook their heads. I asked them if they would take a note to Jimmy.

'Right,' said one of the men. Or it might have been 'write', which I proceeded to do anyway, requesting a little of Jimmy's time. Half an hour later I was walking through a courtyard towards a small house, dozens of bare-breasted women looking up from their washing and cooking chores to cast me shy smiles. In the semi-darkness of the house a bearded, grandfatherly figure was sitting at a bank of radio equipment speaking pidgin into a microphone. I understood 'over and out', before he turned to me and shook my hand.

What followed was a two-hour interview in which Jimmy Stevens explained how he was determined to give the people of Santo their independence, separate to the independence that would be coming to the New Hebrides nine months later. Jimmy was charismatic, there was a gleam in his eyes and he left me in no doubt he would not be backing down. Yes, it was true that he was 'affiliated' to a group of Americans who wanted to build a resort there, but their plans and his were not linked. I found that hard to believe. In any case I had my story—the first interview with the rebel leader. Before I left I asked if I could take a picture of him with his wife.

'Which one?' he asked.

Then he swept his arm around the village square in an arc that took in all the women who were washing and cooking.

'These are all your wives?' I asked incredulously.

'Oh no,' he said, grinning.

'Phew, that's a relief, for a moment I thought that …'

'The others are in the gardens picking vegetables.'

Jimmy had 26 wives. I gathered up as many as I could for the photo, along with some of his henchmen and their weapons. The picture was used well in the *Daily Mail*, which then syndicated it around the world.

Observers believed that Jimmy's stand-off with the central government was little more than a storm in a coconut shell and would soon blow over. But diplomatic relations between Britain and France disintegrated. Britain had citizens on Santo and so did the French, who outnumbered them. Fearing for the safety of the Brits, London asked the New Hebridean government to sort out the problem on their northern island and so did the French. But with a small force of military police who were reluctant to go in heavy-handed against their own people, nothing was done—and Jimmy Stevens' grip tightened.

At 7.15AM on 28 May 1980, Jimmy announced over his short-wave radio that Espiritu Santo had seceded from the New Hebrides and had formed the Vemerana Federation, of which he was prime minister. To emphasize his control, his men, armed with bows and arrows, spears and old rifles left over from World War II, paraded through the streets of Luganville, many of them wearing stolen police hats. What had started out as a relatively simple story for me was now turning into civil war, with the French preparing an invasion of sorts.

Paris put 55 combat police from the Garde Mobile, stationed in the neighbouring Pacific nation of Noumea, on stand-by to fly to the New Hebrides to sort out the mess on Santo. 'Hold it right there,' said Britain. 'We have a say in all this.' But the French turned a deaf ear and the troops landed in Port Vila. 'Go no further,' said the Brits again, 'we have citizens in Santo and we don't want them harmed. We'll send our own troops up there and they'll sort out it.' 'Non!' responded the

French and they were still saying it when 120 men from the 42 Royal Marine Commando arrived. A diplomatic stalemate ensued. The French troops were ordered to remain in Port Vila and soon the message came from London to the Brits: stay put.

Meanwhile, back in Australia after the Jimmy Stevens interview, I received my own phone call from London: 'Get back out there.'

So along with French, Australian, British and American journalists who had been pulled away from their otherwise routine jobs, I found myself fighting for a vacant hotel room in Vila as we all prepared to fly to Santo on the first available flight—a forlorn hope, considering that Jimmy's men had taken over the airport and had placed oil drums along the runway to prevent any 'outsiders' from landing. There was only one way to get to the island and that was by sea. Even then space on any vessel heading to Santo was restricted because many people from the island who were working in Vila were desperate to get back there to be with their terrified families. But I found a couple of feet of space on the good ship *Kombito*, a dodgy-looking 35-foot (11-metre) passenger vessel that plied the islands. The cabin had been taken over by 32 tribal chiefs, one of whom had tethered a black boar to the deck to kill and eat with his family later. I had to share the deck with the boar and dozens of men, women and children.

As we headed north, the weather turned foul. Rain lashed the deck, waves splashed over the bow. Those of us on the deck were soaked.

'What the bloody hell am I doing in this godforsaken place?' cried a desperate voice, in a very posh English accent. 'I live in Hollywood. I interview stars.'

The distressed passenger was Ross Benson, the West Coast show business correspondent for London's *Daily Express*, who, years later, would become a senior feature writer on the *Daily Mail* until his untimely death in 2005 at the age of 56. The *Express* had worked out that Benson and the photographer Derek Hudson were closer than anyone on the newspaper to the New Hebrides and so, like the gardening correspondent in Evelyn Waugh's *Scoop*, he'd been sent to cover a war well beyond his brief. Although, as it turned out, perhaps the ensuing events fell well into the entertainment category.

Suddenly there was another cry—or rather a chorus—of despair on board the *Kombito*. The boar had broken free! Now it was jumping and stumbling over screaming women and heading straight towards Ross. He and Hudson scrambled to their feet and, in a seemingly choreographed movement, each grabbed the side of the wheelhouse and hauled themselves onto the roof. And there they remained, in the lashing rain until our first port of call, refusing to come down even though the boar had been restrained once more.

'Listen old boy,' said Ross as we made our way to a hut to spend the night, 'do you not question what we're all doing here? I mean, I was sent to this … this … wherever we are, to cover a war, but I can't even find the bloody thing. Where, I ask you, is the war?'

I assured him it was on its way but in the meantime we had to be patient.

Luganville was like a ghost town, Jimmy was 'not available' and no Brits could be found. So two days later Ross and Derek got back onto another ship and sailed back to Vila. The other journalists, it transpired, were still awaiting a passage to Santo, so that left me on my own there once again.

I wondered if Jimmy might remember me from our earlier meeting and gave a note to a taxi driver, asking him to drive around everywhere that he could think of and hand it to Jimmy if he could find him. Meanwhile, with the entire staff missing from the small Hotel Santo, I checked myself in, found a key and showed myself to my room. Dinner that night was in a small restaurant next to the hotel, run by an extraordinary French woman called Lulu, who had decided to defy the bad boys beating up the town and serve whoever happened to be brave enough to step out for the evening. So I was the only diner. Even so Lulu decided to entertain me, her huge breasts heaving, her thickly painted lips pouting as she stood on a table and sang a repertoire of what I presumed to be popular French songs—I didn't know, or certainly didn't recognize, any of them. When, much later, I watched the British television comedy 'Allo 'Allo, Rene Artois' wife tuneless singing to German officers reminded me of Lulu, bless her soul.

The following morning I was driven to a house on the outskirts of town where Jimmy's Na Griamel Party had set up temporary headquarters. Yes, he remembered me and no, he wasn't going to surrender to British, French or any other foreign troops the government might send to put down his rebellion.

'I'm the prime minister of Santo and that's how it's going to be,' he insisted. 'Tell Britain and France to send in their boys. I won't be backing down.'

Now that was a good exclusive story. But I had a problem. I had heard that a ship full of newly arrived journalists was on its way to Santo and they, no doubt, would track down Jimmy and hear his same defiant words. I had to stay ahead. However, I could not get my story out from Santo because all the phone lines had been cut. I had to get back to Vila before the opposition arrived. But no ship was available. I learned that Jimmy had given permission for a light plane to take off carrying a couple of injured people to Vila and tried desperately to get a seat. 'Sorry,' the English pilot told me when I tracked him down at the hospital a couple of hours before he was due to take off, 'no room'.

I had to do some quick thinking if I was to get my story out. The pilot said he would be willing to fly back to Vila with my despatch. But I still needed someone I could trust in Vila who would make a reverse-charge call to London and dictate the story to a copy-taker. I could not risk asking another journalist to do it— experience had taught me that was how exclusives became non-exclusives.

I racked my brains. Who did I know in Vila who was trustworthy and smart enough to follow 'how to file a story' instructions? A vision of a beautiful dark-haired woman with a big smile and a quick wit came to me. Filling in as a waitress at Ma Barker's restaurant, where journalists and British and French army officers mingled in the evenings, she was a magnet for all eyes. I remembered 'Isobelle', the daughter of an English Royal Navy officer and a New Hebridean mother, regaling us, as she swirled around the tables, with stories of growing up on a coconut plantation her retired father had run on the island of Malekula.

I passed my handwritten story to the pilot, along with instructions for Isobelle and implored him to find her as soon as he landed in Vila. I watched him take off on a wing while I said a prayer. It was a risk, but I had no choice.

'Dear Isobelle,' I'd written. 'I don't know if you remember me, but could I impose on you to read the attached story to the *Daily Mail* office in London. What you have to do is …' There followed instructions on how to dictate a story, a few words at a time, to a copy-taker.

Three days later I managed to get a flight back to Port Vila—just as the other journalists arrived at the Luganville wharf.

So I was ahead of them.

But did my story reach London? I called the office. Yes, it had made a whole page. Isobelle had done it. When I finally caught up with her, I realized the extraordinary lengths she had gone to in order to help out a relative stranger.

A few hours after he arrived in Vila, the pilot asked Isobelle if she had received the story. What story? It transpired that he had passed my hastily written copy to a French woman, Monique, who said she expected to see Isobelle that afternoon and would give her my notes. But Isobelle had not seen Monique. Realizing that a newspaper story would be urgent, she immediately set out to find her friend. She finally found her at the Intercontinental Hotel in bed with one of the French army officers. Monique was not happy about being disturbed but at least Isobelle received my story and telephoned it through to the *Daily Mail*.

The least I could do was take her out to dinner. Isobelle was beautiful, intelligent, well-read (quote her a line from any of the classics and she'd know it—or, to be honest, she could quote a line from any of the classics and I wouldn't know it). After that first dinner beside the lagoon under a stand of pandanus trees, we met often, although I had to keep my eye on the job, of course. But under a tropical moon, romance blossomed.

In between meeting Isobelle at every chance, I followed the activities of the British troops and watched as Papua New Guinean soldiers were eventually flown to Santo to put down Jimmy Stevens' rebellion. Only one life was lost—a young man who, as fate would have it, was Jimmy's son, hit by a stray bullet. But it was my blood that was the first to flow in the 'coconut war' in the New Hebrides when I was struck in the head by a plate thrown by a Korean fisherman at a man he was arguing with. A medical strip stemmed the flow while my colleagues roared with laughter.

It all ended with Jimmy and his lieutenants being jailed, the British and French troops flying away without firing a single shot and the flag of the new nation, Vanuatu—red, green and black with a curled pig's tusk and a yellow 'Y' to signify the shape of the chain of islands—fluttering from a hilltop over Port Vila. I flew back to Melbourne. Isobelle was just a week or two behind me.

When Isobelle joined me in Melbourne that's when all the fun—and dare I say madness—really started.

CHAPTER 7

Princess Margaret Patted the Sofa and Said, 'Come and Sit Beside Me'

We bought a cottage, one of a terrace of four, with a jasmine arch over the pathway in the suburb of North Carlton, an architect on one side and an elderly Italian couple called Charlie and Rosa on the other. We hardly ever saw the architect, who had kept the front of his house looking like a wreck to deter robbers, while the back part was state-of-the-art design.

Charlie, a retired builder who had migrated with Rosa to Australia back in the 1950s and with other migrants had helped to turn Carlton into a Little Italy, was constantly inviting us in to have pasta with them. Their specialty was spaghetti with a sauce of olive oil and garlic and clams from a tin, a seemingly simple enough concoction which tasted pretty good but which I was never able to successfully copy. Charlie did all the talking because Rosa could still hardly speak a word of English. In time I learned to understand his own version of the Australian tongue. In the middle of summer he would say something like, 'Inna nighta, verra hotta anna oped the win,' which you can probably work out.

Across the road was a small pizza restaurant run by a balding Italian called Santos. He did takeaways and dine-ins and on the wall were autographed photos of famous people who had dropped by, including Sophia Loren and Gina Lollobrigida. Santos drove a big black Cadillac and was reputed to carry a loaded shotgun under the front seat. If he wanted to play the part of a Mafia don with a sly grin and connections in high places, he certainly succeeded, although how much of the image was real and how much was creation I never really established.

He invited Isobelle and me to his house one evening—a fake mansion in the northern suburbs of Melbourne. It had tall corrugated pillars straight out of ancient Rome at the entrance and polished marble floors. The hard stare of stone goddesses seemed to follow you as you walked through the hallway and into the living room. Santos was a charming host but I couldn't help wondering as we dined on yet more pasta why he had invited us. Of course, there was a catch—he wanted me to write a story for 'all the magazines in the world' about his wonderful pizzas. From that day on, what started out as a friendly wave across the street and a casual inquiry as to whether anything had yet been published, turned into an increasingly hostile and unsettling glare. That reputed shotgun … that was the worry. Then one morning we found two empty .22 casings on the front doorstep. There were no holes in the house—but these were used casings, so who or what took the bullets? The mystery was never solved but by coincidence Santos began smiling at us again from across the street. He seemed to have accepted that there would be no write-ups in the glossy magazines of Europe about his little place in North Carlton.

During the stand-off with Santos we were receiving daily visits from another colourful character: 65-year-old Bill Sinclair who had been convicted in Thailand of being the Mr Big in a heroin smuggling racket. He had been sentenced to 33 years and eight months in a Bangkok prison, but managed to win his appeal and was released after just under four years. I had been commissioned to write his book and it was agreed he would come around to the house and describe the living hell he had endured. He couldn't face the memories of his cramped cell, the mosquitoes, the drug-crazed prisoners, the stinking latrines without drinking his way through a bottle of brandy each day. Getting the story out of the silvery-haired survivor of the notorious Bang Kwang jail became an ordeal as he shouted in frustration at the lost years—so loudly that Charlie and Rosa could hear him through the party wall. On one occasion he jumped from his chair, rage sprawled across his face, and smashed his fist down hard on a bookcase, bringing the whole thing crashing down from the wall and smashing a glass table. Who said the life of an author was quiet and simple? I couldn't wait to get back to some relatively soft journalism!

One evening as I was typing up Bill Sinclair's story, I noticed a face peering in through the window—a grey, furry face. I slid the window up and in jumped a cat. He looked a bit thin and I put out some milk. He lapped it up and jumped back out through the window. He was back the next night, and the night after that and, against our better judgement, we bought a can of cat food. In time we realized Boy, as we'd started calling him, didn't belong to anybody.

When we moved to a new house, two streets away, we worried about Boy because it seemed we were the only people feeding him. The removalists came, the furniture went out and our home became an empty shell. There was no sign of the cat. When I went back a couple of nights later he was sitting on the front window ledge looking in. My heart sank. He was looking for us. I went back to the new house, got together some scraps and returned but by then he had gone. I left the food on the windowsill and the next morning it had disappeared. That evening he was back on the windowsill. This time I was ready with the food which he wolfed down and disappeared. And so the routine continued.

'This is crazy,' Isobelle said. 'What's going to happen when the new people move in up there? You can't go walking into their front garden to feed the cat. We'll have to bring him here. We can't abandon him.'

So a new routine began. We would pick up Boy from his lane, drive him to our new house, feed him and then drive him back. One evening he simply curled up on a chair and went to sleep. He'd had enough of roughing it in the lane and so he became Our Cat.

◆

But Boy had to live without me for a week or so when the *Daily Mail* asked me to pick up the trail of Princess Margaret, who had become the black sheep of the royal family and had been described by MP Willie Hamilton as 'swanning off on less than savoury adventures'. She had been accused of squandering the royal purse on lavish parties in the Bahamas in the wake of her divorce from Lord Snowdon, and a relationship with Roddy Llewellyn, the son of an Olympic champion horseman, which had started in 1973 when he was 25 and she was 43.

Against a background of an uncertain public image at home and abroad, two years after her divorce Princess Margaret set off on a tour to promote British interests in the Philippines, Singapore and Malaysia and to regain her own self-confidence. I joined other British correspondents on the Philippines leg but very little of the copy I sent back was used in the London newspapers. She went to this rubber plantation, that factory—it was all very boring and it was a struggle to get anything out of it. By the time we reached the Malaysian capital, Kuala

Lumpur, the photographers and reporters had dropped away and I was the last man standing. Only a couple of days left and she would be on her way home. There wasn't even enough material for me to write about the success her trip had been. She had impressed me with her confidence—such a contrast to the dark woman who had been portrayed in recent years—but it just didn't add up to a good story. I needed to pull out something amazing.

On an impulse, I passed a note to a hotel courier, asking if he would deliver it to the princess's private secretary, Lord Napier—a rather cheeky note, in fact, but there was nothing to lose—in which I wondered whether Her Royal Highness would grant me an interview. The royals absolutely did not give interviews. It was a given. Journalists who asked were given the royal 'phoo-phoo' like someone shooing away an annoying dog. Forgetting the note almost as soon as I had handed it to the concierge, I walked around the city at a brisk pace. Sweating from the humidity, I bought a soft drink, ate a bowl of noodles, wandered around a bazaar and then set off at a brisk pace back to the hotel. In the foyer I was surprised to see Lord Napier pacing up and down in his spiffy grey suit, glancing impatiently at his watch.

'The princess is obviously keeping the poor man waiting,' I thought. I almost reeled backwards as he saw me and exclaimed, 'There you are! Where on earth have you been? Her Royal Highness has agreed to see you. You're keeping her waiting!' he said.

'But I'm not ready!' I protested. 'Look at me, Lord Napier, I'm dripping with sweat.' I didn't draw his attention to my soaked T-shirt and shorts or my trainers, which had seen better days. And I had no notebook or camera.

He escorted me into the elevator and along the corridor to the double doors of the appropriately named Royal Suite. 'You do realize the importance of this,' he whispered. He didn't need to add that the royals never give interviews—but I didn't even know if this was to be an interview. Perhaps this was the princess's nice way of saying, 'Thanks for following me around, I need some good publicity,' and then she'd politely show me the door. In fact, I knew she would show me the door once she'd taken one look at me.

Two ladies-in-waiting looked rather askance at my totally inappropriate clothing but hid what they were probably thinking with quick smiles of greeting.

Princess Margaret was standing at a large window, her back to me, gazing down across the Kuala Lumpur racecourse, which lay in the shadow of the hotel. As she turned I saw that she was smoking through a thin gold holder.

'Ah, there you are,' she said with a warm smile. Her eyes remained on mine—not on my clothing. I started to apologize for keeping her waiting and for the way I was dressed but she interrupted.

'What would you like to drink?'

'Well, er, ma'am, I, er …'

'I'm enjoying a gin and tonic.'

'Well, I'll have the same, thank you, ma'am.'

'And none of this ma'am. You may call me "Margaret". Come and sit down.'

Dressed in a long cream dress embossed with pastel-coloured flowers, she led the way to a semi-circular couch and patted the space beside her. I surreptitiously brushed my hand across a drip on my nose and, wishing I'd had the chance to spray myself with deodorant, took my seat beside the queen of England's younger sister.

'I do appreciate your sparing a little of your time for me,' I ventured, not daring to ask whether I could have a pen and a piece of paper to take notes with. I didn't want the princess to exclaim something like, 'Oh, you're not going to write anything down are you?' I'd cross that bridge later, I decided, as I accepted the gin and tonic proffered by the suite's butler. It was so generously loaded with gin the first sip nearly took my head off.

I told Margaret that I'd been impressed with the dignity and poise she'd displayed throughout her short tour and that those who had criticized her back in the UK should now be prepared to eat their words.

'Oh, I suppose one does one's best. I've done my best and personally I'm very happy with the way it's all gone,' she said. A cliché, perhaps, but I was left in no doubt that she meant every word.

Her Asian visit had gone virtually unnoticed in Britain, but it was obvious that for her and her entourage, from her private secretary right down to her personal hairdresser, it had been a tour of great significance. She had reached a crossroads before setting off for Asia: if she couldn't overcome what had been a painful and emotional period and regain her pride and self-confidence she would remain, in the eyes of British people, the black sheep of the royal family with a frumpy housewife image, who would soon be marking her 50th birthday.

Sitting beside me, however, was a slim, attractive and happy woman who had undergone a drastic change of appearance and personality—a bright and competent ambassador for Britain.

'I should have gone to the National Museum but I just didn't feel up to it,' she said. 'But I'm determined to visit the Girl Guides before I leave. They've come a long way to see me and I won't let them down. No-one's surprised that I've picked up a bug out here. Apparently it's almost expected. But I'm feeling very well because I believe I've turned a corner'—an obvious reference not to her current sickness but to the dark days that had engulfed her.

She smiled appreciatively when I told her that local photographers hardly recognized her from file pictures that were three or four years old.

'When I was in this part of the world a couple of years ago, I was nearly dead,' she said, referring to an emergency flight which took her from the South Pacific to Australia after she became very ill with a virus.

Princess Margaret had set off for the Philippines, the first leg of this tour, with an uncertain public image. It was the big test. She was to be the guest of presidents and prime ministers. Sitting beside me in her expansive suite, she displayed royal authority, British pride and warmth.

'I say,' she suddenly exclaimed as I was struggling to keep the conversation recorded in my mind, while refusing—in vain—a second gin and tonic. 'Wasn't that a great coup? The Iranian thing in London. I mean, it really was a great feat. Did you see the film of it on television? Oh, do tell me all about it. Did they blow it up?'

Just five days previously SAS commandoes had ended a siege at the Iranian embassy in London, which had been taken over by Iranian separatists who took 26 hostages. On the sixth day of the siege, the kidnappers killed a hostage, press attaché Abbas Lavasani, and threw his body outside. At that point, Prime Minister Margaret Thatcher gave the go-ahead for the SAS raid. Commandoes, backed by snipers, blew in the doors with demolition charges and fired tear-gas canisters in a dramatic finale. All but one of the remaining hostages were freed and five of the six terrorists were killed.

It was unusual for a member of the royal family to comment publicly on anything political, particularly involving a foreign country, but Princess Margaret was clearly moved by the drama which had been played out on TV around the world.

I was tempted to ask about her relationship with Roddy Llewellyn but instinct told me that would bring an abrupt end to our conversation. Lord Napier was hovering behind the couch, waiting, no doubt, for me to ask an inappropriate question.

My chat with the princess—with Margaret—came to an end in any case. She laid down her cigarette holder when one of the ladies-in-waiting ostentatiously checked her watch. It was time to go and meet the Girl Guides.

She rose and offered her hand. 'So nice to meet you,' she said.

The chat had not been filled with political talk or any great revelations, but it was the first time a royal had sat down with a reporter and chatted away as if she was talking to a friend about everyday events. It was a good old-fashioned scoop.

In the corridor Lord Napier caught my arm. 'Look, thank you for not raising any of that Roddy stuff,' he said, confirming my earlier instincts. 'I should have reminded you that that would have been out of bounds.'

'Oh, I didn't even think of it,' I said, deciding that diplomacy was the most appropriate reply.

I hurried to my room and sat at my portable typewriter. What a strange event. One minute I had been trudging up a dusty road, trying to cope with Kuala Lumpar's humidity, and the next I was sitting on a couch drinking gin and tonic with the Queen's sister.

I made myself a cup of tea, cursing the effects of the gin and tonic in the middle of the day, and tried to replay every moment of my extraordinary meeting. Slowly, word by word, the conversation returned as I typed each sentence from the start of our meeting. Then I shaped it all into a feature. The *Daily Mail* was delighted and gave the interview a big run.

Later that month, covering a visit by the Queen to Australia, I was pulled aside by one of her ladies-in-waiting. When a reporter is asked for 'a quiet word' away from the 'royal rat pack' it can often mean a scolding.

'I just thought I'd mention that Her Royal Highness Princess Margaret was very pleased with your article,' she said, before adding with a smile, 'And she was impressed that you had remembered every word.'

I wondered at first if that was a stab—that I hadn't remembered every word. But she had said the princess was very pleased and so I accepted that, despite the gin and tonics, I'd got it right.

Sadly, Princess Margaret failed to retain the confidence that she had exuded on that morning of 8 May 1980. The abiding image, before her death 22 years later at the age of 71, was, as the *Daily Mail* commented, of 'a sad, enfeebled woman in a wheelchair, the celebrated eyes hidden by dark glasses and her slight body wrapped in a rug.'

She had smoked and drunk too much and made the wrong choices in love, but I had been privileged to have met her in that brief moment when everything was right.

CHAPTER 8

A Missing Baby and a Dingo in the Desert

On a chilly evening in August 1980, a mother left the barbecue area in a camping ground in central Australia and walked towards the tent she and her husband had set up nearby. Suddenly her screech filled the desert darkness and became embedded in minds around the nation and the world:

'My God! My God! It's got my baby! A dingo's got my baby!'

This cry uttered by Lindy Chamberlain at that campsite near Ayers Rock seems to have endured. Lindy, then aged 32, and her Seventh Day Adventist pastor husband Michael had taken their two sons, Aidan, six, and Reagan, four, along with 67-day-old Azaria, for a winter holiday.

Reagan was in the tent with Azaria while Lindy, Michael and Aidan were at the barbecue area a short distance away. They thought they heard a baby cry. Lindy went to check the tent. And that's when her unforgettable shriek rang out into the night.

Lindy told police she had seen what she thought was a dingo leaving the tent as she approached—and when she looked inside Azaria was missing. This was a legendary moment in Australian criminal history. A mystery—because I, for one, believe to this day there are curious, unexplained elements that have never been resolved. But there's no doubt that public opinion has changed. Everyone, it seemed, was against Lindy in the months and years that followed, convinced that a dingo was not involved in the baby's death. Then, with Lindy's later release from jail under what were bizarre circumstances, public opinion swung the other way. These days the 'Lindy Chamberlain' case is highlighted as an example of how twisted justice can be. But I remain worried.

A big search followed Lindy's cries, the torches of campers flashing through the desert scrub, but there was no sign of the dingo or the baby. Eight days later the child's bloodstained, crumpled jumpsuit was found some 65 feet (20 metres) from a dingo's lair, a crevice in the base of Ayers Rock, which is now known as Uluru. Dingos were shot on sight, but their stomach contents revealed no sign of a consumed baby. Azaria had vanished, never to be found again.

The event had all the elements of a great Fleet Street story: a pastor and his wife, a missing baby, a dingo, the Australian outback, Ayers Rock, a mystery … it was all there.

I was not to know as I flew to Alice Springs to work on the story that I was to become closely involved in the ensuing events. The affair intrigued me. I wrote three books about it and drew my own conclusions. It was a sensational story. Other journalists who were despatched to the Rock and remained on the case through the following weeks, months and years also drew their own conclusions whether Lindy and her husband were telling the truth about that night. I should say now that the couple were both ultimately exonerated—but clearing them of any crime does not mean the many questions surrounding that night have gone away.

I checked into the rather grim motel that was the only accommodation I could find nearby. It was where Lindy and Michael Chamberlain had spent the Sunday night in the hours after Azaria's disappearance and then the following night. I was surprised that the couple had checked out on the Tuesday and driven back to their home in Mount Isa. Campers told me the Chamberlains had not joined in the search for their baby. They said Lindy and Michael had already accepted that Azaria was dead. Equally surprising, they had stopped at the local store before their departure because Lindy wanted to buy a few mementos: teacups and T-shirts with Ayers Rock motifs on them.

Some of the campers and local people questioned what the couple were thinking of, bringing a tiny baby to Ayers Rock in the middle of the Australian winter when temperatures at night drop to zero. As the controversy over the couple's behaviour continued, the search went on for the child, with park rangers and Aboriginal trackers leading the hunt.

Eight days after Azaria's disappearance, Wally Goodwin, a 34-year-old tourist from Victoria, was walking around the base of the Rock taking photographs when he noticed a jumble of clothing: a bloodstained baby's jumpsuit, diaper, singlet and booties. The singlet was inside out, there was blood around the neck area of the jumpsuit and the singlet, and there were rips, also around the neck area. Wally told me that his first impression, from the way the garments lay, was that the child had been eaten out of the clothes, for there was absolutely no sign of the baby. Curiously, though, there were no body parts. Grim though it was, the general feeling was that if a dingo had eaten the baby, it would, surely have left something.

I listened to the locals as they began voicing their scepticism. If a dingo had taken the child, were they expected to believe that it had undressed her and then carried her naked body away somewhere to eat it? The clothing, they suggested, would have been ripped to shreds as the dingo savagely tore into the child.

By the time I left Ayers Rock there were no answers. Azaria Chamberlain was missing, her parents had gone home. We were left with a mystery. But no-one could have foreseen the incredible events that were to follow as the months and the years went by.

◆

On 20 February 1981, Australians sat glued to their television sets as the Alice Springs coroner and former detective, Denis Barritt, created legal history by allowing a live nationwide TV broadcast of his findings into the disappearance of Azaria Chamberlain. The *Daily Mail* wanted my story within minutes of the verdict. Like the rest of the nation, I sat at my TV, recording the astonishing verdict.

A dingo, he decided, had taken Azaria from the tent and, as it was tugging at the baby in the tent doorway, it was holding her by the neck or head and at that point she would have sustained multiple fatal injuries. From the absence of dingo saliva on the jumpsuit, he concluded that Azaria was being held by the head or neck at all times. And he agreed with the evidence of a police sergeant that cuts to the sleeve and neck of the jumpsuit were caused by scissors while the clothing was under tension.

'On the probabilities, I find that at Ayers Rock a pair of scissors would be a tool used by a white person rather than an Aboriginal. From the evidence of lack of damage to the clothing, particularly the singlet, which would have been a difficult garment for a dingo to remove undamaged, the absence of dingo saliva plus any large number of hairs, I find that the dingo's possession of Azaria was interrupted by human intervention …' said Mr Barritt.

This was possibly one of the most bizarre verdicts ever to be brought down anywhere, but there was more to come. 'I am satisfied', said Mr Barritt, 'that at some stage the clothing was buried in the plain or dune country, subsequently dug up, rubbed on undergrowth near the base of the Rock and placed by a person or persons unknown at the spot where it was later found.

'It may have been that whoever rubbed the clothing on the undergrowth had some knowledge of botany, but again, this is speculation. It would appear the clothing was meant to be found. This may have been to support the proposition that the child had been fully eaten, that it had been taken by a dingo having its lair or den in that area, thus concealing the offending dingo's identity for a number of reasons.'

Mr Barritt gave his official verdict, finding that Azaria had met her death when attacked by a wild dingo while asleep in the family tent. Neither her parents, nor either of their remaining children, were in any degree responsible for the baby's death. But he added: 'I find that after her death, the body of Azaria was taken from the possession of the dingo and disposed of by an unknown method by a person or persons, name unknown.'

The Chamberlains were in the court for the verdict. Michael stood as if in prayer, hands clasped in front of him, staring at the floor. Lindy rose and stood beside him. They had been at the centre of the country's attention for months, the subject of intense gossip and speculation. Now, vindicated by the coroner, they could resume their lives—or so they thought.

◆

I owed a favour to Steve O'Baugh, the wonderfully humorous chief of staff of Melbourne's *Sunday Press*—who was to die of a heart attack in his 40s—because he had arranged an interview for me with Charmian Biggs, wife of the Great Train Robber, Ronnie Biggs. I told Steve if he ever needed a helping hand he could give me a call. So when a report came in that a body had been found in a house in the Dandenong Hills, to the east of Melbourne, he asked if I could check it out.

From what I was able to establish from the police, the body was that of an old woman. It didn't look as though it was much of a story but further investigations turned up an interesting scenario.

A father and son out on a burglary expedition had broken into a creaky old house, straight out of *The Addams Family*, while the occupants were out. The son, in his teens, had opened up a window seat and found a mannequin wrapped in polythene.

'Hey Dad,' he called out to his father, who was rifling through drawers in another room, 'come and have a look at this dummy.' The father took one look at the 'mannequin' and shrieked, 'That's no dummy, you dummy! That's a body!'

They fled, but felt obliged to tell the police, risking a charge of breaking and entering with intent to steal. My inquiries revealed that one of the dead woman's daughters, a former beauty queen, could not bear the loss of her mother, who passed away from natural causes.

Although the daughter had called an undertaker, the thought of her mother's body rotting in the earth was too much. She had instructed the undertaker to leave the body, now sealed in a coffin, in the house before the burial. Then she and a relative had prised open the lid, removed the body and filled the coffin with logs to make up the weight before replacing the lid. The coffin was lowered into the grave—but the old lady's body had been placed inside the window seat, wrapped in polythene. For the next few nights, the grieving daughter had unwrapped the body and, assisted by the relative, carried it back to bed. She placed portraits of her mother around her head and by the flickering light of candles imagined the old lady being alive.

The burglers' discovery resulted in charges of interfering with a body. Steve was amazed at the way the story had come to life.

◆

Later I worked on another story for Steve, which was to result in me writing a book. It was an investigation into the death of a poverty-stricken old lady who had vanished from her decaying mansion, set in the middle of a swamp in the rural Gippsland area, south-east of the city of Melbourne.

A bundle of old bones had been dug up by a bulldozer driver in 1980 a few miles from the once-splendid mansion. Experts were unable to establish whether they were the remains of Margaret Clement, who had become known as 'The Lady of the Swamp' or the bones of an Aborigine woman who had been buried there centuries earlier.

Margaret's was an incredible story. She and her sister Jeanie had been born in the late 1880s into great wealth. Her father had struck it rich in a gold mine. The sisters bought the Gippsland mansion, travelled the world together and returned with fabulous objects—tiger skins, Persian rugs, Chinese tapestries. Their home became something of an Aladdin's cave. But thieves were milking their bank account and swapping their good cattle for inferior animals. In time they lost everything. The house began to fall into ruin around them and the open drainage system that stopped the paddocks from flooding became clogged and water covered the fields. When Jeanie died in her cold and lonely bedroom, the undertaker and his team had to walk through miles of swamp to collect the body, carrying it on a stretcher through the water at twilight. Margaret vanished two years later, in 1952. A neighbour, Stanley Livingstone, was suspected of knowing something about her disappearance but he denied all knowledge.

My role was to piece together the story. I needed to find people in the neighbourhood who remembered her from 30 years earlier. I did find a few, but the key to pulling her tale together was a nephew who at one time was regarded as a suspect in her disappearance. His name was Clement Carnaghan, but there was no clue where he was. I ploughed through the electoral rolls but could find no trace of him. So I went back a decade and began searching through the rolls all over again. Once more, I drew a blank, so I repeated the process with the lists for another decade earlier. This time I found a person of that name at an address in St Kilda in Melbourne. I doubted very much if Clement was still there—but was stunned to find that he was. He was living with a woman who described herself as his carer.

He lay, pale and thin, on a broken-down sofa in a room that was filled to the ceiling with old television and radio sets. His carer explained that he had been an electrical engineer but now was extremely ill and was not expected to live much longer. But he nodded his agreement to talk to me. For the next three hours I listened to his painstaking account of his relationship with his aunt. I had to put my ear close to his lips because he spoke in a hoarse whisper, sometimes spraying spittle into my face, but I gained a very good impression of the problems Margaret had endured in the later years of her life.

Clement handed me a bundle as I was about to leave. They were letters Margaret had written to her mother. Reading through them, I was able to follow much of her life: descriptions of her travels in the wonderful bygone days and, towards the end, begging her then aged mother to send another food parcel to Gippsland because she and her sister were starving.

Years later, in 2009, I returned to Gippsland where the old mansion, Tullaree, had been transformed by a young family. They had returned it to its days of glory, when the Clement sisters had hosted garden parties for the landed gentry of the neighbourhood and wealthy families who had travelled down from Melbourne. As I walked through the fabulously restored mansion, it was not so difficult to imagine, Margaret strolling through the corridors a century earlier.

◆

Back in the modern world, the *Daily Mail* asked me to assess for British—and Australian—readers whether I thought Prince Charles was the right man to take on the role of Australia's governor-general as a build-up to his ultimate position as king of England.

Hey, what did I know? But I took up the challenge as the prince ended a tour of New Zealand and Australia in April 1981. I had to ask myself whether he had shown himself to be a man of the people or whether his matey association with the public was cheapening the status of the monarchy. When he allowed himself to be kissed by a former go-go dancer in front of 5000 onlookers was he winning the hearts of the masses or making the monarchy look ordinary? When he fell from a polo pony and landed, undignified, on his head, was he proving that he was willing to have a go—or was he making a downright idiot of himself? And when he was abused by a mob of anti-royalist students, should he have ignored their violent demonstrations or walked through the thick of them, as he did in Melbourne, putting himself at risk and giving his security officers an eight-minute nightmare?

In my opinion, and I told *Mail* readers so, he had been found wanting. Australians were traditionally loyal to the Queen. Thousands of boats crammed Sydney Harbour when the royal yacht steamed in four years earlier.

But Prince Charles, who had worn himself out trying to make friends in Australia, had not attracted that same enthusiasm. Children and the elderly had lined the streets and waved their Union Jacks and their Australian flags, but the essential groups, the majority in the 20-to-50 age bracket, had been missing. They considered that allegiance to the throne was old hat—something to be enjoyed by elderly migrants who recalled the days when royal tours were splendid reminders of home. The new generation of progressive voters felt it was time to sever all links with the British monarchy. Prince Charles was welcome at any time, but I felt he would not be a popular choice for governor-general. Not that he had not done his best to show a love of Australia and its people. After all, in his teens he had attended an Outward Bound school, Timbertop, north of Melbourne, which was part of the exclusive Geelong Grammar boarding school.

The basic problem was that the jovial 32-year-old prince, however much he engaged in sport and public life in Australia, was a Pom. And in a society that had found its own identity with few reminders of old Commonwealth bonds it meant he was simply not the man for the job.

My predictions carried little weight against the sensational claims that were to emerge in early May of 1981. A freelance journalist claimed that he had been passed a number of taped recordings of phone calls between Prince Charles and his then fiancée, Lady Diana Spencer. Allegedly, the recordings were made by an Australian republican group and were said to include disparaging remarks by Prince Charles about Australia and the then prime minister Malcolm Fraser. The story, written by the *Mail*'s chief reporter David Williams in London and me, was the front-page splash—and there was no doubt that its publication would have put paid to any chances of Prince Charles becoming governor-general.

◆

Within a few weeks I moved from staying in fine hotels as I followed royalty around to sitting in a chilly hospital corridor hoping to hear the cry of a couple of newborns. The *Daily Mail* had 'bought up' a husband and wife who were about to become parents of the world's first test tube twins.

Rodney and Radmila Mays, both in their early 30s, were, they freely admitted, just an ordinary couple from the outer suburbs of Melbourne. After trying unsuccessfully to have children naturally, the couple had agreed to enter the in-vitro programme at the Queen Victoria Medical Centre. The twins, Amanda and Stephen, were born in early June 1981, but were immediately separated because Stephen had to be rushed away for a delicate life-saving heart operation. I sent the world exclusive story back to London while photographer Chris Barham, who had been flown out from the UK to join me, waited patiently for the next few days for the chance to take photographs of mother and newborns together.

Our role was more than reporter and photographer. We had to ensure that no other paper got close to the parents for even the simplest of quotes—we would have been strung up by our necks if an opposition newspaper managed to get pictures of the couple.

Rad was a woman with a warm personality, but she suffered from acne. 'What on earth am I going to do with her?' asked Chris just before we entered the private ward. 'They're looking for glamorous mother and twins pictures in London. Dear God, she's going to need a lot of work.'

'I heard that!' came a cry from inside. Whoops. Rad had overheard Chris's remarks. At that point she could have decided to have nothing to do with us, but as we rushed through the door to make our apologies we saw her sitting up in bed, a grin all over her face.

'You're right,' she said. 'I do look a mess. Get out the grouting and fill in the holes!'

Those were the days before Photoshop and we were still using black-and-white film and sending the pictures by wire to London. We smuggled a make-up artist into the hospital and turned Rad into a glamour queen. The photo of her and the unique twins made a spread in the *Mail*.

We managed to get the couple out of the hospital and put them up in a 'safe house' for several days in order to prevent other newspapers breaking our exclusive. As the couple's official 'minder', I was constantly looking over my shoulder and watching for any long lens that might be pointed in our direction. Rad and Rod were such a humble couple that when Rad felt well enough to entertain the thought of a celebration dinner—with the babies left in the care of a relative—they shook their heads in unison at visiting a 'posh' restaurant. Instead they insisted on going to a very average 'all you can eat for $20' establishment, where they helped themselves from the smorgasbord and Rod ordered a bottle of beer.

'No champagne?' I asked.

'No thank you,' said Rad. 'We're very comfortable as we are, aren't we Rod?'

'Yes,' he replied. 'We're very happy as we are, aren't we Rad?'

As I said goodbye to Chris at the airport he said: 'I can't believe Rad and Rod. They're huge news. They've gone into the history books: the parents of the world's first test-tube babies. Their story's gone around the world. They could have gone out on the town for days on end at the *Mail's* expense, but they settled for a couple of beers, a salad and a meat stew.'

♦

I did send a bottle of champagne around to their house later, but whether they got to drink any of it I never did find out because I had to be on my way to New Zealand where ugliness had hit the streets. The 1981 South African Springboks rugby tour had begun and anti-apartheid protesters were out in force. There were running battles with the police, fists and feet flying in the mud and rain as the first match against the All Blacks got under way in Gisborne. The violence continued in city after city but nothing could match the extraordinary events of 12 September when a kamikazi-style pilot, Marx Jones, accompanied by a 'bombadier', Grant Cole, flew a Cessna over the rugby pitch at Auckland's Eden Park and bombed the New Zealand and South African players with paper bags full of flour. The aircraft swooped down towards the rugby field in several passes and came terrifying close to the main stand, where I was, before lifting the nose at the last moment.

Several people were hit by the one-pound (450-gram) flour bags, but none seriously. All Black prop Gary Knight was actually floored by a direct hit to the head, but again he wasn't badly hurt. It was more the spectacle rather than the threat, although there was the worry that the pilot might lose control and smash into the pitch or the stands.

But that dramatic protest wasn't the only aerial storming planned during the violent anti-Springbok clashes. World War II fighter pilot Pat McQuarrie, who knew he was dying from a serious heart complaint according to his friends and neighbours, stole a Cessna 172 plane. Police were later convinced he intended to fly into the grandstand packed with fans. Before he could cause any deaths or damage, a police plane and helicopter forced him down in the centre of a small racetrack some 20 miles (30 kilometres) from the Hamilton rugby field. As it transpired, the match was called off after protesters invaded the pitch.

♦

Very little publicity has been given to an assassination attempt on the Queen on her New Zealand tour in October 1981 when she was visiting Dunedin. Most of the royal rat pack who had flown out from London to cover her tour were waiting at a museum she was due to open. I had wandered away to stand among the crowd.

An air of excitement grew among the flag-wavers as word spread that the royal limousine was due at any moment. Then I heard the shot. No doubt about it. One or two people looked around, but then their attention was taken by the arrival of the limousine carrying the Queen. Nobody was interested in the bang they had heard moments before. As cameras clicked away at the museum, I noticed police officers hurrying around a corner. I followed but by now there were so many people running around hoping to get another look at the Queen that I lost sight of them. I saw a senior officer and asked if he had heard the shot and questioned him about the police I'd seen hurrying away.

'No drama,' he said. 'All you heard—all we heard—was one of these,' and he kicked over a metal portable 'No Waiting' sign. It clattered as it hit the ground.

'No,' I said, 'that wasn't what I heard.'

'Well, that's what it was,' he insisted.

I knocked on doors. Some people had heard a bang—could have been a shot, could have been a car backfiring, could have been anything. I got nowhere with my inquiries, official or unofficial, and reluctantly hurried to the airport to catch up with the rest of the royal reporters and photographers who were preparing to leave for the next leg of the tour in Wellington.

Years later it emerged that a shot was fired by a deranged 17-year student called Christopher Lewis. He had come to police attention a year earlier when he had established a self-styled fascist group known as the National Imperial Guerilla Army and, with two other members, held up a post office in Dunedin, stealing $10,000. Then he decided to shoot the Queen. Armed with a .22 rifle he found a window overlooking the royal route and as the Queen's vehicle approached he either had cold feet or pulled the trigger accidentally. The shot he fired—the bang I heard—hit the road, the bullet miraculously not hitting anyone.

Lewis was charged with discharging a firearm near a public dwelling, unlawful possession of firearms and aggravated robbery, and was sent to jail for eight-and-a-half years. He escaped a year later, but was recaptured. A string of offences followed, the worst being the murder of 27-year-old Tania Furlan, who was found battered to death in her home in Auckland. Before the case could go to court, Lewis electrocuted himself with wires pulled from a TV aerial in his cell in Mount Eden prison in Auckland.

◆

Above: This is me at eight (on the right). I visited my mother in Bristol and discovered I had a half-brother John and two (headless) half-sisters, Susan and Linda. I haven't seen John since but was reunited with Susan and Linda decades later.

Left: Playing table tennis for Devon in the early 1960s. When I got into North Korea in 2011, I challenged a female minder to a game, believing my old prowess would show those communists a thing or two. I was humiliated by her wily serves and forehand smashes.

Above: My first job on Torquay's evening paper, the *Herald Express,* in 1962. Those were the days of 'sit-up-and-beg' typewriters, which filled the newsroom with their clattering. I learned how to touch-type, which has served me in good stead in the age of the computer.

Left: I set out to cover a 50-mile (80-kilometre) walk across Dartmoor for the *Herald Express* and for some reason decided to join the competitors. To my surprise, I ended up winning. I was awarded a pewter mug but the biggest thrill was writing about the event for the paper!

Right: One of my stories for the *Herald Express.* I was the first reporter to be given a by-line on the paper.

Below: The Lambretta motor scooter I used for my rounds when I was working for the *Herald Express.* I have no idea who the dog is! I bought the scooter from a friend for £50, fell off on ice a couple of times (no crash helmets in those days) but it proved a reliable steed to get me to breaking stories quickly.

U.F.O.'s seem to have a taste for Dartmoor

by Richard Shears

ARMED with binoculars, maps, cameras and special detectors, 20 people will go hunting on Dartmoor this summer.

Their mission: To spot and shoot—on film—flying saucers.

According to a South Devon saucer-spotting group, the Torbay Astro-Research Society, unidentified flying objects have been spotted several times over Dartmoor.

And the group predicts that there will be more sightings of unidentified flying objects in Devon during 1967 than in any previous year.

SIGHTINGS

Mr. Richard Farrow, the society's associate director of research, says: "UFO are giving Devon a fair share of their visits.

"There have been several dozen sightings, including landings, in the past few years, but as most sightings are not reported it is difficult to judge accurately how many there have been."

In the last two years the society, formed in 1963, has investigated over 20 sightings in Devon, mostly from Dartmoor.

It claims that of these, five were definitely flying saucers, and the rest were "other types" of UFO.

In two cases the saucer landed, one for only a few seconds and the other for 40 minutes.

In the first case, in 1965, a saucer of 20ft. in diameter was seen by six people to land on Berry Head. It is claimed. A few seconds later it shot upwards at a terrific speed and disappeared.

ON THE MOORS

The other landing was in 1965 on the moors a few miles from Ashburton.

It was about 50ft. in diameter and was observed from close range. It hovered just above the ground for 40 minutes before speeding away, but it is said to have returned for a brief visit five weeks later.

Several people in the Ashburton district claimed to have seen a number of UFO during 1965-66. These included as many as 18 large glowing discs seen at one time in the same area.

Last summer two people saw a large cigar-shaped object travelling over Plymouth. It suddenly changed direction to come down very low over some houses and remained still for some time.

It then started to glow until it became such an intense white light that the witnesses had to turn away. When they looked round a few seconds later the object had gone they said.

Members of the society have studied many hundreds of reports from all over the world and consequently have acquired a good knowledge of the many types of UFO and their characteristics.

When a local report it received two members of the committee interview witnesses and are usually able to judge whether to class the report as genuine, or a case of mistaken identity.

Full reports are kept in the society's files and are treated in the strictest confidence.

Says Mr. Farrow: "The society is interested to hear from the public any information on UFO seen in Devon.

"We have specialists in a number of scientific subjects, but still need more, particularly in electricity, radio, geology and metallurgy.

Above: The last night of the *Daily Sketch* on 10 May 1971, as the entire staff listen to the news that the paper is closing and will be merged with the *Daily Mail*. I'm sitting on a desk towards the rear centre with those long sideburns!

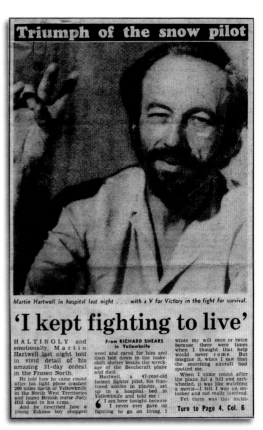

Triumph of the snow pilot

Martin Hartwell in hospital last night . . . with a V for Victory in the fight for survival.

'I kept fighting to live'

HALTINGLY and emotionally, Martin Hartwell last night told in vivid detail of his amazing 31-day ordeal in the Frozen North.

He told how he came round after his light plane crashed 200 miles north of Yellowknife in the North West Territories and found British nurse Judy Hill dead in his arms.

And he described how a young Eskimo boy chopped

From RICHARD SHEARS
in Yellowknife

wood and cared for him and then laid down in the makeshift shelter beside the wreckage of the Beechcraft plane and died.

Hartwell, a 47-year-old former fighter pilot, his fractured ankles in plaster, sat up in a hospital bed in Yellowknife and told me:

❛ I am here tonight because ❜ I never ever gave up fighting to go on living. I

wrote my will once or twice because there were times when I thought that help would never come. But imagine it, when I saw that the searching aircraft had spotted me.

When I came round after the plane hit a hill and cartwheeled, it was like watching a movie—I felt I was an onlooker and not really involved.

Yet there was this night-

Turn to Page 4, Col. 6

Above left: My New York press pass.
Above right: One of my first stories from New York was an interview with the British pilot who ate part of a dead nurse to survive after his plane crashed.
Left: Heading through the coconut trees with my typewriter during the uprising on Espiritu Santo in 1980.
Opposite top: Rebel leader Jimmy Stevens and some of his warriors on Espiritu Santo.
Opposite bottom: Chief Jack from a tribe on Tanna Island in the former New Hebrides which worships the Duke of Edinburgh as a god. The duke sent them this signed photo of himself clutching a war club the tribe had sent to him.

Above: I take on the role of a royal photographer for *You* magazine, part of the *Daily Mail* group, during the Prince and Princess of Wales' visit to Australia in 1988. I found it hard work! *Right:* My press pass for the trial of French agents involved in the bombing of the *Rainbow Warrior* in Auckland in 1985.

R. SHEARS
DAILY MAIL
Accredited for 049 'Rainbow Warrior' hearing
NEWS MEDIA

On 20 November 1981, Australia—and a fascinated section of the western world—was startled by the announcement that police did not believe the verdict given by coroner Denis Barritt, who had decided that a dingo had taken baby Azaria Chamberlain from the tent at Ayers Rock. A new inquest was to be held. Police had uncovered what they believed was sensational evidence pointing to the guilt of the Chamberlains in the baby's disappearance and death.

As before, I headed for Alice Springs. I watched Lindy and Michael come and go from the coroner's court and listened to astonishing evidence from a series of expert witness relating to what had happened that night on 17 August 1980.

As the coroner had suggested, it was alleged that scissors or some kind of cutting instrument had made the cuts in the baby's jumpsuit after she had been fatally injured, but this time more details were given: the edges of strands of wool where the cut had been made showed no blood, meaning that the blood had already dried on the garment before it was cut. Then there was the inside of Michael Chamberlain's camera bag: it was far too clean, suggesting it had been thoroughly washed, perhaps of Azaria's blood after she had been hidden in the bag before being buried somewhere in the desert. The interior of the couple's yellow Torana car had also been wiped clean, but in the bolts holding the passenger seat to the floor scrapings of foetal haemoglobin (baby's blood) had been found.

One witness, a burly, sandy-haired man, had flown across the world from London. Professor James Cameron was one of the world's leading forensic experts with a string of big cases to his name, including solving the mystery of a criminal's head found in the River Thames and a 1980 fire in which ten West Indians died when a firebomb was thrown into a house in one of London's south-eastern suburbs. Based on his findings in the Azaria case, the police had been ordered to reopen investigations, although unofficially these had been under way for some months. They had taken possession of the Chamberlain's Torana car and called in a forensic biologist, Joy Kuhl, from the New South Wales Health Commission's Division of Forensic Medicine. Her evidence stunned those sitting in the second inquest.

Professor Cameron told the inquest that, after studying the stains on the front and rear of the jumpsuit, he believed Azaria had died after her throat was cut. He used a doll to illustrate how the baby might have been held while the deadly act was performed—and it was his opinion, based on his interpretation of the bloodstains, that she had been held by a small human hand 'that was bloodstained'. He added that Azaria, 'Met her death by unnatural causes, and the mode of death was by a cutting instrument, possibly encircling the neck or certainly cutting the vital blood vessels and structures of the neck.'

His dramatic evidence suggested that somebody, or some thing, wanted Azaria dead.

But there was more: 'There is little, if any, evidence of involvement with members of the canine family,' said Professor Cameron.

'There is evidence, however, to suggest that a human being, with wet, bloodstained hands of the same blood group as the blood of the infant, held the jumpsuit in an upright position whilst the blood was still flowing onto the clothing. That is to say, the blood, in my opinion, flowed circumferentially; that is, all around the neck and not from isolated points'.

He told the court he had had difficulty finding an area of skin exposed in a child that remained to be grasped without damaging the material of the neck of the garment. 'Examination of the jumpsuit which I was presented with confirmed that bleeding had occurred when the jumpsuit was buttoned up to the top and that the neck [of the garment] had been cut at or about shortly after by a cutting instrument such as scissors or a knife, but on closer examination it's more consistent with scissors'.

He added that, assuming dingos acted much the same way as ordinary domestic dogs, he would be surprised if there were no saliva or grip marks on the cloth. That comment was to be used by Lindy's defence, which claimed that the baby had been wearing a matinee jacket over the jumpsuit. But where was it? A thorough search around Ayers Rock had failed to find it.

Professor Cameron's was not the only damning evidence to be presented against Lindy Chamberlain and her husband, now the key suspects in Azaria's disappearance and death.

Joy Kuhl told the court that dark stains she had found in the Chamberlains' car had been caused by foetal blood, which exists in babies of six months and under. A pair of scissors belonging to the Chamberlains had evidence of blood of foetal origin on the cutting edge, in the hinge area and around the handle, she said. In the car she had found foetal blood on brackets, bolt holes and hinges around the front seats, and on the carpet.

Foetal blood, she went on, had stuck a ten-cent coin to the car floor. Ms Kuhl said the blood would have been at least 12 months old when she examined it in September 1981, 13 months after Azaria's disappearance. There had been positive findings, too, of baby's blood on the underside of the glove box and on the console.

It was the blood she said she found under the glove box that was to have major significance in the case against the Chamberlains.

But for the time being, coroner Gerry Galvin had heard enough. In February 1982, he announced his bombshell verdict. While the evidence had been largely circumstantial, 'it is my view that a properly instructed jury could arrive at a verdict'—and he committed Lindy Chamberlain for trial on a charge of murdering baby Azaria and her husband for being an accessory after the fact of murder.

I sat staring at them as, with heads bowed, perhaps in silent prayer, they were granted bail of $5000 each. When I left the court that day I was convinced of one fact: a dingo had not killed Azaria Chamberlain.

The Azaria case was typical of stories that were to remain with me for months and sometimes years. There would be a development that might lead me to believe that was finally the end of the matter, and then it would bob up again. Mysterious deaths might result in a murder charge, a committal hearing, a trial, an appeal— the processes could drag on for a very long time. Often, as soon as I got my teeth into a story, I would have to drop it and turn to something else which needed immediately attention—as was the case of Isaac.

◆

Isaac was a cyclone. In early March 1982 it hit the tiny Pacific nation of Tonga, flattening everything in its wake. As Tonga was a former British colony, the *Daily Mail* was keen on me getting there.

There was a problem. The airport was closed. No commercial flights. Then I heard that the Royal Australian Air Force was planning a food flight in a Hercules and they had been given permission to land. I contacted the air force base at Richmond, west of Sydney, and was told that, yes, they could take me on board and they were taking one other British journalist, Ian Ward of the *Daily Telegraph*. Ian, based in Singapore, was a longtime friend, an expert on south-east Asia and had covered the Vietnam war. He happened to have just arrived in Sydney when the cyclone hit Tonga and, like me, had been asked by his paper to find some way of getting there.

We were given one hour to get to Richmond. I picked Ian up from his hotel and we set off in a race against the clock. Within minutes of arriving at the base we were being hurried onto the Hercules. There was nowhere to sit except on sacks of rice, which we clung to as we headed across the stormy Pacific.

Tonga had been badly hit. Even His Majesty, King Tauta'ahau Tupou IV was moved out of his palace to a safer haven shortly before the storm bowled over huge trees and laid them across the lawns. Windows in the palace were smashed and sentry boxes were blow apart like matchboxes.

Ian and I decided to call on the residence of the British high commissioner, Bernard Coleman who, for UK newspaper purposes, was referred to in our stories as 'Our Man in Paradise'. The British papers loved such descriptions—they conjured up colourful visions of old Empire and the writings of Somerset Maugham. Mr Coleman offered us a warm beer with the deepest apologies.

'I'm sorry I can't offer you anything cooler but the fridge is off. The phone isn't working either and goodness knows when we'll be able to wash in the bathroom again. Life for Sonia'—his wife—'and I has been uncomfortably sticky in the past day or so and we've been told it will be many weeks before electricity is fully restored. Still, one must keep a stiff upper lip.'

Ah ha, that was a quote for London without a doubt.

Other Brits in Tonga were doing it even tougher. Fisheries adviser Cliff Radcliff and his wife Monica and their two children, from Penzance, took to the roof of their house as the sea smashed through the beachfront wall, while Hildegarde Catterall, wife of the Cable & Wireless manager, confessed that the first thing that came into her mind as the sea threatened to engulf the house was to save the piano. 'I managed to tip it on to the bed above the water level,' she said. 'Whether it's been affected I won't know until we try to play it again. Dear oh dear.'

Of course Ian and I would not be doing our jobs if we did not attempt to interview the King. We approached one of the government buildings that was still standing and where the King's household staff were temporarily housed. When we told a stern-faced official that we would like to talk to His Majesty about the terrible storm, ask what his thoughts were about it and what his hopes were for the island nation's immediate future, the aide looked us up and down with disapproving eyes.

We did not look our best. We were both in shorts, our legs and arms were spattered with mud, the sole of Ian's once-shiny leather shoe was hanging off after he'd crunched it against a rock, and our clothing was soaked.

'I will not even begin to consider your request unless you can return suitably attired,' we were told by the official in the most immaculate Queen's English. Suggesting we return that afternoon, he shooed us away.

Ian had grabbed his packed suitcase for the Hercules flight. I had simply snatched up a backpack and stuffed in a T-shirt, a spare pair of jeans, shorts, underwear and a spare pair of trainers.

'This is a problem,' I said when I brought my backpack around to Ian's hotel room to sort out what clothes we had. 'I don't even have a jacket.'

'And I don't have any shoes,' he said.

We agreed that we should try to mix and match, swapping each other's clothes to the best effect. Fortunately, Ian had a suit in his luggage, plus a spare jacket. Unfortunately, I was tall and slim and he was much shorter and more burly. Our fitting session was not the best.

When we approached the government building later that afternoon, Ian was wearing my trainers, but because he took a size 8 and I took a size 11 he had great difficulty in walking in them, picking up his feet and slapping them down like Coco the Clown in oversized shoes. They just didn't go with his neatly pressed suit.

I looked like the village scarecrow—the jacket Ian had lent me was enormous and hung from my frame like an empty sack of potatoes. All I had on under the jacket was my spare T-shirt emblazoned with the motif of a Balinese god.

Sadly, we were confronted by the same official.

'I was wondering if …' I began.

'… we might ask you again if …' continued Ian.

'… his Majesty might …' I went on.

'… agree to giving us an interview?' Ian concluded.

Five minutes later we were walking back to our hotel.

'I didn't think it would work,' I said.

'No,' said Ian. 'Neither did I.'

CHAPTER 9

Some Like It Jungle

Papua New Guinea is more than 450,000 square miles (1,165,00 square kilometres)—over four times the size of the United Kingdom—of mostly inhospitable jungle, a dark and dangerous land where tribes fought one another to the death with spears and bows and arrows. A place where some tribes had little or no contact with the outside world. The thick rainforests are alive with deadly snakes, like the taipan which can inflict multiple bites as fast as a pecking bird, not to mention the death adder and the highly toxic black snake. And the poisonous funnel-web spider. There are bird-eating spiders with webs as thick as wire netting, blood-sucking leeches and malaria-carrying mosquitoes.

It was 1981 and this was the location of my assignment. The story seemed highly unlikely—impossible, in fact, in territory that offered no comfort to a reporter with a pen, notebook and camera. But I couldn't fail. You must never fail on an assignment for the *Daily Mail*. Failure was a word that had to be avoided at all costs.

The helicopter lifted me from the goldmining camp in the Star Mountains in western Papua New Guinea and threaded its way along a winding river valley that sliced through the surrounding jungle. I was looking for a western man reputed to be making his way through the rainforest, carrying a double bass, which he unstrapped from time to time to play to remote tribes.

I had no idea where he was. Just a name: Christopher Roberts, an American. The *Mail's* Picture Desk had told me he might be travelling from east to west, but then again he could be going the other way. Or north to south. Or he might not be there at all. Nothing like precise instructions in a country with virtually no infrastructure, where it could take days to walk from one village to the next.

'There we are—down there,' said the Aussie pilot through the intercom. I could see a patch of mud through a tiny space in the thick tree canopy.

'Gee,' I said. 'You certainly can fly. That's not much of an area to land on.'

'Who said anything about landing, mate? I can't put her down anywhere around here. Get ready to jump.'

'Jump! You want me to jump?'

'It's soft, mate. You can see water glistening on it. It'll be a bit swampy but you won't hurt yourself. Trust me. You told me you didn't know where you were going, so it's as good a place as anywhere.'

'But haven't you got a rope or a ladder or something?'

'Just jump.'

So I jumped. It seemed an eternity before I plopped into the mud patch, sinking up to my knees. No broken bones. The chopper pulled away, the pilot grinning and giving me the thumbs up. I half-heartedly returned the signal, then listened to the aircraft throp-throp-throp away down the valley.

Then there was silence.

This was madness. Chasing a stupid story that had been picked up by a wire service from a newspaper in Papua New Guinea, which had run a few lines about this mysterious white man playing an oversized violin to long-lost tribes, or rather to tribes that had had little contact with westerners. Even if this man existed, all I had to go on was a vague report of him being seen in the region bordering neighbouring Irian Jaya, which was part of Indonesia. The forbidding jungles of Papua New Guinea weren't exactly bursting with tour guides or anyone who would be waiting for someone to literally drop out of the sky. Like me.

To add to the madness, the word was that the double bass Christopher Roberts was carrying was the very same instrument that had been used in the 1959 comedy *Some Like It Hot*, starring Jack Lemmon, Tony Curtis and Marilyn Monroe. Jack is seen running from gangsters who unleash a volley of machine-gun bullets at him. Four bullets strike the double bass but Jack escapes. Now, it was rumoured, this crazy American was hacking his way through the rainforests carting the instrument with him. It had to be the figment of someone's imagination. Slow news day.

Dragging myself from the swamp, I saw what appeared to be a narrow bush track. The pilot had said there would probably be a path down here 'somewhere' and if I followed it I'd reach a village and then I could 'ask again', like stopping someone in the high street for directions to the local pub or cinema.

I set out along the wet, slippery track. I was carrying a small backpack containing a bottle of water, a camera, a notebook, a chocolate bar, T-shirt, undies and socks. I was wearing jeans—a minor deterrent against mosquitoes—a short-sleeved shirt and trainers.

Gradually the jungle came alive. Birds screeched, insects buzzed, all happily going about their business. This was their environment. They were all at home. Like my colleagues in London covering 'comfortable' stories like interviewing celebrities or sitting in courtrooms. Lucky buggers, I thought. A century earlier, intrepid reporters from *The Times* headed into the rainforests of Africa accompanied by teams of porters before scribbling out their reports and despatching them by ship back to London. But this was August 1982 and Fleet Street had come a long way since then.

Trees with enormous roots and thick vines wrapped around them towered above me. I was aware of all the nasties that were lurking under the wet leaves that slapped against my face … the snakes, spiders, leeches. I decided the best defence against fear was to pretend they weren't there.

Progress was slow. Mud sucked at my trainers as I followed the track up hills and down into dales. Every incline turned into a test of balance. I clung to bushes to haul myself up one slope, then slipped and slithered down the other side. I was caked in clay. Sweat seeped from every pore.

Despite the thick tree canopy, which turned bright day into semi-darkness, I realized that the sun was dropping. What on earth was I going to do if total darkness fell and I hadn't reached the promised village? Malaria! I'd forgotten the mozzie repellent! Or a net. And I hadn't taken any anti-malaria pills. Plough on with courage, old boy, like those intrepid *Times* reporters of old.

I stopped dead. Blocking the path, caught in a shaft of sunlight, was a creature that put the fear of God into me. A feathered dinosaur! Huge eyes glared above a terrifying beak, wearing what appeared to be a small crash helmet. And there were claws, like scythes. I'd never seen a cassowarie—a distant and more aggressive relation of the ostrich, with a brick hard skull—and this was the very worst place for an introduction. I was in its territory. Defenceless. Then it was on its way— straight towards me. I scrambled behind a tree, which seemed to confuse it for a moment, until it worked things out. I ran for another tree where I found a chunk of wood, which I hurled at the huge bird. This dashing and dodging battle continued for a good ten minutes of terror before the bird grew tired of the game and trotted off into the undergrowth.

The light was now very dim. I smelled smoke. Civilisation? Perhaps.

I broke through into a clearing. There were huts, a fire. And wide-eyed bare-breasted women staring in astonishment—and then fear—as they took in the filthy apparition that I had become. The women ran, followed by their screaming children. Then the men fled. 'It's all right,' I cried —and then, as if it solved everything—'I'm from the *Daily Mail!*'

The only reply was the crackling of the deserted fire.

I didn't know what to do, except faintly call out 'Hello? Hello? Does anybody speak English?'

Eventually a small man emerged from a hut. He was stark naked except for a penis gourd and a feather in his hair. Yes, he spoke a bit of English, he said, but it was hard to understand him because it was a mixture of pidgin and pure English. I'd learned enough pidgin from Isobelle to understand most of what he said and he seemed to be able to understand my words. His name was Jacob. I introduced myself and, trying to hide my feelings of foolishness, explained my mission: trying to find a white man who was wandering through the jungle with a big musical instrument.

'Yes,' said Jacob. 'He is coming here.'

I thought I was hearing things.

'You mean here, to this very village?'

I could hardly believe it. Finding this village, which I learned was called Bultem, home of a hundred Wopkaimin tribal people, had been pure chance.

'When? When is he coming?'

Jacob shrugged. My heart sank. He could be weeks, months away. My efforts to find out more were in vain. Darkness had descended. Men and women emerged from their huts, finally convinced I was not the devil, and sat with me and Jacob around the light of the fire. They gave me meat and rice, a straw mat to sleep on and a hut to sleep in. In the pitch darkness mosquitoes buzzed and bit as I swatted at them blindly in my half sleep.

Someone was shaking me. The dim light of dawn was seeping through the doorway. Jacob was grinning down at me.

'Masta, he come,' he said, using the pidgin form of master or mister.

'Who?'

'Masta.'

I sat up, realising what he was saying. The white man was close to the village. He'd be arriving that very day. I couldn't believe my luck.

But it still had to happen.

At mid-morning, Christopher Roberts from the US of A, stepped out of the jungle. He was a tall, thick-bearded man, his hair a tangled mess. On his back was the double bass. I glanced at the villagers. If I'd frightened them, this figure would surely send them scurrying to the distant hills. But it turned out they'd seen him before because he moved around in that immediate region, something they hadn't told me the night before.

In fact, the only person who looked astonished was Christopher.

'I'm from the *Daily Mail*,' I said. Heaven only knew why I felt that this was a magic phrase that would bring peace and reassurance to worried strangers. When Christopher had overcome his astonishment and, with the men and women gathered around us, he was ready to share his extraordinary story.

It had its roots in New York's Carnegie Hall, he said. He would be playing his double bass before audiences who sat poker-faced throughout the performance until at last came the applause with the finale.

'I appreciated their appreciation but I just wanted more input from them. They were afraid to cough or they were scared they might clap at the wrong time—if they clapped at all.' Christopher was a Juilliard School graduate and was on track for a traditional classical career but 'I wanted something more and I couldn't be sure what.'

Strolling through Los Angeles one day he saw a double bass for sale in a shop window. He found out that the instrument had played a star role in *Some Like It Hot*. He handed over $100 and it was his.

'See, it's still got the holes,' he said pointing to four plugged marks at the top of the bout, the upper part of the 'body'. 'They're the work of a Hollywood carpenter's drill. But they prove that it's the same instrument used in the movie.

'The reaction I've received has been incredible. I've been walking into villages, setting up the instrument and giving them a good old dose of Johann Sebastian Bach. They yell, they sing, laugh and dance.'

He had been lugging the instrument through the jungles for months. He saw Papua New Guinea as a kind of outdoor concert hall and thought some people might be scared when they first saw him—just as they'd been frightened when I'd walked in on the tribe. But the reaction was quite different.

'When I burst in among them with the double bass strapped to my back they fell down screaming with laughter. They'd never seen a string instrument before— their music comes from drums. When I played a bit of a Bach cello suite they cheered and clapped all the way through and afterwards they indicated that they wanted me to stay in Papua New Guinea. Food and lodges were provided and I found myself playing three times a day. They've even given the bass a name—my "tiringmingi".' In return for Chris's music, the tribes people sang to him, songs that outsiders had never heard, accompanied by the beat of their elongated drums.

It was time for Chris to put on a show for the Wopkaimins. But not before he'd prepared some pancakes for breakfast. With flour provided by his hosts, he turned the bass over and used it as a benchtop to flatten out the pancakes with his hands before they were cooked in a pan (now where did that come from?) over the open fire.

Then it was time for a recital. Using partial sign language, I asked Jacob if he could organize the women for a few photographs. Could they put on some tribal dresses perhaps? No problem. And Jacob and the rest of the men would change into custom dress.

When the women emerged from their huts I couldn't believe my eyes. The main feature of their tribal outfits were western bras! 'Whoa,' I cried to Jacob. 'This doesn't look very primitive.'

I was from the *Daily Mail*, after all. The picture editor wouldn't want them dressing up in Marks and Spencer-style underwear. This was the jungle. He was going to want grass skirts, and grass 'tops'. Britain had its preconceived notions about the jungle—and bras were not part of that picture.

'I explained to them you were going to take a photo that would be seen all over the world and they are very shy about that,' said Jacob. They were happy to sit bare-breasted with Chris and me, but modesty prevented them showing off their bodies to the rest of the world. The missionaries were to blame. They'd warned about the dangers of being seen naked and handed out boxes of bras along with Bibles. So bras and feathers of the bird of paradise it had to be for the pictures.

The men were a little more undressed. Those who had been wearing loin cloths had changed into penis gourds and added a few feathers to their hair. The gourds were just pieces of string holding up wooden sheaths containing their manhood. Some sheaths had curly ends.

Christopher started playing, the men beat their drums and the women hummed a harmony in the background. I wondered what the stars of *Some Like It Hot*—Jack and Tony and Marilyn—would have made of it. Or the even more bizarre sight of one of the local men giving Christopher his drum to play while he took up the bow and scraped it across the bass strings. It was not a happy melody, but the locals loved it and shouted for an encore.

It was time to leave. The helicopter was due to come back for me—with a rope ladder—at the end of the day.

I thanked my hosts, wished Christopher all the best with his career and headed back along the torturous jungle track. I barely made it to the pick-up point an hour before dusk. I waited with increasing panic as darkness descended. The helicopter didn't show. What was I to do? It was pitch dark and the village was too far away. I made a space on some dried leaves and tried to sleep, hoping that the helicopter would arrive the next day.

Thankfully it did but not until mid-afternoon. I was hungry, thirsty and pickled with mosquito bites, so I was more than grateful to be hauling myself up the rope ladder. No, the pilot insisted, there was no arrangement to pick me up the day before. No, he hadn't got the days mixed up. But it didn't matter—I had a story I had thought would never materialize.

The *Daily Mail* ran the article and pictures as a spread across two pages under the headline, written like musical score: 'Down in the Jungle, Something Stirred'. They used a big photo of Christopher grinning as one of the tribesmen played on the double bass. But—hello—something was missing. Women in bras: yes. But the curly penis gourds had been tactfully airbrushed out. That was not a sight for the eyes of the gentle womenfolk of middle England.

I tracked down Christopher recently. He was living in Seattle. He had earned a doctorate in composition and double bass in 1990, then travelled to Taiwan as a Fulbright scholar and studied the ancient Chinese classical instrument, the gin. But he did not forget his earlier links with the Pacific tribes. He began documenting the music of the Amis tribe of Korea, distant relatives of the Kiriwina islanders of Papua New Guinea. Inspired by what he had learned in the islands he made a CD called *Betel Nuts*. He was also the subject of a documentary film, *Songs of a Distant Jungle*.

He sent me the following email: 'The *Some Like It Hot* bass still lives in its custom-made New Guinea case, with all the extra zipper pockets and aluminum carrying frame, packed and ready for another adventure. It was on this bass that I composed the bowing pattern to evoke the sound of hornbills in flight, a sound so characteristic of Papua New Guinea, but so new to me when I first arrived.

'I had sketched the sound in music notation upon hearing it while on walkabout in the Star Mountains, but the key bowing pattern to make this sound happen came in a dream—I was standing there in my village house in the dream, playing this unusual bowing pattern on the bass. When I awoke, I grabbed my bow and rosin (the resin compound applied to the bow) and tried it—and it worked, just as in the dream. I made a fire, and coffee. Soon I was joined by others from the village, including the ritual leader, Gesok. I showed him the bowing on the bass—he declared it the sound of the hornbills!'

◆

Through September and October 1982 I sat among other reporters in the Northern Territory Supreme Court in Darwin, watching the couple in the dock: Lindy Chamberlain and her husband Michael. Their murder trial was hearing much of the same evidence presented at the second inquest. This time, though, Lindy was pregnant, two months away from giving birth to her fourth child. Her eyes widened just a little as Ian Barker QC told the court: 'When the mother commenced to walk to the tent, the child Azaria had not long to live.'

The Chamberlains' lawyer, John Phillips QC, attacked the evidence of Professor Cameron and forensic scientist Joy Kuhl. Referring to glass plates on which blood had been tested that had been destroyed, he asked the jury: 'How would you like to be tried on the basis of opinions based on hard evidence which is destroyed?'

The three women and nine men on the jury retired to consider their verdict at 2PM on Friday 29 October. In a few hours, at sundown, the Seventh Day Adventist sabbath would begin.

The hours ticked by. The jury returned at 8.30PM. The Chamberlains walked back into the dock, Michael in a red-and-blue striped tie and white shirt, Lindy in a turquoise-and-white smock with white ruffled sleeves. They watched tight-lipped, as the jury took their places in the jury box.

'Do you find the accused Alice Lynne Chamberlain, guilty or not guilty of murder?'

'Guilty.'

The journalist sitting beside me, Malcolm Brown of the *Sydney Morning Herald*, who had befriended the Chamberlains throughout their ordeal of the inquests and the trial—and had even gone running with Michael—almost shouted aloud. In any case his cry was heard by those in his immediate vicinity.

'Bastards!' he said. Fortunately neither the judge nor the lawyers heard him.

Michael was found guilty of being an accessory.

Justice James Muirhead addressed Lindy Chamberlain. She had been found guilty of murder, he said. There was only one sentence he could pass. 'You will be imprisoned with hard labour for life.'

The shock appeared to hit her then. There was a frown and her eyes flashed with anger. Her husband looked disbelievingly at the jury who had convicted them.

The judge was talking again. Michael Chamberlain would be released and brought back to the court later so that submissions could be made on his behalf. An orderly opened the door behind the stunned couple and, as one, they rose and turned to their right and walked away from the sea of faces in the public gallery. In those last few seconds, Lindy looked close to tears.

Outside, it was dusk. Her sabbath had just begun.

CHAPTER **10**

Love on a Desert Island

As a freelance correspondent, holidays were out of the question. I remained tethered to an invisible phone line, linked around the clock to the *Mail*'s Foreign Desk. No stories, no pay. I read all the daily papers, listened to all the radio news bulletins, and watched the evening news, flicking from channel to channel. Aside from the need to keep earning, I really enjoyed my work, proud of the fact that if there was 'anything going on' in Australia and the South Pacific region, I knew about it right away.

But there was one exception to my 'no holiday' rule—and I paid dearly.

Isobelle had been a tremendous support to me from the day we set up home together in Melbourne. Occasionally she would break away to visit friends in the US or family members in Vanuatu, but one day the chance came for us to both go away for a few days—and for once it wasn't for the *Daily Mail*. My friend on the *Sunday Press* newspaper in Melbourne, Steve O'Baugh, said a 'freebie' was available: a trip to Norfolk Island, which lies in the Pacific east of New South Wales.

'Take a few days break,' he said. 'All you have to do is write 800 words about the trip and the hotel. Nothing's going to happen while you're away.'

'Just relax,' said Isobelle later as we sat in a cosy little restaurant on Norfolk Island, me sharing a bottle of wine with myself because Isobelle doesn't drink.

'I'm trying to hear what those two women are saying,' I said, nodding towards a couple sitting at a nearby table.

'Yes, I just caught a bit about it on the radio,' one of them said.

'How many did he shoot?'

'Oh, it was more than 20.'

I couldn't resist. I walked over to their table.

'I'm sorry to bother you, ladies, but I couldn't help overhearing your conversation. There's been a shooting?'

'Yes, in Melbourne.'

My heart gave a jolt.

'And he's shot a lot of people, and they're saying there must be at least ten dead.'

I couldn't believe what I was hearing. 'When was this?' hoping they might have been referring to an incident years earlier.

'Just a short time ago.'

I sped back to the hotel with Isobelle. As I feared, there was no-one on the switchboard. Norfolk Island is a beautiful place but it's also a backwater that closes down around 9PM. There was no way I could make phone calls to Melbourne to find out more. But there was a phone box in the main street. We gathered all our coins and I rang a *Sunday Press* reporter, Dennis Williams, who hadn't heard about the incident. But in the seconds before the coins ran out he said he'd get onto it right away and would file a story to London. Quite rightly, Dennis got a big byline in the *Mail* while I was stuck on a tiny dot in the Pacific cursing my bad timing and missing one of Melbourne's most dramatic crimes. Julian Knight, armed with a Ruger rifle, a Mossberg shotgun and an M14 military rifle, had shot dead seven people and seriously wounded 19 others.

'I'll never go away to a remote island again,' I told Isobelle.

'What is it they always said in Fleet Street when things like this happen—sod's law?' she asked. If anything can go wrong it will.

'You've got it. This is sod's law personified.'

I was still using a typewriter in 1983, my Remington portable, which had pummelled out heaven knows how many words but was still holding up well. I also carried a camera, an Olympus OM1 and a couple of zoom lenses, but if a photographer travelled with me I left that equipment at home. Dedicated newspaper photographers hated reporters carrying cameras. On the other hand, being so far from London, it was virtually impossible to get hold of a freelance photographer in Australia who could drop everything and travel with me. If I didn't carry a camera while travelling alone on an assignment there would be no picture—and a story without a picture had far less impact. As time went by and newspapers began running their own web pages, a story without a picture meant the story wasn't run at all unless it was world-beatingly sensational.

I was, in fact, more than a reporter who picked up a camera. I had taken pictures from the early days when my 'uncle' Cyril worked in a photographic processor's, and had learned how to develop them. My earlier cameras included a Rolliflex, a Fed—a Soviet copy of a Leica M3—and a Yashica Lynx. I'd also held two exhibitions in Melbourne, one of photos I'd taken in Papua New Guinea and the other of images from India and Japan. So I considered myself a true photo-journalist.

Although I vowed never to be stranded on a remote island again, it was perfectly fine if the *Mail* had sent me to one. As happened in the extraordinary case of Martin Popplewell.

A stringy, tousle-haired youth, he was 15 in 1986 when he saw the film *Blue Lagoon* in his local cinema in Cambridge. It starred Brooke Shields and Christopher Atkins and told the story of two young people who fall in love while marooned on a tropical island.

'I want to do that,' thought Martin. 'I'll find myself an island and a girl to go with me, and I'll live off the land.'

He began a quest to find a 'Girl Friday', while also writing to the heads of small island nations in the Pacific asking if they could find a deserted island for him to live on. The reject letters poured in. No-one wanted to be responsible for a crazy English teenager who was going to risk his life on a dot of land in the middle of the world's biggest ocean. Undeterred, Martin advertised in his local paper and on the radio for girls to come forward and tell him why they were suitable desert island companions. Just as the island nations had rejected him, so he turned down the young women who answered his ads—until along came Helen Freeman. She was a schoolteacher from Nottingham, 12 years older than Martin. But she shared his sense of adventure. At least she thought she did.

When news reached the *Daily Mail* that a young English couple were living on a desert island—Martin's appeals had finally been heard by a Pacific government— I was told: 'Find them. They must have quite a story to tell.' They were living on a remote dot of land near the island of Mog Mog in the Caroline Islands north of New Guinea. Well, there was an exotic dateline for a start.

It was early 1989. Back in London the *Mail* was settling into its new headquarters in Kensington, having moved the previous year from its creaky old building, New Carmelite House, a street back from the Embankment. The new premises had a towering 115-foot (35-metre) atrium, a domed roof and more than 60 tons of glass. It was the beginning of a revolution, with 'silent' technology taking over from the clacking of typewriters on the editorial floor. The linotype machines of old were dismantled. Other national papers were moving, or had already moved, from Fleet Street, following the dramatic decision by Rupert Murdoch to move his four papers—*The Sun*, the *News of the World*, *The Times* and the *Sunday Times*—to a new fortified plant in Wapping in 1986, and in the process breaking the power of the print unions. Fleet Street, the dear old mother who had embraced untold numbers of journalists over the decades, had passed away. The bars where journalists like myself had once gathered closed, the camaraderie that had existed between writers from rival papers evaporated— spread out as they now were, it was no easy matter to slip out for a quick beer with a mate from another paper. But I had, of course, already moved on to a different kind of world.

By definition, foreign correspondents are in control of their own world—to a point. While the strings are still pulled by foreign editors, news editors and occasionally by the Man at the Top—the editor himself—foreign correspondents can work to their own hours as long as they meet all deadlines. I could ask for help from London, but usually time differences and lack of local knowledge make it difficult for someone there to get me to a city or country on time. As for getting to Mog Mog—well, even with what I thought was a fairly good knowledge of the Pacific, I had to look it up on the map.

Apart from the basic facts—teenager Martin Popplewell had advertised for a Girl Friday and would be living a kind of modern *Blue Lagoon* lifestyle—little was known about his grand adventure. His initial plan was to tell all about it in *The Times*, with whom he was suspected of doing a deal. But the *Daily Mail* didn't want to read it in that paper first. It was down to me to get there and find out how he and Helen were faring after several weeks on Mog Mog.

After much plotting, I flew to Guam, which is under US administration but part of the Federated States of Micronesia. Mog Mog, I was informed, was administered from the island of Yap, so off I flew again. The Yap tribes used to trade in stone money: pieces of it, with holes in the centre, can still be purchased as souvenirs. A friendly official in the local government office informed me that I would have to wait for permission from the local chief on Mog Mog before I could fly there. It might take 'a day or two'. I had to wait around for a week in the local hotel, dining on fish and rice, before word came back that permission had been granted.

On a sunny morning I climbed aboard a Pacific Missionary Aviation plane, which flew me to an airstrip on Ulithi Atoll. As the plane approached the crude runway I noticed a boat speeding below. 'That's the boat that will take you on to Mog Mog,' said the pilot. 'There's nowhere to land there.'

On touchdown I helped the three islanders who had come to meet me unload two sacks of rice, a kava root and a large bag of salt. I had been warned not to fly to Mog Mog without these gifts for the village chief. I jumped into the open boat and half an hour later we were walking up a concrete wharf at Mog Mog, population 300. All I had to do now was find Martin Popplewell, although I was wondering about all the islanders who were standing on the shoreline watching me. I thought Martin and Helen were supposed to be on a deserted island.

I felt like an intrepid explorer of old as I was escorted to the visitors' reception centre—a large hut in the middle of the village—followed by 'porters' carrying my gifts for their chief. Women laughed as I banged my head on the low doorway. Sitting in a dark corner was a portly man dressed in a wrap-around lap-lap.

'Welcome my friend,' said Hosey Sogruy, adding in good English, 'I'm just the acting chief, so I'll have to do.'

At least he had a sense of humour. My gifts were laid before his bare feet as he listened to the purpose of my visit.

'Well, you won't find that crazy man Martin here,' he said. 'Oh don't worry, he's not far away. He's on Patongros, a nearby island which has nothing on it except rats, coconuts and a few wild hens. And Martin and Helen, of course. Why do you think we are all living here on Mog Mog and there's no other soul apart from those crazy English over there? That island is the pits. I wouldn't stay there for a minute. The mosquitoes drove all our earlier generations away—apart from the fact that the island is haunted by the spirits of our ancestors and the ghost of an American coastguard who accidentally shot himself with a spear gun after the war.'

After morning tea with Chief Hosey I was back on a boat heading for an inconspicuous, small dark shape on the horizon. The two boatmen began whistling as we crossed the flat sea. Suddenly we were surrounded by leaping dolphins. Their whistles, they said, always attracted the dolphins, which would rise up to escort boats through these waters whenever they heard the sound. Half an hour later I was standing, shoes in hand, on the beach at Patongros. The boatmen promised they'd be back at dusk. It would be stupid, they'd told me in various ways, to think about staying the night there.

All I had to do was find Martin and Helen. I didn't have to wait long. Out of the line of coconut trees fringing the beach came a gangling figure, so thin you could see all his ribs, a coconut in one hand, a machete in another.

'You must be Martin,' I said, which was rather silly.

'And who are you?' he demanded. His tone suggested that this native was not friendly.

When I told him I was from the *Daily Mail*, he raised his machete high and yelled: 'Leave! Leave! I am not talking to you!'

'But Martin, I've come all this way—and I bring greetings from all the people of Britain.'

Many years earlier a respected Fleet Street reporter had told me that if I ever found an 'uncooperative' subject about to close a door in my face, a good line to use is: 'But I've come all the way from London specially to see you.'

It's never worked for me. All it does is give the person an opening along the lines of: 'Well, you can just bugger off back to London again, can't you?'

Here I was confronted by a hostile adventurer in the middle of the Pacific. My 'greetings from Britain' line was a downright lie and he saw through it.

'I'm under contract to *The Times* and not only am I forbidden from talking to you, I do not care to talk to you. You've arrived unannounced and that's bloody rude.'

I wasn't going to argue about how on earth I could have let him know I was on my way. I tried a different tack: I didn't want all his story—just enough to tickle the fancy of *Daily Mail* readers who then would be dying to read his full account in *The Times* when he got around to writing it. Finally he agreed to show me around his encampment until the boat came to pick me up. He turned towards the trees and called, 'It's all right, Helen, you can come out now.'

She was a sad, slumped figure in a white T-shirt and shorts. She had red hair and the complexion of someone who would burn easily. She was as red as a lobster, but not so much that the mosquito bites—also bright red—didn't stand out all over her skin.

'Hello,' she said softly. She smiled at Martin, but said nothing more as he led me to their base camp. It was a large tent which they shared. Even before I could ask a question about 'hanky panky', Helen whispered, 'There's nothing going on. He wants to … you know … but I've made it very clear to him that I have a boyfriend back in England and there's no way I'm going to betray him.'

'What does Martin think about that?' I whispered back.

'He's very unhappy about it. I think he wanted sex on a desert island from the moment he saw that film. But I made it clear I was coming here for the adventure, not for any kind of relationship, if you know what I mean.'

I knew what she meant. When Martin ran off to look for coconuts, Helen, who had spent the two weeks since they arrived weaving palm fronds to make a bigger shelter, poured out her heart.

'He's a vegetarian so he's happy to eat nothing but coconuts and a few strange vegetables he's been able to find, along with rice we brought from Mog Mog. To be honest, I'm starving. There are a few wild chickens running around, as well as rats, but I don't think I could bring myself to catch one of the chickens and kill it. I dream day and night of all the things I had at home—curries, chocolate, fish and chips.

'There are six months to go and I'm going to try to stick it out. But it's going to be far harder than I ever imagined. Not that this is a life-threatening situation—we can send up a flare for the people on the other island to come and rescue us. But the only worry I have is Martin. I'm scared he's going a bit "troppo". All he does all day is run around like Tarzan, eating coconuts and drinking coconut water.'

On cue, Martin returned with a coconut for me, deftly slicing off the top and inviting me to drink the warm juice. 'Nothing is going to distract me,' he said. 'I've been planning this for three years and only a major accident will force me away from here.'

Patongros was three miles (five kilometres) in circumference, fringed by a coral and sand beach with thick undergrowth covering the flat interior. Martin's reference to a 'major accident' could mean a sting from one of the thousands of deadly stonefish which lurked in the shallows, an encounter with a shark or even a cracked skull from a falling coconut.

When Martin ran off into the jungle again—I was expecting to hear a Tarzan-like yodel, but instead it was just a 'Yes! Yes!'—Helen repeated how hungry she was. The first thing that came into her head in the mornings was 'find food'.

But she had tonight's dinner lined up. She led me to an old oil drum on which stood a large jar. From it, she pulled a small fish, no more than six inches (15 centimetres) long. She had caught it that morning. She didn't know what kind of fish it was but she was going to roast it over a fire that night, her only meal of the day. No wonder I thought she wasn't going to last the distance. She had dreamed of an adventure in paradise but I just saw sadness. I waved them goodbye when the Mog Mog men came to pick me up at the end of the day. Martin waved back, like an excited child. Helen seemed to barely have the enthusiasm to lift her arm.

I spent the next three nights on Mog Mog, waiting for the missionary plane to return to the atoll on its weekly schedule. There was absolutely nothing to do apart from wander around the tiny island taking photos of the locals, who were happy enough to pose. I was itching to get my story out.

Worse, a London journalist working for the *Sunday Express* had turned up with a photographer he'd hired in the Philippines. It had started out as a no-pressure story, but once I'd persuaded Martin to talk to me the appearance of another newspaper team, who had also got enough out of the couple to write a big piece, meant that I had to maintain the initiative and get into print first. I had to get my story into the Saturday paper or the opposition would hit the streets first on the Sunday. It was still the middle of the week, but with no way off the island I had to sit out my frustrations.

We ended up picking straws for who could have the two beds in an abandoned doctor's surgery—and who was the poor sod who would have to sleep on a stone slab. That turned out to be me. Sod's law again. I was first there, but I get the stone bed. It was impossible to nod off, so I clambered onto the rusting operating table—the head and the feet ends dropped down at 30 degrees, but at least it kept me off the floor. It was a restless night, though, mostly spent ensuring I didn't roll off and smash my face in. The next night I drank copious amounts of tuba, the distilled sap of the coconut tree, thinking it might help me get a better night's sleep. It tasted great and I gulped down several large glasses which, I realized when morning came, was about the equivalent of swallowing a bottle of scotch. Not only that, the juice solidified in my stomach and I—and the others, I was glad to learn—remained constipated for the following fortnight.

A motorized canoe took us across the lagoon to the airstrip and from Yap we flew to Guam and then on to Manila, where we could send out pictures through the Associated Press agency. Throughout the journey to Manila the *Sunday Express* journalist tried everything to prevent me filing my story on the Friday, when we would arrive in the Philippines. He even tried friendly bribery, at the suggestion of the *Sunday Express*. They would pay me exceedingly well if I would hold off sending my story until Sunday, allowing the *Sunday Express* to come out first. I didn't think of the ethics and I certainly didn't begin to consider how much they would pay. I just knew that I had a damn good story and nothing was going to stop me getting it out first.

Further dirty deeds were afoot in the Associated Press office. The Filipino photographer knew the darkroom man and I saw the two of them chatting and looking across at me as I waited on the editorial floor. Horror suddenly swept over me. What if my film 'accidentally' became exposed to the light? I insisted on being present in the darkroom while the film was processed. My competitor's film was developed immediately, whereas I had to wait for mine. Then there was an unexpected delay in getting my pictures wired. But I was still a day ahead of the *Sunday Express* deadline. I could not have been more relieved to learn that the *Mail* had run my story, datelined Mog Mog, Western Pacific, Friday, as a centre-page spread under the headline: 'The Blue Side of the Lagoon'. Understandably, the *Sunday Express* team were not happy, but the only grumble I heard when I joined them for a farewell drink in a seedy Manila bar was from the photographer. He complained about the picture he had taken of Helen with another fish she had caught.

'You took a picture of her holding up the fish and you focused on her face,' he said. 'I focused on the fish and I think your picture was better than mine. I should have realized she was more important than the fish.' It was a curious comeback when I was expecting a surly response about them being beaten into print.

My prediction about Helen not being mentally or physically fit to last the distance proved true. Within weeks she was back in England.

But the Martin Popplewell story was far from over. He managed to get a message out through the missionary service calling for another Girl Friday. This time, his companion was 19-year-old Rachel Stevens, a former sixth-form college classmate in Cambridge. She would be living with him, not on Patongros but on a nearby island, Dorenleng. It was a new start for Martin after Helen failed to stay the course. New surroundings. A new companion. Finally the real beginning of his adventure. Or so he thought.

The *Daily Mail* bought their exclusive story. I have no idea what happened to his deal with *The Times*, although I suspect money had something to do with it. The *Mail's* idea, for their exclusive arrangement, involved Martin and Rachel keeping diaries in which they had to comment on their companion's behaviour …

the problems of living with another person on a desert island, the unanticipated difficulties encountered, their best and worst moments, and so on.

The adventure was planned for eight weeks and it turned out to be a disaster. They ended up deeply disliking each other, bordering on hatred. Like Helen, Rachel suffered from hunger and sickness. But she also knew physical terror when she and Martin sailed to Mog Mog to pick up rice, the only food supplement they had allowed themselves. Alone in a hut there and topless, following the local tradition, an islander came in and demanded she show him all of her body. She was threatened with gang rape, but fortunately Martin returned at the right moment.

'Rachel was attracting a great deal of attention among the male population of Mog Mog,' Martin noted in his diary, 'and one villager asked me if he could have her. Another confided that he could hardly contain himself when he saw her beautiful white body and he would be quite willing to trade me two local girls for her.'

I returned to the Pacific to pick up their diaries. The *Mail* had sent freelance photographer Brendan Beirne ahead of me to take pictures of the couple on their island. Martin had refused to cooperate until Brendan could prove that he was from the *Mail* and insisted on 'holding' film while Brendan searched through his bag for a note I had given him.

Later I sat in the hotel in Yap reading through the diaries. It was clear that sexual tensions and hunger had created a deep rift. On Friday 14 July 1989 Martin wrote: 'Managed to get a letter away today after flagging down a passing boat. After a row with Rachel, I left the tent and slept much of the night beneath a moon and stars so bright I could have read a book by them. It is times like these that I do wish Rachel and I were lovers.'

Six days later Rachel recorded: 'It is very hard to sustain a conversation with Martin which isn't just packed with information and practicalities. Feelings aren't shared, which makes things very lonely sometimes. He tends to wander off for hours without explanation, giving the impression he is sulking.'

'Two Strangers in Paradise' blared the headline accompanying my despatch in the *Daily Mail*. The story ran for three days. But if I thought that was the end of my links with Martin and his dream island I was mistaken. He returned to Mog Mog and the surrounding islands in 2001 to film a documentary called *The Real Castaway*—and once again the *Mail* sent me off into the Pacific to find him.

I caught up with him in the Federated States of Micronesia after his whirlwind visit to his island. He was a changed man. Martin had grown from the gangling youth I had first met on that beach in Patongros to a confident broadcaster and journalist, presenting the news on the BBC News Channel Five, BBC World and Sky News. We sat on a beach with the Pacific lapping at our feet and chatted about those crazy days, a time that he said he did not regret because it gave him a perfect grounding for his career—if he could cope with two women on a desert island, he could cope with anything that people could throw at him!

By coincidence, at one stage Martin worked as a researcher for British Tory MP Alan Duncan, who the *Mail* asked me to track down in 2009 while he was on holiday 'somewhere in Bali' with James Dunseath, the man with whom he had a civil partnership. His gay relationship was not the point of the story—that had been covered to saturation point by the British press. Rather, he was reported to have flown off to a luxury resort in the wake of a row over MPs' expenses and allegations that he had claimed more than £4000 in expenses for gardening. It took four days of phoning and visiting every resort in Bali before instinct led me to the nearby island of Lombok. Freelance photographer Cameron Laird and I found Mr Duncan relaxing in the sun with his partner in an exclusive resort in the far north of the island. He refused to be interviewed. Unlike his former researcher Martin Popplewell all those years before, he did not give in and agree to talk to me eventually.

Some you win and some you lose.

◆

Back in Melbourne after my difficult pursuit of Martin, things were also becoming a little strenuous. Isobelle's mother Madeline had advanced Alzheimer's disease and Isobelle was caring for her around the clock. Then Isobelle's Aunt Dorothy, who was in her late 70s, arrived from Norfolk Island and moved in with us. Aunt Dorothy sat on the sofa with her knitting and expected to be waited on hand and foot, as if Isobelle did not have enough to do looking after her mother. And then there was the ever-increasing number of animals Isobelle had rescued from death row: Ruggerlug the white rabbit, Lucifer the black rabbit, the cats Boy and Pompey and an earless former feral we found on the highway called Miss Mouse, Rolly the Maltese terrier and Rolly's sister Sassy. We decided to move this human and animal menagerie to Sydney so that Isobelle's father could be closer to his wife.

In moving to Sydney, I was also thinking of my career. There had been a wealth of good stories in Melbourne, but the harbour city was the more recognisable

'Aussie' base for foreign correspondents—and most of the other British papers were there.

By now I had entered the world of high-tech journalism … of a kind. I acquired a Tandy TRS-80, a beige machine about the size of an iPad, with black keys and a narrow, flat screen that displayed six lines of LCD text. It was considered the world's first laptop computer and I loved it. Although I couldn't send through pictures or do anything else apart from write on it, for journalists constantly on the move it was a boon. I wrote my copy, then sent it digitally to a computer at the *Daily Mail* office. The connection was via an acoustic coupler, a device about a foot (30 centimetres) long and six inches (15 centimetres) wide, with two rubber cups on the upper surface. Once I heard the computer in London deliver its welcoming fax-like screech, I would fit the mouthpiece and earpiece of a telephone in the coupler. Then I would watch my words move down the Tandy screen as they sped on their way to London—in a way, this was the world's first form of email.

One of the most tragic stories I pounded out on the Tandy was the hanging deaths of two young men who sacrificed their lives for a stupid drug-carrying operation. Kevin Barlow, who held British and Australian passports, was 27 when he died and his Australian friend, Brian Geoffrey Chambers, was 28. Because of the British link, the *Daily Mail* wanted me to follow events after their arrest at Penang airport in November 1983. Kevin's parents, Barbara and Wilf Barlow, were 'ten-pound Poms', Britons who paid just £10 a head to migrate to Australia under an assisted passage scheme, and who found themselves struggling for cash when they eventually set up home in South Australia. Brian Chambers had been on several drug runs for a criminal group and had made good money, but needed an accomplice on what would be his final run. Kevin Barlow had his doubts but eventually agreed when one of the drug cartel's heavies promised that he would be paid $2000 and if he tried to back out his girlfriend would be disfigured. That, in any case, was what Kevin told his mother when she raised the money to visit him in the Malaysian prison.

As is virtually always the case, the 'Mr Bigs' of drug operations sit in the shadows while their couriers end up behind bars. Those who try to smuggle heroin through an airport in Malaysia are gambling with their lives, risking the mandatory death penalty if caught. Often the people doing the selling will tip off the police, collect a fee for their information and the drugs will go back onto the streets again in readiness for the next dupe.

Whether Barlow and Chambers, who had picked up the heroin from a contact in their hotel room, had been fingered by a police informant has never been established but they were doomed in any case. When they arrived at the airport with their suitcase containing 5 ounces (141.9 grams) of heroin lying underneath a towel, they bypassed the X-ray machine and went straight to the check-in counter. Kevin was sweating, edgy. Whether or not they were tipped off, Kevin's apparent nervousness alerted undercover airport police. The two men were escorted to an interview room, the suitcase was opened—and the slow march to the gallows began.

I sat in the court as Barlow and Chambers went through the long legal process in Penang. Barlow's defence lawyer, Mr Karpal Singh, insisted that his client was an innocent patsy who had been tricked into carrying the drugs. The suitcase wasn't his—it belonged to Chambers. But Chambers said the suitcase belonged to Barlow. They blamed each other because they realized they were fighting for their lives. If convicted of trying to export drugs, they were facing the death penalty because 15 grams (half an ounce) of heroin was the cut-off point used to distinguish users, who could expect leniency, from traffickers.

Both men were found guilty on 24 July 1985. A week later Barlow, who was leaning on crutches because of a groin injury, and a pathetically thin Chambers stood before the trial judge as he pronounced sentence. They would be taken from prison to a place where they would be hanged from the neck until they were dead. No-one in the court could help but feel a chill running through them at those words.

Barlow and Chambers were flown under heavy guard to Kuala Lumpur, where they were imprisoned in Pudu Jail, aware now that their only chances lay in a series of appeals. Prominent Melbourne lawyer Frank Galbally flew to Malaysia to assist Mr Singh with Barlow's appeal. But there were ugly scenes when, at the close of one of the court sessions, the two lawyers clashed over a legal point. Mr Singh stormed from the room, warning Mr Galbally not to criticize Malaysia's British-based legal system or suggest that the system in Australia was superior. Singh tried to have Galbally charged with contempt, but peace was restored when the Melbourne QC apologized the following day.

But the damage was done. Mr Galbally left the country after the row, claiming that if his argument had been allowed—introducing medical evidence to prove that Barlow's shaking at the airport was due to a groin injury and not because of fear of getting caught—his client would have been found not guilty. When an ongoing series of appeals and pleas for mercy failed, the *Daily Mail* asked me to return to Kuala Lumpur. They wanted me to be there the morning the two men were put to death—it was a moment that would serve as a dire warning to others.

I checked into the Hilton Hotel in Kuala Lumpur, where Barlow's mother was staying. The last time I had been there I was sitting beside Princess Margaret in her suite. Now I was writing about the mother of a condemned drug courier who was staying in a standard room. I wanted to count the hours down, just as she would be doing in her room one floor above.

She told me later that she knew it was over when the hands on her clock reached 6AM. Her son and Chambers had dropped through trap doors side by side. Most of all, she remembered his chilling words to her during a visit: 'They came to weigh me today, Mum. I'm 47 kilograms.' The hangman had wanted to be sure that Barlow was sufficiently weighed down so he died quickly at the end of the noose.

According to his wishes, after his execution Barlow was cremated and his ashes sprinkled under a gum tree in the heart of Tasmania, a place where his family had once all taken a holiday and which Kevin had loved. Barbara and her husband laid a black marble slab there, engraved with gold lettering which read:

KEVIN JOHN BARLOW

BORN 12–10–58

MURDERED 7–7–86

'We drank some billy tea,' Barbara said, 'just as Kevin loved to do on the family jaunts into the bush, and then Wilf planted some bluebell bulbs around the gravestone. "They'll be up in spring," said Wilf. "They'll look beautiful," I said. "They will that, love," he said.'

CHAPTER 11

The Schoolboy 'Spy'

Whenever I think back to the time I met Charles Evans, I can't help comparing him with Major Gowen, that rather confused military gent who's a resident of Fawlty Towers. They looked alike, dressed alike and spoke alike.

But there the comparison ends. Charles was a hero who had made it onto the front pages of the British newspapers. He was 67 when I met him and since 1949 had lived in Australia with the secret of his wartime activities unknown even to his wife. Now separated and living in Melbourne, he told a British paper that he had operated as an undercover agent within Germany military intelligence circles for most of World War II.

'I was probably the only ex-British public schoolboy on their books,' Charles said. 'My cover was so good that it even survived two random checks by the Gestapo. While I was serving as one of the Third Reich's apparently faithful high-ranking army officers, I was passing many secrets to British intelligence. Those secrets included the date Hitler intended to occupy the Channel Islands and the date, within 24 hours, that the Germans planned to invade Russia.'

There was much more.

He said he had given London information about the German coding device Enigma, learned of the German V-1 flying bomb that was to be launched against London in June 1944 and had obtained secret designs of the Tiger Tank. He had also told the British about the spy Cicero, who was stealing documents from the British embassy in Ankara. To his dismay, though, Charles believed that much of his information might have been ignored by the British because it could not be corroborated.

However, he was still in possession of the Iron Cross given to him by the Germans, an honour he remained proud of because it confirmed his skill as a spy. His undercover activities had begun, Charles said, when he was recruited for MI6 by the intelligence service's head, Admiral Sir Hugh Sinclair, while still in his teens and attending Marlborough school in Wiltshire in the 1930s. His role was to adopt the identity of a German student who had also been educated at Marlborough—and arrangements were made for him to study medicine at Heidelberg University.

When he graduated from Heidelberg in 1940 he was recruited into the Abwehr, Germany's military intelligence organization. After sending information to London through a network of anti-Nazi Germans, in 1945 he was ordered by the British to escape. Wearing a British uniform, he joined a column of prisoners of war. After four months of captivity, he was released by allied troops and in November 1945 flown home to England to a hero's welcome—a secret hero's welcome in MI6 headquarters.

'You must find this man and talk to him at length,' the *Mail* instructed me. 'A lot of it has been told, but the truth is we smell a rat. And why do we smell a rat? Because his brother has told us that Charles has gone potty. His brother says that Charles must be a fast traveller because if he was working for the Brits behind German lines, he came home to London for tea every night.'

The *Mail* smelt rats in many fantastic claims. I had to agree with them about this one. But what a wonderful hoax, if that's what it was. It was my job to find out, even though Charles had spoken to other British papers and convinced them of the veracity of his claims with documents and photographs. Then again, we all remember the Hitler diaries, a forged bundle of documents that fooled Germany's *Stern* magazine and major newspapers in 1983.

Dozens of phone calls, a search through the electoral rolls and many door-knocks later, I was sitting in a restaurant called the Ritz in one of Melbourne's swanky hotels. Opposite me was the pensioner who was front-page news in Britain. Wearing a blazer, his silvery hair combed back and his eyes almost hidden by a pair of dark glasses, Charles took a swig of German wine and said he was happy to answer any questions. I decided to go straight for the throat.

'People are saying that your story is a load of bunkum. Are you a hoaxer?'

Charles swallowed an oyster, adjusted his maroon silk tie and retorted, 'Certainly not, old boy! I don't care whether people believe me or not. I have the Iron Cross to prove my work behind German lines. There were others like me—heroes all!—but we tend not to talk about it. Someone found out about my work as a spy and the next minute it's all over the news. So I decided it was time to speak up. If there's false gossip that's starting up, it doesn't worry me. I've faced a lot more in Germany than listening to idle chatter.'

'So there will be official records, either in Germany or in Britain, that will support your story?'

He smiled, pulled at the crease of his grey flannels, and shook his head as if that was the stupidest question.

'The point is, old boy, all records concerning my background have been deliberately tampered with by those who wanted to protect my identity. Even my own family have been fed a version of my wartime exploits which weren't exactly true. I'm not setting myself up for hero worship when I say I did my country a great service. The only reason for me coming forward is to clear allegations that Sir Hugh Sinclair was not prepared for the outbreak of war.'

I felt it was time to point out that Charles appeared to have a bad memory about his schooldays. He claimed he had attended Marlborough school, but his brother had come forward in England to say he had gone to Kilburn High in north-west London.

'I don't know why he would say a thing like that. I've never heard of Kilburn High. How do you think I was able to get my Old Marlborians' school tie?'

Well, how did he get it? 'I'll tell you the truth about that,' said Charles. 'I bought it for three quid in a shop in Marlborough two years ago. But of course I had to explain that I had the authority to buy it from Mr Thompson of the Old Marlborians' Association.'

He took another sip of the white wine that he said always reminded him of the dear friends who helped him in Germany. I mentioned his brother, who had said that Charles was lost in fantasy land.

'Look, old boy, whatever my brother says is absolutely true—as he has heard it. He and every other member of my family were fed a version of my life after I was signed up by British intelligence in 1933. British intelligence could not take risks for the sake of those in the field. That's why you won't find my name in the records at Marlborough. I was enrolled under my real name, but while

I was attending there I was given a new identity and the old me was wiped from the records.'

Now, about his father: why had he said his father had been a secret agent in World War I when, in reality, it seemed he was a turf accountant, a bookmaker.

He chuckled. 'There's a very simple answer. My father was a great humorist. On my birth certificate the registrar should have written that my father was a "commissioned agent—a spy—but the registrar must have misheard and instead wrote "commission agent", which is, of course, a turf accountant. When my father saw what had been written he laughed his head off and thought it was so funny he wouldn't correct it.'

All right, how did Charles explain his brother's insistence that he trained as a ship's purser when Charles himself says he was at Marlborough?

'Again, the official version, old boy. My cover was so well done that somewhere I could probably produce some ships' documents showing that I served on two liners, although I was never really there—I was in Germany at Heidelberg University, studying as a doctor.'

Did he get a degree?

'No, not a degree exactly. I had a certificate stating my qualifications, but all that was surpassed when I was enlisted into German intelligence.'

But, I insisted, how could he prove he was actually in Germany … ever?

To my astonishment, he pushed his chair back and hoisted a leg onto the clean white tablecloth, almost knocking over the bottle of riesling. He yanked back his trouser leg and pointed to a small scar on the shin. Other diners stared in amazement as he struggled to keep his balance on one leg.

'See that? Shrapnel wound from an RAF strafing. I was in a POW camp at the time after I had served my espionage duties and a German saved my life by pushing me into a dung heap. I was also hit by Russian machine-gun fire, which left two scars across my stomach.'

He constantly referred to the Iron Cross the Germans had given him for military work on their behalf. Just when did he get it? And who presented it to him?

'Do you know, old boy, and I say this with great embarrassment, I can't remember a thing about that. You must understand that I was under severe pressure and only got out of Germany by putting on a uniform that had belonged to a dead British prisoner of war.'

He sat back down, took another sip, and went on, 'I'm afraid to say that the period from the early 1930s to 1946 is pretty much a complete blur. All I recall is that my brother found the Iron Cross at the bottom of my kitbag.'

If things were such a blur, I asked, could the Iron Cross—like the old school tie—have come from a second-hand shop in England, assuming that it was a real Iron Cross.

'Oh, come, come. I have no doubt what I did and what rewards I reaped. The Iron Cross was definitely given to me. I can vaguely remember an officer presenting me with it and making a statement along the lines that I had been very brave.'

He slapped his forehead. 'Of course, I'd entirely forgotten. I have photographs of me behind German lines. Would that dispel your doubts?'

He reached into his inside pocket and laid out four black-and-white postcard-sized photographs of what appeared to be leather-coated Gestapo officers posing beside a car. The men in the photo and the whole atmosphere of the shot seemed genuine enough, but there was something about the quality of the paper on which it had been printed. I turned it over and could just make out some rubbed-out lines. The pictures were postcard-sized because they were postcards! It seemed that Charles had been shopping once again and had found the postcards on which wartime photos had been transposed, for sale to current-day tourists. He, or someone, had then made rather a hash of trying to wipe out the lines to write the addresses on the back.

Charles, a $200-a-week pensioner, lived in a modest flat in the Melbourne suburb of East St Kilda, where I had first tracked him down. He had an electric train set which filled almost the whole of one room—the main station was called Peddlehome—and on his bedroom bookshelf were works by novelist John le Carre, famous, of course, for his spy novels.

Charles did not have many kind words to say about the author of another one of the books on his shelf, espionage writer Nigel West.

'He has pushed me further than I wanted to go. I wrote to him to set the record straight in one of his books and he came rushing over here and started lining me up for interviews with news organizations and asking vast amounts for my story. I haven't received a penny from anyone. But everyone is after me for more. *Stern* magazine in Germany is offering a great deal of money. But I'll have to give the reporters from Germany a security check. It's possible that neo-Nazis, upset with the work I did, will abduct the reporters and come over to Australia posing as them and my life will be in danger.'

Charles finished his wine. The interview was over. There was a car waiting for him. His agent, Barry Moignard, a justice of the peace, he said, would be controlling just who he spoke to. I walked out into the street with Charles. Barry Moignard's car—a Mercedes, fittingly—was waiting. Charles got into the back seat and off it went into the night.

I noticed the number plate and could hardly believe my eyes. It was 'BM 070'—close to the code name for James '007' Bond—an appropriate salute for the spy who almost was.

◆

When Isobelle's father died of pneumonia it was decided we should move into the family home, a three-bedroom house on a corner block directly opposite Taronga Park Zoo. There we were joined by Isobelle's sister, Cynthia, a teacher and single mother of two young children. The occupants of Whiting Beach Road now consisted of me, Isobelle, Madeline, Cynthia and her two children, Aunt Dorothy, Boy, Pompey, Miss Mouse, Rolly and Sassy, the white rabbit, the black rabbit—and Dennis.

Yes Dennis, dear God. He turned up early one morning, an old friend of Isobelle's and Cynthia's, driving in from the country in a battered orange 'ute' with enormous bull bars on the front and spotlights on the roof. A lanky figure with a shock of white hair down to his shoulders, he greeted Isobelle and Cynthia with a 'Hi Izzy, hi Cynth' and marched through to the kitchen, carrying his 'swag' (a canvas sheet in which he had piled his entire possessions, including a small cooking stove and a thin, rolled up mattress). I explained there was nowhere for him to sleep, but by then he was looking out the kitchen window and eyeing up the garden shed.

'That'll do,' he said and hurried out the back door. I watched as he tugged open the shed door. It had been locked, but that was obviously no impediment for Dennis.

I tried to find out from Isobelle and her sister how long they had known this curious visitor from the bush. The best I could get from them was, 'Ages and ages—we've told you about him a million times', which they hadn't.

Dennis, it seemed, had been living in and around Dubbo, a country town north-west of Sydney, where he had been a jack of all trades. Now, he explained over a mug of tea, he had decided to try his luck in the big city. Did he have a job lined up? Not as such. Did he have anything to live on? Not as such.

Isobelle, always full of kindness, offered him a chair but he said he had to stand. 'That drive has brought on the agitation.'

Don't ask him, I silently pleaded. Don't ask him. Cynthia was likely to do just that. Don't ask him about the agitation.

'What agitation is that?' Cynthia asked.

'Haemorrhoids,' he replied quickly. 'I'm going to have to get them seen to while I'm here. You can't imagine—oh bugger!' he suddenly cried. 'I forgot about the bloody 'roo!'

He was out through the front door and back again with a sack he'd hauled off the back of the ute. He dumped it on the kitchen table and carefully peeled it open.

A small brown head appeared.

'I found it in its mother's pouch on the way down,' he said, as the joey peered wide-eyed around the kitchen. 'The mother'd been killed by a car. I was driving by and saw the joey's head and legs, pulled it out and here we are.' He patted it on the head. 'Aren't we mate?'

Isobelle pulled the sack away and lifted the small creature into her arms. Its long baby legs stuck up in the air, much as they would have in its mother's pouch.

'You dear little thing,' she said. 'Are you sure it's not injured?' she asked Dennis.

'Not unless it banged itself up in the sack,' he said. 'It's been in there for a few hours and I could hear it crashing around as it tried to get out.'

'Lucky we're just across the road from the zoo,' I said, unable to resist giving it a pat. 'Let's take it over there now and they'll sort out what to do with it.'

'Yes, I'll do that,' said Isobelle. 'I'll just give it some warm milk, let it settle down a bit and then we'll take it over.'

Famous last words.

CHAPTER 12

The Sinking of the *Rainbow Warrior*

While my time with 'spy' Charles Evans had been fun, the spy story in which I became engrossed in New Zealand was no laughing matter. It was the scandal of the French government sending a team to Auckland to sink the Greenpeace ship *Rainbow Warrior*.

The event still reads like a spy novel or the plot of a movie thriller—and the French almost got away with it.

My faithful radio news informed me late at night in July 1985 that Greenpeace's flagship, a converted trawler moored in Auckland harbour, had been blown up and sunk. There were no more details but the *Mail* was demanding a full and immediate story.

I began making calls to every news organization I could think of in New Zealand. But it was the early hours of the morning, newspaper staff had gone home and there were only one or two people manning the news desks of radio and TV stations. In one bizarre call I unwittingly found myself talking on radio. Not realising I was on air I asked the host if he had any details about the bombing of the ship. He laughed and told me to stop mucking about. As the one-sided conversation continued, it dawned on me that he hadn't heard about the attack and had decided I was one of the late-night nutters who called in regularly.

I arrived in Auckland the following day to piece together what I could. But the story became so big that I felt compelled to begin writing a book about it. I was not to know that at least two other books were in the making, one by the *Sunday*

Times Insight team. The first book to come out about a news event is usually the bestseller. A race to publish was up and running.

I continued to feed material daily to the *Mail* while writing my chapters. It was not easy to pull the story together from the authorities because the affair had become a major diplomatic incident. The New Zealand government was furious that the French had sent a sabotage team into the country to blow up a ship. The story became bigger by the day and, with little to work on from official channels, I had to pull it together from whatever witnesses and clues I could gather.

The sabotage team had arrived by submarine off the northern coast of New Zealand, were picked up by a yacht, sailed into a small bay in North Auckland and had made their way down to Auckland, posing as tourists. A frogman reached the *Rainbow Warrior* using special re-breathing apparatus, which allowed him to swim underwater without sending bubbles up to the surface, as would have been the case had he used an oxygen tank. The saboteur attached two limpet mines to the hull of the *Rainbow Warrior* and then swam clear and was picked up by a Zodiac inflatable.

The French believed the ship had to be disabled—or sunk—because it was due to take Greenpeace protesters into the Pacific to disrupt nuclear tests on a tiny atoll called Mururoa. What the saboteurs did not know was that the *Rainbow Warrior* was not unoccupied when the limpet mines went off. Nine crew were sleeping on board. British engineer Davy Edwards yelled at everyone to abandon ship after the first explosions rocked the vessel, and it began to go down. All but one got off: 35-year-old Portuguese photographer Fernando Pereira, a father of two who lived in Holland and was a veteran of several conservation campaigns. He had gone below decks after the first blast to get his cameras and make sure everyone was out. He was caught by the second explosion.

Suspicion quickly fell on the French—they were the intended target of the *Rainbow Warrior*'s voyage. A massive nationwide hunt got under way for any French citizens who were in New Zealand. Had it not been for the arrest of two of the sabotage team there might have been no hard proof that France was behind the outrage. But greed was their undoing. Captain Dominique Prieur, 36, and Major Alain Mafart, 35, were caught. They had rented a van to travel around the North Island as part of their 'tourist' cover. Having returned the vehicle, they vanished. Frustrated police accepted they could be anywhere but incredibly Mafart returned to the car rental depot to claim a refund over a discrepancy in the paperwork. The French couple were grabbed when an employee at the depot called the police.

Prieur and Marfat were originally charged with the photographer's murder. They pleaded not guilty to manslaughter in the Auckland courthouse and were ordered to serve 'prison time' at a French military base on the tiny Pacific island of Hao, where, outraged peace group members said, they would live a life of luxury, enjoying fine French foods and wines.

Had there been a trade-off between New Zealand and France? New Zealand prime minister David Lange denied a deal had been struck, but I had no doubt, as I watched the smirks on the faces of the French spies in the Auckland court, that there had been a great deal of international bargaining. Had the murder charge remained, the spies would have undoubtedly pleaded not guilty, resulting in a lengthy trial which would have shed further light on the ugly affair. And that would have caused even greater embarrassment to French president, François Mitterand, who had already lost his defence minister to the scandal.

So it was over … almost. An unknown number of the sabotage team remained at large and are believed to have escaped by yacht before being picked up by submarine near the French Pacific territory of Noumea and taken to Tahiti.

Isobelle went through my manuscript with a fine toothcomb and the book was the first of many to be published on the bombing. It was called the *Rainbow Warrior Affair*.

◆

Dennis from Dubbo, I regret to say, was still with us, complaining of ongoing haemorrhoid problems. Whenever I returned home from an assignment, I would hope the orange ute would not be parked outside the house. Inevitably it was. One day, alighting from a cab, I saw a huge dent in the door of my car, which had been parked outside the house. As I approached the front door, I noticed wire netting stretching from the side of the house to the garden fence.

Not only was Dennis still with us, so was the kangaroo. It was now a monstrous beast, hopping around the garden and trying to jump over next door's fence. The wire told me Isobelle was making strenuous attempts to keep it safe and secure.

I dropped my bags inside the door and walked down the hall, catching sight of Aunt Dorothy sprawled out on a bed, her mouth open, her contented snores filling the room. The Maltese terriers were asleep at her feet with Pompey the cat. Most reporters come home to a wife and children. I seemed to be returning to increasing madness.

Isobelle sat me down in the kitchen and waited for the question. 'What happened to my car?'

'Well,' she began. I cut in.

'Has Dennis got anything to do with it?'

'What happened was this: Dennis was trying to turn around and he didn't see your car and backed into it. He says he's sorry and that his insurance will pay for it.'

'And where is Dennis now? Still in the shed?'

'That's where he's sleeping still, yes, but he's not there now. He's gone running up the road with Cynthia.'

'Running? He's not the running type and Cynthia certainly isn't. Why are they running?'

'They're trying to catch Rover.'

'Rover? Who the hell's Rover? Don't tell me you've got another dog!'

'The kangaroo. You know that we called him Rover. He got out. They're trying to round him up before anyone reports this to the police.'

I had a horrible vision of Rover hopping along the main street of Mosman, one of the snootiest suburbs in Sydney. At least, for the first time in my life, I'd be able to write a story that supported the British impression that kangaroos hopped through the streets of Australian cities. The only problem was that this particular animal was ours.

I brought my hands to my eyes and when I lowered them I saw the pile of long-stemmed grass on the kitchen bench. Kangaroo fodder, which Cynthia had been out collecting that morning.

Thankfully, Cynthia, Dennis and a handful of understanding neighbours caught Rover and he was brought back, most obediently for a kangaroo, on the end of a rope. Isobelle promised in front of everybody that she would get the zoo to pick him up the next day.

Dennis, whose voice always seemed to carry a very long way, promised he would get onto his insurance company and arrange for my car to be repaired. I thought Isobelle had said arrangements had already been made. And there was something about Dennis that seemed different, but I couldn't put a finger on it.

Anyway, before we could go into the fine details about my car, he was out the door and I heard his ute roaring into life.

Then it struck me. 'Isobelle, why is Dennis wearing green eye shadow?'

'He's going through a bit of a crisis, I think,' she said. 'He was wearing stockings one day and from what I can gather he's been going to some strange clubs in Sydney and staying there all night.'

I went to the fridge to take out an orange juice, but the container was empty. Why would anyone put an empty container back in the fridge?

'That's Cynthia,' said Isobelle, removing an empty milk carton. 'She's only being thoughtful. There's always a tiny drop left because she doesn't want to be the one to use it all up.'

I found another bottle of juice in the pantry and opened the freezer to add some ice.

'What the hell is THAT?' I howled.

Resting among the ice cubes was a human hand, white, totally drained of blood, its withered fingers reaching up as if to grasp anyone who came within reach.

'So that's where it is!' Isobelle exclaimed. 'Dennis has been looking everywhere for it.'

She closed the door. 'Better leave it where it is,' she said. 'I'll let him take it out.'

Before I could say anything she continued: 'It's his rubber haemorrhoid glove. He uses it to …'

'Stop! What is it doing in our fridge?'

'He keeps it hygienically clean with some special solution but he's been told to keep it away from any kind of contamination so he thought the fridge would be the best place. He must have forgotten he'd put it in the freezer.'

I slumped back down onto the kitchen chair. Then I said very softly: 'Isobelle, can I just ask if you could take care of a few things? Can you please get rid of that glove? Can we find out how to fumigate a freezer? Will you kindly remove the kangaroo once and for all. And most important of all, can you get rid of bloody Dennis!'

But Dennis was just one of several waifs who turned up at our door at around this time, all of them in the footsteps of Isobelle. There was the mad bloke she found sitting at the kerb as she was walking to the shops one Sunday morning. He was crying and he had a large cardboard box beside him. Something was moving inside. It turned out that the box was filled with six kittens and that the man—I'll call him Sergeant Joe because Isobelle and I have deliberately forgotten his name—had been thrown out of his flat, along with his wife and the kittens, that very morning and he had nowhere to go.

When Isobelle brought him home—yes, she brought him home—he said he was very grateful that she was putting him up for a few days, words which rang alarm bells. Placing the cardboard box of kittens at his feet, he pulled a walkie-talkie unit from his pocket, switched it on, made it squeak, then said into it: 'Transport. D–46. Transport required.' He then rattled off some unintelligible numbers and letters, checked our address, and told us that his 'transport' wasn't immediately available and that his wife would have to come by taxi. She arrived an hour later, a thin, meek woman who seemed to be very much under the thumb of our guest.

Over dinner he explained he was a military intelligence officer working on a number of top-secret missions. Shades of old Charles in Melbourne. He would interrupt himself by pulling out his walkie-talkie and arranging for transport at a certain time but later he would repeat the process, changing the time. He was totally nuts. They left after a month, leaving behind four of the cats, all of which went down with severe cat flu. He and his wife, he said, were heading to New Zealand on another mission.

'Isobelle,' I said. 'Where do you get these people?'

'Well, you meet them in your job. I meet them in my life,' she said. I had no answer. Especially when she added: 'They all need a little help along the way. It's not much to give, is it?'

It seemed that hardly had we had this conversation when another guest took up residence. Doug was a burly, bald Scotsman who had migrated to Australia many years earlier and was earning a living as a process server. He was the kind of man you wouldn't want to argue with if he came round to collect a debt. But he was always polite in our company.

I don't know where Isobelle had come across him. But he slumped down on our couch for weeks. He said he had been a cook in the British Army and, I have to give it to him, he knocked up a mean soup and would regale us with stories of characters he had met in the shadowy world he operated in.

Like Dennis, Doug would often disappear into the darkness of Sydney at night. Sometimes he would fly off to the Philippines and we didn't have to guess what he was up to over there—he would return with tales of slinky women in gloomy bars and hotel rooms that could be rented by the hour. The enduring memory of him was the way he spoke. An ambulance on his lips was an 'ambolince', the police were 'pleece' and a hospital was an 'ossie-pittal'.

◆

Thankfully, I had to leave Doug and Dennis and the other permanent/temporary human and animal members of the household behind, as I hurried to the airport to follow up a sensational news flash: the matinee jacket Lindy Chamberlain had claimed was being worn by Azaria at the time she disappeared had been found. She had been telling the truth all along, the Northern Territory authorities agreed—and it probably supported her claim that no dingo saliva had been found on the baby's jumpsuit because Azaria had been wearing the matinee jacket over the jumpsuit.

In a sensational move, the authorities opened the gates of Darwin's Berrimah Jail on 7 February 1986, and Lindy walked free—or at least she was free pending a new investigation into the case. During the four years she had spent behind bars she had given birth to her fourth child, Kahlia, but the baby had been taken from her and given to her husband Michael to care for.

The circumstances surrounding the discovery of the matinee jacket were curious. The police announced that the jacket had been found beside the body of a British tourist who had fallen to his death while climbing Uluru in a prohibited area. I began checking into the circumstances of 31-year-old David Brett's death and located a phone number for his mother, Mrs Doreen Brett, in Hartley, Kent. What she told me left me dumbfounded.

'I'm convinced that Azaria and my son have been the victims of some black magic cult,' she said. I assumed these were the ravings of a mother filled with grief over her loss. She added: 'When David came back to Britain last year, his parting words to me were: "If anything happens to me, I have been made a sacrifice".'

Well, something had happened. His death had gone virtually unnoticed by the Australian and British press, but I was determined to find out more about him. His mother promised to send me some of the letters he had written from Australia and when I began reading them I was inspired to investigate. They were the ravings of a disturbed young man, but what seemed to have driven him was curiously linked to the Azaria Chamberlain case.

David had grown up in Kent and stayed on at school until he was 18, before announcing to his parents and two sisters that instead of going to university he wanted to travel. He worked his way around the world. It was 1973 when the last of the hippies were heading across Asia to Europe—just 18 months before I made my own trip in my Ford Transit—and when the final platoons of American soldiers were leaving Vietnam.

Before David Brett left, he went to a tattooist in Chatham and had his buttocks branded with a Union Jack and, underneath, the words 'Born to Lose'.

When he returned to England in 1979 he carried close to £10,000, which he had earned in the iron ore mines at Mount Newman in north-west Australia. After hanging around in England for a while he decided to head back down-under. He had a plan to buy a property in the Queensland mining town of Mount Isa, which he had visited on his earlier trip—and where the Chamberlains were living. Did he ever meet them, or attend Pastor Michael Chamberlain's Seventh Day Adventist church? That I don't know. David arrived in Perth and stayed for a month with Nina Castle and her husband, whom he had met previously. For the next three years he played his guitar and drifted around Western Australia. Eventually he moved into a flat on the top floor of the eight-storey Lakeview Apartments in Claremont, a Perth suburb.

Back in England, Doreen Brett assumed all was well with her wandering son who by then, in 1985, was 31. In fact, he was having serious problems. He wrote to his mother in tiny, spidery handwriting telling her that 'something strange' was happening and he hoped to return home to England soon. In a phone call, he told her, 'You're not going to believe what's happening to me. It's really freaking me.'

Doreen implored him to explain, but he hung up. The following month David approached Mr and Mrs Castle in a local supermarket. 'I need some help,' he said. His hair was tangled, his clothes dishevelled. 'Please, you've got to help me.'

They took him home. 'I'm possessed by a demon,' he said. 'It's in my stomach. It's living in my stomach.'

The Castles had always thought David was a level-headed young man, but they agreed later that he was having a nervous breakdown. A friend of theirs mentioned the curious affair to Pastor Milton Gabrielson. The Congregational minister thought he knew what was wrong. He believed that many who displayed signs of mental torment were possessed and the only way to help was to challenge the evil spirit to leave the body.

I travelled to Western Australia to find out more. A stocky man in his 50s, Pastor Gabrielson explained that the foundation for his beliefs was, of course, the work of Christ. As the Gospels taught, Jesus Christ had met a man called Legion, who had been driven by the devil that possessed him to wander into the wilderness. Christ commanded the spirits to depart from Legion—they entered a herd of pigs which then, according to the Book of Luke, 'ran violently down a steep place into the lake, and were choked.'

Back in Hartley, Mrs Brett and her daughters were becoming desperately worried about David. He told them in a phone call, 'I'm seeing a priest for an exorcism. But if I don't arrive home, you'll know that I've been sacrificed.'

Pastor Gabrielson and a church deacon met David at the Castles' home on 6 June. 'David's eyes were glazed and his face was white' the pastor said. 'The first thing I thought was that David was in the grip of an evil power. He wasn't crazy or suffering a breakdown, but he was without doubt under the influence of something linked to the occult, to something that was not of this world.

'He was like a man struggling with an inner force. He said "they" were chanting in the flat next door. They were trying to kill him. They wanted him to jump from the balcony. "They chant, chant, chant. I can't sleep. The other night I pulled the blankets over my head and my body lit up, shining bright and luminous. When I got into the shower, the devil came in with me. I fought with him with the water flowing down around us." I know I'm going to be killed. They want me to die.'

Gabrielson decided to perform the exorcism. With the lights in the room remaining on so that he could look David straight in the eyes 'and stare at the spirit which possessed him,' he commanded the devil to leave the Englishman's body in the name of Christ. It sounded like a scene from *The Exorcist*.

It went on for two hours, and Pastor Gabrielson felt he had not been entirely successful. Whatever was troubling David, he believed, remained with him. More time was needed. But David did not turn up for a second session.

Instead, he flew home to England where he shocked his mother and sisters by telling them, 'I died out there. They have my brain, you know. But I'll never go back. That exorcism, it's just made things worse. It's taken all the good from me. I've only got evil left … only evil.'

Doreen told me that David began walking around the house, telling his family that he was tormented by voices, by the faces of the devil. Very slowly over the following days, she learned a little of what David thought had happened in

Australia. Two men had been living next door. Hearing David playing his guitar, one of them asked David to teach him, but after the lessons began David realized the man wasn't paying any attention. Instead, he seemed to be studying David. Not long afterwards, the chanting had begun, followed by tapping on the wall. He felt certain that the bricks and mortar were going to fall in on him. Items started to vanish from his flat. He began to lose his appetite.

Back with his family, he sat around the house reading the Bible and reciting the Lord's Prayer. His family sought medical help and in August David was admitted to a general hospital in Dartford, Kent. But doctors could find nothing wrong with him, suggesting that he just needed a break. But he suddenly declared that he had to return to Australia. 'I have to go back. I must go back!'

His sisters reluctantly drove him to the airport. 'You know,' he said, 'I don't really want to go. It's just that I have to. And remember, if anything happens to me, you'll know I've been sacrificed.'

He moved into a flat in Sydney, but people he met or shared accommodation with felt worried about being in his company because he continued to talk about the demon in his stomach. He tried to leave Sydney to travel to Perth four times, but never got any farther than Liverpool, 12 miles (20 kilometres) west. On 15 January 1986, he said goodbye to a group of new acquaintances and this time he didn't come back.

Bert Cramer was the only dairy farmer in the Alice Springs district. He had arrived in 'The Alice' in 1957 looking for work and always remembered how the locals took him in—since then he had tried to help anyone who passed his way. Although not a regular churchgoer, he had a Lutheran background and believed in the unseen forces of good and evil.

On the afternoon of 24 January a man with a small backpack arrived at the farm asking for milk. Bert gave him a pint and the traveller asked if there were any jobs on the farm. Bert thought the stranger was reasonably well presented, although he had a look in his eye that Bert couldn't quite place. His visitor said he'd done farmwork before, although Bert reckoned from his hands that it must have been some time ago.

Bert told David he could follow him around, the best way of learning the routine of things. As they moved around the farm, unloading hay, checking the cattle, David asked, 'Do you believe in evil spirits?'

'As a matter of fact I do,' said the farmer. 'Why do you ask?'

'Because I have been exorcized.'

Bert wanted to question David a bit more about it but was interrupted. He gave the Englishman a couple of chops and showed him to a shed that had been fitted out with a primus stove and a few utensils.

The next morning Bert found David sitting under a tree staring blankly at the horizon. He hadn't eaten the chops, hadn't even cooked them.

'I won't be able to start work yet,' David said. 'But will it be all right if I come back and make a bit of a home out of that shed?'

'Yes, sure, mate,' said Bert. 'Where are you going?'

David looked intently at Bert and the farmer thought the Englishman wasn't quite seeing him. Then David said he was going to Ross River, a cattle station which also operated as a tourist village, some 75 miles (120 kilometres) east of Alice Springs.

Bert gave David a three-and-a-half pint (two-litre) water bottle and said that if he was planning to hitchhike he should wait for a lift at Emily Gap, the last water hole, about four-and-a-half miles (seven kilometres) from Alice Springs.

'You shouldn't walk anywhere in the desert round here,' said Bert. 'It's dangerous—the sun will burn you up.' Bert told me that David had been like a man on a mission, someone who had been mysteriously guided to a place.

Gary Glazebrook, manager of the Ross River Station, found David on the road some six miles (ten kilometres) out from the station. David said he was heading there to camp. Gary gave him a lift and showed him the camping area. The next morning, however, there were no signs David had spent the night there.

On Saturday 26 January, David bought a one-way coach ticket from Alice Springs to the tourist resort at Yulara, near Uluru. The bus arrived at Yulara at 2PM. A couple of hours later local journalist Tony Wells saw a lone, hatless man walking unsteadily towards Uluru. He wouldn't swear to it one hundred per cent but it seemed there was something weird about the man's eyes.

A little after 8PM David was 660 feet (200 metres) up the face of Uluru, unaware that he was being watched by Tanya Armstrong and Edwin Edwards, who were returning from the sunset viewing area. They thought they had better tell the rangers about the man climbing the rock in the twilight and so far up.

David climbed up over the lichen. Some of the bits broke away as he climbed. He was a long way up. Later Pastor Gabrielson pointed out a biblical passage because he read into it a relevance to David's fate:

And the devil; taking him up into a high mountain, showed unto him all the kingdoms of the world in a moment of time.

And the devil said unto him, All this power will I give thee, and the glory of them: for that is delivered unto me; and to whomsoever I will give it.

If thou therefore wilt worship me, all shall be thine.

And Jesus answered and said unto him, Get thee behind me Satan; for it is written, Thou shalt worship the Lord thy God, and him only shalt thou serve.

Early in the morning of the following Sunday 2 February, Paul Robinson, a tourist from Victoria, was strolling around the base of Uluru when he came across a body. David's backpack was still attached but his right arm, left hand and right foot were missing, apparently taken by dingos.

Line searches of the area were carried out with the aid of Conservation Commission rangers and Northern Territory Emergency Service volunteers. If there were body parts still around it was the decent thing to try to find them. As the searchers spread out from where the shattered body had been found and walked through the nearby desert undergrowth, about 150 paces away, a shout went up. Somebody had found something.

The searchers gathered around. It was cloth, a garment—woollen clothing of some kind, soiled and stained as if it had been lying out in the weather for a long time.

Somebody said it looked like a baby's jacket. A strange feeling came over many of them. Some said later that their blood had run cold, as their minds went back five-and-a-half years, to the time when a baby called Azaria, whose name means 'for whom Jehovah aids', had vanished in the black night of the desert.

CHAPTER 13

A Thorny Time for Colleen

After being stranded on Norfolk Island years earlier while Julian Knight went berserk killing people in Melbourne, I wondered what would happen if I ever had to go back, for with the whole of the Pacific as part of my patch, a return one day was a certainty.

It is home to descendants of the *Bounty* mutineers, many of whom carry the names of the British crew who turned against their captain, William Bligh, and set him and 18 others adrift in 1789. There are Christians, Buffets, Adams—oh, and there's Colleen McCullough.

She, of course, is the famous Australian novelist who gave us *The Thorn Birds* and many other classics. Among them is a short novel called *The Ladies of Missalonghi*, published in 1987. It was popular, made suddenly even more so when a sharp-eyed reader noticed apparently remarkably similar passages in Miss McCullough's work and 1926 novel *The Blue Castle* by the Canadian writer and author of *Anne of Greengables*, L.M. Montgomery. It was claimed the plot and character details were nearly identical. In short, Miss McCullough was being accused of plagiarism.

Would McCullough talk to me about the claims? It was a chance I had to take. At the tiny Norfolk Island airport I was greeted by a wandering minstrel. It was, and is, a tightly knit community and I wondered, as I made efforts to find out where Colleen McCullough lived, just how well she fitted in. It did not take long to realize that she had been happily welcomed as 'one of us', which was not particularly surprising because her novels had made her into a multimillionaire and a decent amount had gone out into the community. It took some persuasion before a taxi driver agreed to take me to her home, a simple house on a hilltop.

Far from the 'go away' I had expected, she threw open the door and asked me to follow her, a large woman with red hair in a flowing gown, through to her conservatory where she said she did her writing.

'Would you like dinner?' she asked. 'I'm about to start cooking so let me know what you would like.'

This was a surprise—I had found that usually people accused of doing something wrong tended to keep well away from the media until they'd had time to come up with a good explanation. But as she cooked us steaks she was ready to answer anything I could put to her. Yes, of course she had heard the accusations of plagiarism and her unease had grown by the minute.

'No, I'm not a thief. Neither am I a fool,' she said. 'I have too many wonderful ideas of my own to have to steal from another writer. They can throw at me what they like—tell me again that they hate my books, set me up once more as the Aunt Sally to be knocked down at the coconut shy—but never, never accuse me of being a plagiarist.'

She admitted quite openly that she had read Montgomery as a child, along with some 40 other books a week.

'Perhaps because I loved her work best of all, my subconscious recorded something. But she was writing in a certain genre, she was writing in a period—and so was I. There are bound to be similarities because that's the way things happened in small towns.

'I know what it was like to be poor. I know what it's like to suffer the slings and arrows of spinsterhood because I was 45 before I married. I was never a repressed old maid, but I know what it was like to be alone out there, young and plain. Let's face it, I'm no Miss Australia to look at. And it was because of my own personal experience that I have had a particular fascination with the old maid.'

A room adjoining the conservatory was adorned with sheets of paper pinned to the wall. They were research notes for her next major project, a series of novels on the Roman empire, which she admitted was an enormous task.

She was keen to talk about old maids, however, given the crisis she was facing. 'Four of my five novels—*Tim, An Indecent Obsession, A Creed for the Third Millennium* and then, of course, *Ladies*—have unmarried women as heroines or villains. The life I gave Missy [the protaganist in *Ladies*] is based on my own experiences and those of my mother, who really had a tough time of it. The idea of a woman setting out to catch a man on the basis that she was dying came to me a long time ago. I have known at least half a dozen women who have resorted to this tactic. In fact, it was this woman who knew damn well she wasn't dying who set me off. I started to put the story together as light relief when I was writing *Creed*. Then the publishers asked me if I would write a ghost story for them, one of a series of novels they wanted to bring out, and I told them I had just the thing.'

Yes, she admitted, there were some similarities between her book and Montgomery's. All the comparisons that have been drawn, McCullough insisted, were there because she and L.M. Montgomery captured the way of life of the time as they both experienced it: both heroines hate oatmeal porridge, both have uncles who own a country store, neither woman is permitted the companionship of a cat. The Australian Hurlingfords attend the Church of England and the Canadian Stirlings are staunch Anglicans.

'Oh dear,' sighed Miss McCullough, clearly exasperated as I pointed out the similarities. 'My family had to be something because each town's leading family was either Church of England or Catholic, and I had used Catholics in *Thorn Birds*.'

But then there was the similarity of the enviable, desirable, tall, golden-haired cousins in the spinsters' lives, Alicia for Missy, Olive for Montgomery's Valancy. 'But you see,' said the author, 'there had to be a contrast of characters and being tall and blonde was a great mark of beauty in the days before the peroxide bottle. Do you know what I think? I think that Lucy Montgomery, who comes through in her writings as a really nice person, wouldn't be upset at all by my book.'

So that was Colleen McCullough's case for the defence. She hoped I would put it out to the world and help clear her name. I thanked her for the nice dinner. She insisted before I left on giving me a number of signed copies of her books. Among them was *The Ladies of Missalonghi*. She had written on the inside page: 'This is the contentious one!'

◆

Back in Sydney, a wonderful battle of a different kind was taking place between Lady Susan Renouf and her husband, Sir Frank. It gave me and *Daily Mail* readers an insight not only into how the other half lived, but revealed the eccentricities of their daily lives.

Lady Susan was no stranger to the high life, having been married first to Andrew Peacock, leader of the Australian Liberal Party, and then to British racehorse owner and pools tycoon Robert Sangster. Then along came New Zealand-born Sir Frank, from whom she gained her title. They set up home in her magnificent multimillion-dollar harbourside mansion, purchased for her by Mr Sangster. If TV viewers, gripped at the time by the US soap opera *Dallas*, thought they had seen it all, the best drama of all was about to hit their screens. Princess Diana was visiting Australia, but it was Lady Susan who stole the show and was the lead item on the evening news.

For two months, from November 1987 to January 1988, Lady Susan and Sir Frank had been waging war inside the mansion. It began when she stormed out of the property after, it was said, she accused him of losing a fortune on the stockmarket. The figure of $25 million was being bandied about. She stayed at her home in the country until her father, Sir John Rossiter, died in late January and, seeking compassion, she returned to the Sydney house she knew as Toison d'Or, meaning Golden Fleece. Sir Frank later renamed it Paradis-sur-Mer (Paradise on the Sea) but it had not been anything like that since Lady Susan returned.

Despite what seemed like a reconciliation on Australia Day, 26 January, when Sir Frank was seen to give her a friendly tap on the head with his tennis racket, the relationship plunged downhill. I was outside the gates when Sir Frank approached from the inside.

'What's happening in there, Sir Frank?' I asked. He was surprisingly, well, frank.

'The rumours that you might have heard suggesting that I have been trying to starve her out of the house are completely untrue,' he said. We hadn't heard anything about starvation. 'But she can jump into her car and go off as soon as she wishes.'

What added to the mystery, however, was the presence of 'his and her' security guards. She couldn't come and go without getting his guards' permission and the opposite applied to him. And any goods delivered by local stores and tossed over the wall had to be logged by both groups of guards in a 'goods received' book.

Lady Susan, wearing a dress that was printed with newspaper stories, picked up a bag of groceries from the gates one day and agreed to speak briefly to reporters through the gates. 'I'm afraid to leave in case I can't get back in. I do have a legal right to the house and if I am free to come and go, as he claims, why are there six security guards here and at the gate and guards inside my house? My legal representatives are not allowed in to see me and I have no access to phones inside the house. I feel completely cut off from everything.'

Rumours persisted that she was being starved out, but the gossip appeared to come from Sir Frank denying that was the case.

It certainly seemed that Lady Susan was trying to cook because, in the absence of maids, cooks and butlers, she had sent palls of smoke across the sparkling blue waters of the harbour as she burned a pan of sausages for the second day running.

And it did seem that she was getting some food because a friend managed to smuggle in a supply of Vegemite, lamb chops, lettuce, biscuits and coffee. She also seemed to be able to manage the washing because most of her underwear was hanging out on the line for all and sundry on passing boats to goggle at.

Sir Frank didn't seem to worry about laundry. He was thoroughly enjoying himself smashing tennis balls at yacht crews which dared to approach the harbourside of the house for a closer look at the scene of the drama enthralling the nation.

Officers from the local police station were having a fine old time, too, as the log book revealed:

Monday, 1PM: Officers respond to a call by Sir Frank requesting removal of his wife from the premises. Police legal branch advise no action, due to pending legal fight between the two in the Family Court.

Tuesday, 11.30AM: Solicitor acting for Lady Renouf complains she has been denied access to the property. Police, again on advice, eventually decided to take no action.

Wednesday, 2.55PM: Private investigators for Lady Renouf allege that a portable telephone has been stolen by Sir Frank's security guards.

Wednesday, 2.56PM: Sir Frank's security guards call the police and complain that one of Lady Renouf's men has trespassed by jumping the fence.

It seemed certain it would all end up in the divorce courts, but the couple later announced a reconciliation. Perhaps Sir Frank should have heeded the warning of one of the local gossip columnists who wrote, 'Hell hath no fury like a woman starved.'

◆

The three decades from 1980 to 2010 were the busiest of my career—and, like just about everyone in the newspaper industry, I could not have foreseen the speed of the changes that were to turn journalism on its head in the years to come. Social journalism, with its unchecked reports and articles and rumours from dubious sources, began to spread. But newspapers struggled on. They followed one another in giving away their stories on the web in the hope that this would encourage people to buy the papers to read more reliable detail. Most of us in the industry began to realize it wasn't going to work like that—except for one paper, and thankfully it was the one I had been working for over the decades: the *Daily Mail*. Its online edition was to become the most popular in the world, and the paper itself was able to hold on to its two million-plus readership.

In general, though, triviality, the creation of 'citizen' journalists operating new-fangled devices, was pushing quality journalism aside. People wanted news fast, but in most cases it wasn't the same kind of news that had fascinated anyone who could read the written word down through the centuries. Text-talk became the order of the day, followed by Twitter notes and YouTube. It was all about entertainment. I've joined that band of communicators because I love technology, but I remain thankful to have been involved in many of the world's big stories when they mattered, at least as far as my 'patch' was concerned. Royal and political scandals, coups, interviews with stars, fun assignments, major crimes—they were all part of my daily routine and to this day, I'm still poised to chase them up.

Many of the stories I've been involved in have links in other countries, one of which was the extraordinary case of Hilary Foretich.

In February 1990 Hilary was aged seven. She had been at the centre of an embittered custody battle since she disappeared in August 1987. At the school she attended in Devon she was known by the name of Ellen and when a friend asked about her parents she lisped her practised lie, 'They have been killed in a car accident.' Shortly afterwards she disappeared from the school. I was among a handful of journalists who staked out a small motel in New Zealand, where Hilary turned up with her grandparents. They had smuggled her out of the UK.

The desperate attempts to hide the girl came about because her mother, American plastic surgeon Elizabeth Morgan, had accused her ex-husband of sexually abusing their daughter during weekend custody visits. A former columnist for *Cosmopolitan* magazine, Morgan insisted her ex-husband, Dr Eric Foretich, should not be allowed anywhere near Hilary, but the courts insisted her father should be allowed to see her. So one day she kissed her four-year-old daughter goodbye at a roadside restaurant in the USA and sent her to Britain, into hiding with her grandparents, in the hope that she would be able to stay with them, undiscovered, until she was 18.

It was a courageous move for a mother, but it cost her her liberty. Dr Morgan was sent to a Washington jail for defying the courts and was only released in September 1989 when President George H.W. Bush signed special legislation to end her imprisonment.

'I can't see my daughter now without endangering her safety,' she said as she left the prison. 'But I know she's happy and she has many friends. She's leading a normal existence and she's had two years of safety from her father—something she has never had in her entire life.' She added: 'On her seventh birthday, I gave her an incest-free day. She has been raped on her birthday before.'

Hilary's father consistently denied the sexual abuse allegations and when his daughter disappeared from the US he enlisted first the help of Scotland Yard and later the aid of British newspapers and TV networks to trace his missing child. Then he received an anonymous tip about the whereabouts of his daughter.

After the discovery of Hilary in New Zealand, her father began making plans to see her.

'I'd never hurt a hair on her head,' Eric Foretich insisted. 'We used to go to the zoo or the park and play on the swings—that sort of thing. I loved that time with my daughter. I'm planning to fight her grandparents for custody.'

To add to the intrigue, Hilary's grandfather, William Morgan, was a 79-year-old former US spy who fought with the French resistance. He and his wife Antonia had looked after Hilary in Plymouth, Devon, and lived quietly in a luxury apartment. But when Dr Foretich asked British police to help him find Hilary, William and his wife Antonia decided to fly as far away from Britain as they could get—to Christchurch in New Zealand.

The *Daily Mail* was anxious for me to get a long interview with the grandparents, or at least take a picture of the three of them together. I had my doubts about both, given the controversial nature of the case and I was surprised when, approached at their motel in Christchurch, they agreed to describe a little of their life on the run.

'It's been strenuous for us, but the only thing that matters is the welfare of Hilary,' said the 80-year-old grandmother. 'We set out to keep her away from her father, and even though we know he is on his way to New Zealand, we will not allow him to see her unless the courts order it.'

Antonia Morgan described an emotional conversation Hilary had with her mother, who was still in Washington DC. 'When she talked to her mother she broke down in tears. She's received letters from her mother through various channels but this was the first time Hilary has spoken on the phone to her.'

The grandparents had been granted interim custody and William Morgan declared that 'If her father tries to approach her I'll call the police. You know, we've lived for years with the fear of a knock on the door or the day Hilary might disappear from the school playground. We've spent all our savings to keep Hilary from her father and we'll fight him all the way.'

Hilary was nowhere in sight when I talked to the Morgans. She was being cared for at a secret address by a trusted family who knew about her background. I asked the couple if I could take a photo of them with Hilary. The answer was what I expected: 'No—we aren't allowing any photos.'

But as I was leaving, Mr Morgan said, 'Antonia and I might be going for a walk in the botanical gardens in a day two. We enjoy watching the ducks.'

Was this an invite? I was given no time, no exact location, and so for the next three days I walked, hour after hour, around the gardens, not really knowing what to expect. And then to my amazement, there they were—Mr and Mrs Morgan and Hilary. They were on the far side of a river that ran through the gardens but it was no trouble for me to get the exclusive photo. A picture of a little girl enjoying a happy hour with her grandparents away from the international controversy raging around her.

Persistence, I'd learned over the years, always paid off.

CHAPTER 14

Confessions of a
Temporary Royal Paparazzo

I may be a journalist for a 'compact' newspaper, but the world of the paparazzi was as foreign to me as it is to the man and woman in the street. That was until *You* magazine asked me to join the royal paparazzi on the Prince and Princess of Wales's tour of Australia in 1988 at the time of celebrations for the country's bicentennial.

I had never worked as a royal tour photographer before. No writer had. Such was the exclusivity of the circle of the permanent royal snappers, built up over the years like a team of masons erecting a fortress, that outsiders could only try to look over the top. Climb the wall I did, but once I had landed on the other side I had some idea of how the Christians felt when they were tossed into the arenas of Rome with the lions. In time the bruises went down and the nightmares faded.

This is an account of the horror I experienced.

◆

Late on the Sunday night before the morning that the royals are due to arrive at Sydney airport, I see a photographer walking through the hotel lobby with a pair of aluminium steps. 'You could get a porter to do that,' I say.

'Do what?'

'Well, change the light bulb.'

'Ha ha.'

When I see another photographer arrive with another three-step ladder even later that night, I begin to catch on. It will never do to ask, of course. But if you're going to do the royals, you need a ladder to get above the crowds.

Desperate phone calls to friends result in plenty of offers of ladders that can get me on to any roof, but a small pair of steps prove elusive. Somebody knows somebody who runs a hardware shop. More phone calls: furtive arrangements are made.

At 1.30AM I stand on a pair of steps in a suburban street. 'I'll take them,' I say to the owner, who has kindly got out of bed to serve me. They are a little on the flimsy side, but beggars can't be choosers.

Nine AM, Monday. The media bus is racing along to the airport for the arrival of the Prince and Princess. My eyes are fixed in horror at the bazooka-like lenses of my colleagues. The ends are as large as full-length mirrors.

The pool for covering the royal couple actually walking down the aircraft steps has been selected. A couple of colour photographers from Britain and Australia, a couple of black-and-white from the two countries, and a TV crew. My name has been on the board at the media room but I am not chosen. In these circumstances, I am assured, you get a couple of frames from the negs of those selected.

Dragging our ladders, we run to the general media area on the tarmac. My lenses smack against each other. I am way behind the others, although I reckon I'm as fit as they are.

There is a technique for beating everyone off the bus. You have to be the first to move away from the previous job in order to get on the bus ahead of the rest so you can grab the seat near the door. Then you can get off in front of everybody else at the next job and set up your ladder in the best position. Elementary.

At the general media area at the airport we all jump onto our ladders, so we are all at the same level we would have been had we not had ladders. This is getting silly, I think.

There she is. The Princess waves and comes down the steps. Motor drives whirr, even from this distance. I touch the button. I am falling, falling. My motor drive shoots away at feet and sky as I take the blow on my elbow. I look up at the camera bag which has knocked me from my ladder. 'Sorry mate,' says its owner. Oh yeah?

Somehow my ladder has been shifted. I'm now on a ladder behind the other ladders. So I drop down low and shoot between legs. The Princess's face fills the viewfinder. But she's fuzzy. Twist the focusing ring—wrong way. Quick, quick, she's moving.

Wow. Instant clarity. She has sparkling blue eyes. I am privileged, honoured, to be so close.

Click … whirr. I have her, even with a wounded arm. A lens smacks on the top of my head. Dazed, I shoot on, like a war hero. And now there's only the back of her hat. She's moving away, getting fuzzy. Like a big game hunter grinning at bagging a prize, I run happily back to the bus.

Three PM. A floating pontoon beside the sail training ship *Young Endeavour*, Britain's Bicentennial gift to Australia. The best positions on the wharf have already been grabbed. The floating pontoon is filling up with ladders. I position mine. The Princess approaches the ship. A police launch passes, creating a wake, rocking the pontoon. My ladder wobbles. A gentle nudge from my left is all that is needed. More knee-high shots.

Tuesday, AM. I approach an Australian tour official. 'Bruce, I'd like to get myself in on a few of these pools.' His eyes flick across to the assembled team of royal snappers from London. 'Well,' he says, and you can almost feel the telepathy at work. Or are they just well-rehearsed lines? Or am I paranoid? There is a problem. 'You haven't come out from London. You'll have to talk to the Australian photographers.'

Excluded from privileged pool positions for Bicentennial celebrations on the steps of the Sydney Opera House, I check out the distance from the general media area to the royal position. It is 75 yards (70 metres) if it's a foot. I need a powerful lens—and I need one fast.

Urgent phone calls. There isn't a standard lens for my camera anywhere in town. But a supplier can lend me an 800mm lens which will fit with an adaptor. The lens comes in a small suitcase, laid out in a multitude of parts. As the Prince and Princess arrive on the dais, I start to assemble the weapon, feeling like the Jackal.

◆

The lens proves impossibly cumbersome as I balance it on the rail in front of me. I decide I need a tripod and acquire one the following day. My luggage now consists of a computer, paper, compacted cardboard boxes for putting film in for airfreighting, an enormous bag of colour film, a multitude of lenses, four camera bodies, the suitcase with the 800mm lens, an enormous tripod to hold the 800mm lens, a fishing jacket bursting with odds and ends like light meters and doublers, and a step ladder.

I think this is bad. Mind you, others have wire machines, enlargers, developing trays, chemicals, and enormous machines for transmitting negatives to London.

Melbourne, 6PM. A media conference. 'About tonight's dance,' says Bruce, referring to a ball at which the Prince and Princess of Wales have agreed to a few minutes of photographs while they dance. 'There's enough room for one member of every organisation covering the tour.'

'Any pooling?' I ask.

'There's no pooling. Just one representative from every organisation.'

No worries. I put on my white jacket and my bow-tie, check my flash and head off in the media bus to the venue. The Prince and Princess come up the escalators, walk through the first-floor foyer—flash, whirr—and up more escalators. We crowd around, waiting to be allowed up for the picture session.

There are media officials everywhere, special people employed to keep a watch on the press. A hand comes across my chest.

'Where's your pass?'

'I'm wearing it.'

'Not your general media pass. Your special pass to go upstairs.' My eyes dart around. All the boys from London are holding little yellow cards. They rush past.

'Bruce,' I yell. 'Bruce.' But Bruce hurries away. I grab a media woman marshal. 'Hey,' I say. 'What's going on?'

'Who are …' Her eyes read my name. I swear two red blotches appear on her cheeks. 'Wait here,' she says. 'I'll be right back.'

But, of course, she never does come back. Neither does Bruce.

Nobbled. Out into the street.

◆

It is 8.45PM. I am sitting on a park bench beside St Paul's Cathedral, feeding pieces of hamburger to a stray cat. I am still wearing my white dinner jacket. Three cameras lie beside me, redundant. Two blocks away the Prince and Princess of Wales swirl across a dance floor to the music of 'In the Mood', illuminated by dozens of flashlights. Flash, whirr, click, flash, whirr … the colour boys and the black-and-white shooters are having a field day.

The cat is eating furiously. Onions, tomatoes, bun. I pick up a camera and frame him. Pop. Captured at ten yards on 100 ASA Ektachrome at f8. The cat runs away.

Nine PM. The dancing will be over now and the others will be heading back to the hotel. Hundreds of frames of majestic tango captured for perpetuity.

On this bleakest of nights I had come face to face with the merciless world of the royal paparazzi … and the utter desolation experienced after you imagine what you are going to get, gear yourself up to it, ride along at fever pitch, then fail to achieve your goal. What would I have done without the cat?

CHAPTER 15

Never Play Golf with an Ape

I don't know why, but spies seem to be drawn to me like lawyers to money. I've lost count of the number of shadowy figures who, with their fingers against the side of their noses, have whispered secrets that often cannot be authenticated. But everyone loves a mystery and whenever possible I've tried to introduce elements into my stories that invite curiosity—perhaps because there are times when I don't know all the answers. Just tell it as it is, present all the available facts and let readers judge for themselves. Yes, spies and con men, for often the two dubious professions overlap. After all, you can't be a good spy, living a double or an undercover life, without being a good con man.

You won't get a spy admitting he's an agent or a confidence trickster, but Peter Foster has been labelled a con man so often that he now happily admits: 'OK, that's me, I'm a con man'.

I have to say this right away: Foster is a loveable rogue who has made and lost fortunes, usually other people's money, but that's because in many cases they've chased dreams that are just too good to be true. I have found him to be intelligent, witty, sharp, highly entertaining and a thorough gentleman.

Peter Foster is the first to admit that he is not the world's most handsome man. He's told me that enough times, yet he had the charm to win the heart of Samantha Fox, *The Sun*'s 'page three girl', in the 1980s. He wriggled into her life at a party and he had all the money in the world to entice her because he had made a fortune selling Bai-Lin tea, which he said had remarkable weight-loss properties.

Samantha helped with the promotion, along with jockey Lester Piggott and none other than Fergie, Sarah Ferguson, the Duchess of York.

He made so much money that he was able to swan around London in a Rolls Royce, Sam Fox at his side. Much later, using his charm, he won the heart of a Miss Australia who was taking part in the Miss World contest in London. He saw her on TV, phoned her, and suggested that as one lonely Australian to another they should meet up. One thing led to another and off they went on a tour of Europe in his Roller.

His lifestory fills a book—and I should know, having spent a month with him writing the manuscript. He's been jailed in three continents for misleading advertising and been thrown into prison in Fiji for allegedly falsifying documents relating to the purchase of a block of land. He also worked undercover for Australian and British police on separate occasions, fingering crooks and drug runners he had information about.

Following his arrest in Fiji, where he was also accused of interfering in local politics, he made a dramatic escape by ship to neighbouring Vanuatu. He phoned me on my birthday in 2007.

'Mate, it's Peter Foster.'

'Peter! Blimey. What're those birds in the background? You sound like you're in the middle of the jungle.'

'I am! I've just swum ashore. I need help. Can any of Isobelle's relatives hide me?'

We couldn't help, of course. Foster was a fugitive and, inevitably, he was caught and thrown into jail in the capital, Port Vila. I was able to arrange some clothing and other basics for him. In time, he charmed his jailers to the extent that he was allowed to slip into town for lunch and hold court with all who came to meet him. On his eventual return to Australia he was jailed for forging bank documents. After his release, I bumped into him on the Gold Coast, having breakfast in an outdoor café. We said 'g'day', lied to each other about how little we had changed since those days nearly ten years earlier when I'd written his book, and I strolled on, the big names that he'd been associated with swirling through my mind.

The biggest, of course, was British prime minister Tony Blair and his wife Cherie. And Carole Caplin, Cherie's health guru, style adviser, friend and companion. Peter Foster had used all that old-time charm once again to win Carole's heart. In an exchange of pillowtalk—so Foster claimed to me later—he learned a great deal of what Tony had told Cherie. His ears had pricked up when he heard that Cherie was trying to purchase a couple of flats in Bristol. Foster told Carole to let Cherie know he could probably swing a deal for her—which he did, allowing Cherie to buy the flats at a discounted price. The prime minister's wife famously sent an email to Foster later, as the *Daily Mail* revealed, saying: 'You're a star'.

There was uproar when it was learned that Cherie had used a con man to negotiate the purchase and, predictably, the affair become known as 'Cherie-gate'. In December 2002, in an unprecedented public statement, Cherie tearfully apologized for the embarrassment she had caused buying property with the help of a man of dubious character.

For Peter Foster the affair, which ended with him and Carole going their separate ways, was all grist to the mill. He later claimed that he had learned other information from Carole and, although it sparked rumours among the British newspapers, none of it came to light. But the interest remained focused on Cherie Blair. So, when she was invited to address a lawyers' conference in Malaysia, I was despatched to see if she had anything interesting to say. She didn't and I wondered what else I could do in the country. That's when I found myself teeing up for a remarkable game of golf with two orang-utans.

◆

I'd heard that they were the stars of a stage show at a hotel resort south of Kuala Lumpur. I thought I'd drive down and have a look. Might be a 'cruelty to animals' story or a fun story or, well, I didn't really know what to expect. It turned out that Ta Ta and his caddy Lucy were very keen golfers. Oh, come on, I hear you say, what a load of nonsense. And what about the animal cruelty thing?

I would be the first to put my hand up to protest the dressing up of animals to perform tricks for humans, but my orang-utan friends were not cruelly dragged into the role of professional golfers. Mr Phong Sathon, an elephant carer from Thailand, had found them in a distressed state in a cage in Bangkok. Smugglers had caught them as youngsters in Malaysia, transported them across the border into Thailand and hawked them around the streets. They had spent all their early years behind bars and later become the star attraction at a travelling zoo, performing tricks for a public who threw bananas and poked fingers at them whenever they were in reach.

Learning they were for sale, Mr Sathon believed he could offer them a much better life than the one they had endured so far. So he handed over his cash and took them back to Malaysia where he found a new home for them in an animal sanctuary south of Kuala Lumpur—but by now they were totally dependent on humans.

The two orang-utans took to Mr Sathon, as he did to them. Told they had no hope of surviving in the jungle, Mr Sathon wondered how he could provide for them in a way that would make them happy. The solution came by chance. One day he noticed Ta Ta striking at some peanut shells with a stick, in the manner of a golfer putting a ball. Mr Sathon found a putter and ball and to his amazement saw Ta Ta neatly strike out. This was obviously something he had been taught by one of his previous owners in Thailand. When he tried to take the putter off Ta Ta there was a screech of protest. The orang-utan wanted to continue playing, hitting the ball around his compound—and Mr Sathon could have sworn the animal was smiling each time he made a good connection.

In time, Mr Sathon took Ta Ta and Lucy to the nearby A'Famosa championship course where, to his astonishment, the ape struck a clean ball—with his putter— off the tee straight down the middle of the fairway. True, the ball did not travel very far, but Mr Sathon could tell that Ta Ta was in his element. Lucy's behaviour was equally astonishing. She grabbed the putter and scurried down the fairway after the ball and stood guarding it until Ta Ta lumbered up to it for his second shot. There was no doubt that Lucy was a born caddy!

When I turned up at the animal sanctuary I was politely informed by Mr Sathon that Ta Ta was not available . He was practising his golf.

'Well, if he's that keen,' I said to Mr Sathon, 'would he be prepared to take me on in a putting contest?'

'Oh, he'll do better than that,' said Mr Sathon. 'He'll play a couple of holes on the big course with you.'

'You're on,' I said.

'But if you lose,' Mr Sathon said, 'you buy the bananas.'

This, of course, had to be a joke. Playing golf with an ape, that is—not the buying of bananas.

I was still chuckling about it the next morning when I turned up at the first hole of the beautifully manicured A'Famosa course. Then I stopped chuckling and gaped. Ta Ta and Lucy, kitted out in the smartest golfing gear you could imagine, were waiting patiently for me in a golf cart. All right, they weren't wearing spikes but that was understandable with huge feet like those.

Mr Sathon insisted that Ta Ta and I shake hands before what was to be a three-hole contest. The ape's handshake was firm. In fact, if it had been any firmer I would have had to retire hurt with crushed bones.

Mr Sathon set about laying down the rules, although it sounded to me more like the law of the jungle. Bringing our heads together like two boxers, his directions, which I sensed were aimed more towards Ta Ta than me, were: 'Keep it clean. No biting, scratching or kicking. This will be a three-hole contest. Anyone who loses a ball, loses that hole. May the best man win.'

At this, the Wild Man of Borneo—as explorers described orang-utans when they first saw them in the Malaysian jungle—turned and scuttled towards the tee. There was no tossing of a coin to establish who would hit off first. Ta Ta had already set his ball on the tee and was lining up his first hit with his cut-down putter.

'He's no good off the tee with a driver,' Mr Sathon whispered. 'He'll use his putter all the way around.'

The putter swept down—and the ball went just 30 yards (25 metres). Straight, but only 30 yards just the same. This was going to be a pushover. I'd show this dumb ape a thing or two.

I picked up my borrowed driver and gave it everything—and the ball sailed straight off into the jungle with such a severe slice that I wondered if there was something wrong with my borrowed club. I took a quick look and found that the head was loose.

'No,' said Mr Sathon, 'you're not allowed to have another shot. You'll have to use an iron next time.'

Something dodgy here, I thought, but not to worry. I'm playing an ape after all. No problem.

A few spectators joined me in what turned out to be a fruitless hunt for the ball.

'It has to be here somewhere,' I cried but no-one could find it. Then I saw Lucy scampering from the trees, a big grin on her face—and a shape that looked like a golf ball in her trouser pocket.

'Hey!' I yelled, but my protest was ignored. My ball was officially lost and Ta Ta skilfully used his putter to keep his ball on the fairway. He then trickled it neatly into the hole, to take first blood.

So that was their game. Ta Ta and Lucy were a couple of conniving bandits.

On the second hole, after double-checking my iron, I made sure I stayed on the fairway and—yes!—I popped the ball in with Ta Ta trailing several strokes behind. Got him. Can't lose, I thought. He's only an ape, after all.

With the score at 1–1, it was all down to the final hole. I picked up the iron. The Wild Man of Borneo was about to find out who was the king of the jungle around here.

Somewhere between the second hole and the next, final, tee, my ball became mislaid. 'Don't worry,' said Mr Sathon, 'we won't count it as a lost ball. Here, I'll set up a new one for you.' He placed a nice shiny ball on the tee. What a gentleman.

'By the way,' he said, as I was just starting my back swing. 'Do you know what they call this hole?'

'No,' I said, halting my swing. 'What do they call this hole?'

'It's the Crocodile Hole. Do you know why they call it the Crocodile Hole?'

'No, why do they call it the Crocodile Hole?'

'Because in that lake up there to your left, and in the water further on near the green, are several large crocodiles.'

'Go on,' I said nervously.'

'Last year, and this is really, really true, we nearly lost one of our visiting golfers when he tried to get his ball back after hitting it into the water. He got bitten on the bum. I'd be very careful if I were you.'

This was a very serious case of gamesmanship. I was not going to be distracted. But I knew I had to get this tee shot right. If I hit the ball into the water, I'd be risking life and limb to look for it. I'd aim to the right side of the fairway, well away from the water.

I drew the iron back, swept down—and although I intended to put a gentle slice on the ball, I had never seen anything like the result in my life. It shot off to the right almost at right angles and disappeared into the thick of the jungle. If I had a suspicious mind I would have sworn there was something wrong with the ball—like being weighted down on one side and being lined up on the tee so that it soared off severely to the right. Had they switched balls as I approached the third tee? I would find out when I retrieved it. In fact, as the seconds raced by and Ta Ta sent another clean ball down the middle of the fairway, I became convinced there had been something wrong with my ball.

I hurried towards the trees to look for my ball and confirm my suspicions—but not before Lucy and Mr Sathon disappeared into the thick bush ahead of me.

'Found it!' came Mr Sathon's voice from somewhere in the trees.

Surprise, surprise, Lucy was standing over a ball, chattering and grinning.

'I think she's telling you that you'll have to try to hit it out from here,' said Mr Sathon.

'Just hold on a minute,' I said. 'Will you allow me to pick the ball up and have a look at it?'

'Yes, of course,' said Mr Sathon. I examined the ball closely, tossed it in the air, felt its weight. Nothing wrong with it. But in Lucy's pocket I saw another golf-ball shape. Before I could ask if I could have a look at that ball, Lucy was scampering away to join her golfer boyfriend on the fairway.

By the time I'd hit the ball out through the trees and then from the thick rough, I was five shots behind Ta Ta. But he wasn't doing too well on the fairway this time and we both ended up on the green for nine. Nine! I couldn't remember when I'd scored so badly—and I still hadn't holed out.

So the Ape v Human championship was down to the putting.

Lucy held the flag as I lined up the hole. Then both Ta Ta and Lucy started laughing. Was it my style? Was it because they had successfully duped me so far? Who knows? But what I do know is that I missed an easy putt, to Lucy's hysterical delight. And yes, you guessed it. Ta Ta holed his. You only have to look at the pictures, see the grin on Lucy's face as my ball missed the hole, to accept that I'm not making this up.

I'd been beaten by an orang-utan.

We posed for a victory photograph. Their victory. My devious friends grinning their faces off with their arms around me as I sat between them.

That photograph found its way into the hands of Trevor McDonald, host of the top-rating TV news show, *Tonight With Trevor McDonald*. It was flashed on the screen for the whole of the UK to chuckle over. What was described as the caption of the week read: 'Mr and Mrs Monkey proudly show off their new son.'

As you might expect, there were roars of laughter among the studio audience. Laughter that was no doubt echoed in millions of homes around the country.

There were further hoots as Mr McDonald suggested that the orang-utans had bred a son who looked like them and added, 'And very successful it was too.'

CHAPTER 16

'The Groom's Eloped with the Best Man!'

Guests flew to Venice from all over the world in April 1990, to witness 36-year-old Anne Margaret Primrose Dunlop, daughter of Australian matriarch Lady Potter, marry her sweetheart, the handsome Prince Giustiniani, Count of the Phanaar, Knight of St Sophia—known to his Sydney friends as Lorenzo Montesini. A weekend of champagne celebrations was planned, leading up to the glittering Catholic ceremony in the basilica of St Peter the Apostle.

The bride, who was nicknamed Pitty Pat, was once public relations assistant to Lord McAlpine, the Conservative Party treasurer, for his Australian hotel chain. He had been invited to host a dinner for 70 in Primrose's honour at the famous Harry's Bar.

This was to be one of the grandest weddings of the year. But wait—something was wrong. It transpired that when the engagement was announced in *The Times* and in Australian newspapers seven months earlier, the champagne set was aghast. There were whispers about Lorenzo's title, which he said dated back to the 15th century and was bestowed on him by his grandmother just before her death. Lorenzo was born in Egypt and his father settled in Australia after arriving there in 1956 as an official for the Melbourne Olympics. Lorenzo claimed he was a descendant of the Giustinianis, a great Venetian family whose hereditary titles were awarded when they were diplomats at the court of the Ottoman Empire in Constantinople.

But he agreed in an interview that his title was not royal because, 'Royalty is considered vulgar in our class. The Italian aristocracy looks down on Italian royalty, who only go back 100 years.' One of Lorenzo's cousins in Australia commented, as the wedding plans were going ahead, that all the claims about a title were a load of codswallop and that he would 'sooner sit down with a pie and watch the telly'.

Nevertheless, the wedding was on. Lorenzo who was employed as a steward with Qantas and lived in a pink-painted terrace house in Woolloomooloo, a harbourside suburb of Sydney, headed for the airport for his date with destiny.

As he flew to Venice, accompanied by property dealer Robert Straub, who was to be best man, Lorenzo's heart was beating with love. But alas, it was not for poor Pitty Pat. He gazed lovingly into the eyes of Robert and told him that he didn't think he could go through with the wedding.

If Lorenzo's and Robert's friends back in Sydney could have heard this conversation, they would not have been surprised. They had been stunned when Lorenzo announced he was getting married—to a woman.

It had all the makings of a disaster. And it came sooner than anyone expected. Shortly before he was due to walk down the aisle with Primrose, Lorenzo—who was also accompanied by friend John Lane, a gentleman's outfitter—telephoned the bride's mother, Lady Potter, and told her that he was eloping with the best man.

Lady Potter was stunned and it was 'only with the greatest difficulty' that she broke the news to Primrose, who became hysterical. Lady Potter next telephoned Father Vincent Kiss—ah, we needed a name like that to toss into this extraordinary story—who had flown from Melbourne to marry the couple, and Father Bruno Carraro, the priest in charge of St Peter's, to tell them the wedding was cancelled for reasons that no-one on God's earth could have imagined.

The bride-to-be, who became the bride-who-wasn't, wept into the night as the dastardly prince flew into Florence with his best man. The two men are said to have met in Vietnam and, although it is not clear if they were in the forces, the action was not of the warring kind.

One of Primrose's cousins, acting as family spokesman, told guests that the families of both the bride and the groom had searched high and low for an answer to an 'inexplicable riddle and a way to redeem the damage, spiritual, psychological and material. To say the bride and her mother are distraught is an understatement. They are utterly devastated—as though a bomb had exploded.' The cousin said the prince's family had handed over generations of jewels and heirlooms to Primrose.

Lord McAlpine was shocked at the news that the groom had run off with the best man. 'Good grief! I had no idea at all,' he exclaimed.

My role in this incredible saga was to try to secure an interview with the jilted bride on her return to Australia. No easy task, because for weeks afterwards she was filled with so much pain and embarrassment she could hardly speak. She knew the entire world was after her story, so she placed her affairs in the hands of Sydney agent Harry M. Miller.

Harry had a reputation for being a tough negotiator. I'd had several dealings with him over the years and found him to be fair and extremely helpful once a deal had been done. In his autobiography he described me as the most tenacious reporter he had ever met—I'm not so sure about that, but it was nice of him to say so. Discussions began with Harry on behalf of the *Daily Mail's* sister paper, the *Mail on Sunday*, and finally an agreement was reached. A world exclusive chat with Primrose 'Pitty Pat' Dunlop, deserted bride of the groom-to-be who had fled with the best man.

We strolled through the streets of Woolloomooloo, where, by coincidence, Harry's office was located and where the vanished groom's terrace house stood. Primrose, at 36, was a tall, graceful woman with long black hair and piercing dark eyes. She looked every bit the aristocrat, a woman with dazzling social connections. She should have been furious, but as she spoke to me, there was no hatred in her voice for what her fiancé had done. Primrose admitted she was still 'very confused about the whole thing'.

But what an astonishing story she had to tell, admitting that Frederico Fellini could not have done it better. Primrose had been staying in the Venetian palazzo of Countess Maria Pia Ferri when she had been told the bad news. Amid her hysterics, her mother confirmed that the groom had done a runner.

'Do you know, I still love him and I'd still consider marrying him,' Primrose said. 'But first we have to talk. I need an explanation. My emotions for him haven't changed. I obviously loved the man to want to marry him. I still love him.'

I had been expecting her to say that she would want to drown her Latin lover in the Grand Canal rather than forgive him. But she wasn't carrying any of that kind of hatred. Rumours of Lorenzo's close friendship with Robert Straub added a bizarre element to the love affair.

Primrose said Lorenzo would have no trouble passing a heterosexual test. 'I wouldn't have been marrying him if I hadn't had a sexual relationship with him. There's nothing wrong with a bit of the old Latin in the blood. It's much better, in fact, than a bit of Australian in the genes.' Nice line.

They had met at the Opera Ball in 1985, when Primrose was danced off her feet by the dashing Lorenzo, then aged 41. Soon the handsome couple were inseparable partners at dinner parties and society balls—but always somewhere in the background was Lorenzo's friend Robert Straub. 'Do you know, I had no suspicions,' Primrose said. 'In fact, the only thing that did enter my head was that Robert was a great womanizer.'

One day, as they dashed into a bank to get coins for a parking meter, Lorenzo proposed in front of the teller. 'My immediate reaction was to question if this man was really serious. But my smile was sufficient answer for him.'

Several months later, when woozy on champagne, Lorenzo rang Primrose's mother, Lady Potter, and formally asked her permission to marry her daughter. Primrose wanted to marry in Egypt, with a camel nearby, but they settled on Venice in springtime with a background of boats. The list of guests was impressive: aside from Lord McAlpine, there was romantic novelist Barbara Taylor Bradford, Sotheby's owner Alfred Taubman, cosmetics queen Estee Lauder's son Leonard and *Australian Vogue* publisher Lesley Wild.

'I and my entourage arrived in Venice a few hours behind Lorenzo and his best man. We stayed at the Countess's 15th-century Palazzo Pisani, which overlooks the Grand Canal. Later we were joined by John Lane and we all dined together and strolled individually or in small groups around the city as the wedding day approached. It was a fun time, going to galleries, champagne, friends dropping in, phone calls and faxes coming in from around the world.'

But slowly the fairytale plot was being rewritten. Lorenzo seemed to be under stress—but Primrose put it down to jet lag (he a flight steward and all) and she also knew he was suffering from the flu. 'He was getting pre-marital nerves and so was I,' she told me.

'What did hurt me was when Lorenzo told me that he was getting calls from vicious people who told him they could not understand why they had not been invited and, worse, they wanted to know why he was marrying "that girl"—as if I were a piece of meat. He was also upset about his relations speaking out against him and the validity of his title.

'What nobody knows is that Lorenzo is a very sensitive person with a sad background. His beloved grandmother and his mother both committed suicide when he was young and his cousins were very unsympathetic towards him. I picked up in his voice that he was worried about the ongoing controversy, but

I never dreamed that the wedding would be cancelled. Later he said in a panicky voice that our passports had been stolen.

'I went upstairs to ring the Australian consulate in Rome and when I came down the Countess told me that the three men—Lorenzo, Straub and John Lane—had taken off. Later he called my mother to say the wedding was off—and he hung up.'

'How did you take it?' I asked.

'I had a brandy. Or two. For 48 hours I felt nothing while the headlines flew around the world about the groom who had run off with the best man. Some people were rather cruel, whispering: 'I told you so.''

I was astonished that she was showing so much grace and kindness towards the man who had let her down, virtually at the altar.

She agreed to pose for a photograph and wrapped an arm around a lamppost as she stared into the lens with huge doe eyes. Her arm should have been around her Prince Charming, but it was not to be.

I kissed the back of her hand and thanked her for her time. Our chat had helped, she said. And as I walked away she commented: 'I'd also like it known that I'd give him another chance—but he may not ask.'

He never did. But we were not allowed to forget Prince Lorenzo because reputedly it was his character who became a feature of a comic Australian TV show, *Tonight Live With Steve Vizard*. He and 'Robert Straub' were shown sitting side by side on a plane each week gossiping away in high-pitched voices—which had nothing to do with the height at which they were supposedly flying.

◆

One marriage that did come off a month later, on 5 May 1990, was between *Crocodile Dundee* creator Paul Hogan and his co-star Linda Kozlowski. It was at Possum Creek, in northern New South Wales, and I, and half the world's press, had about as much hope of being invited to the ceremony at the couple's Disneyland-style mansion as a crocodile had of surviving an encounter with Mick Dundee's dagger—remember the line from the film: 'that's not a knife, that's a knife'?

Trying to get a picture of the couple in the days before the dusk wedding had been a risky business. My photographer friend Brendan Beirne, who had been closely involved with me on the Pamela Bordes' 'High class hooker in the House of Commons' story—more about that later—fitted me out with a camouflage shirt and trousers. Brendan checked my lens was long enough, and we had then began creeping through long grass and thick bushes several miles away in the hope of finding a good vantage point. I suspect at times we crossed onto private land and there were moments when we sent cattle scattering. But each step took us closer to the Hogan mansion.

When I saw the huge brown snake I announced to Brendan, in the calmest voice I could muster, that I would not be proceeding and would be making my way back. Brendan told me later that what I had actually said should never be repeated in print and that he had never seen anyone run through waist-high grass in a manner that would have broken all short-track records. My decision to abandon our commando-style approach, which was supported by Brendan who was hot on my heels, was justified when we learned that the area we had walked through was alive with eastern brown snakes, among the deadliest creatures on the planet, the fangs of which can bring death within the hour.

So we did not get our pre-wedding photos. We had also hoped to snap Hollywood superstars such as Tom Cruise, Clint Eastwood and Madonna, who it was rumoured would be attending but who did not show up after all. 'Hoges' and Linda had agreed to restrict the guest list to members of their families and personal friends. The list, not unexpectedly, did not include Hogan's former wife, Noelene, although she had, like Primrose Dunlop, shown only good grace when she learned that Hogan was deserting her to start a new life with Linda.

Noelene had refused to talk about the break-up, although she did not deny that she received a satisfactory payout for the distress caused from the millions he had earned.

You magazine, part of the *Daily Mail* group, was a great publication which ran lengthy features and fantastic pictures. I'd written for them on many occasions, travelling out into the Pacific and flying all around Australia on assignments which would run for several pages—and more often than not with my pictures.

Noelene Hogan had always fascinated the magazine—the abandoned wife whose husband had become a superstar and had run off with his co-star (no comparison here, though, with Primrose Dunlop and Prince Lorenzo)—and I was constantly asked to work at getting an interview with her, accompanied by pictures. She kept saying 'no'—until one day she said 'yes'. But she wasn't prepared to do any talking in Australia. Perhaps it was too much of a reminder of the country where Hoges had decided to leave her, although she did live there. She was going on holiday with a lady friend to Italy (land of the abandoned woman!) and the interview could be done there.

I thought that all the months spent persuading Noelene to talk would result in a London writer and a photographer getting the plum job, considering the short hop to Rome. But editor Nick Gordon said: 'No, you've got on well with her. Go for it.'

I rang Noelene to say I'd be meeting her in Italy after all. She said she'd be ready to chat after a few days of settling in, which was fair enough. It was arranged that I would meet up with her at the Hilton Hotel in Rome. But after I'd checked in and inquired about her whereabouts I was given a note saying she had left. She and her friend had decided to travel to the medieval walled town of Lucca, 170 miles (275 kilometres) north of Rome, and I could find her at a particular hotel. So the next morning I rented a car, checked out of the Hilton and battled my way through the Rome traffic, going every which-way but the right one, until I finally struck the northbound autostrade.

I reached Noelene's hotel that evening, only to be given another note saying that she and her friend had decided to return to Rome and I could find them at the Hilton. One thing journalism had taught me was to remain calm—or try to—in the most trying of circumstances. Mobile phones were not in widespread use in 1990 so there was no hope of her reaching me by phone, unless, of course she had telephoned the Hilton while I was there to inform me of her plans. But I gave Noelene the benefit of the doubt. Perhaps she and her friend had decided to check out of the Lucca hotel after I had left Rome. In any case, I headed back to Rome, but before re-checking myself into the Hilton I made sure she was in house. She was. But where? On arrival, I tried ringing her room, but there was no answer and she was nowhere to be found. I decided not to keep ringing after 11PM in case she was fast asleep. The last thing I wanted to do was upset her on such an important assignment.

I found her at breakfast the next day. Would this be a good time to start chatting to her? No, not today, she and her friend had other arrangements. But perhaps the following day. I wondered whether she was enjoying all this mucking around. Was this how it was with Paul? I tried to impress on her that the magazine wouldn't keep me in Italy for days on end and it was finally agreed that the following day would be set aside for the words and the pictures.

At last I found myself out and about in the streets of Rome with Noelene and her friend. She talked at length about the wonderful times she had had with Paul, but not a word of criticism—which, of course the magazine wanted—would she utter against him. She thought all those years ago when she first met him at a swimming pool that he believed he had 'a big ticket on himself'—meaning that he thought he was God's gift to the world—but as for the rest of it, Paul had been a wonderful husband and father. I couldn't decide whether she was speaking from the heart or if her enormous divorce settlement included a clause that she would not talk about their life together in any detrimental way.

I took literally hundreds of pictures of her at all the usual tourist places and even got Noelene to pose with her arms around a policeman. The *carabiniero* was most obliging and even allowed Noelene to pose holding his gun, which might have alarmed his superiors if they had witnessed the scene. But I thought at the time that this was the magazine's front-page picture: the contrast between Crocodile Dundee holding up that knife of his and Noelene, enjoying life in Rome on the fortune he had bestowed upon her, holding up a gun.

In those days the photographs were transparencies—slides—and I bundled them all together in a packet and sent them off to *You* magazine, where they would be processed and the best ones picked out. The editor wanted a story in which Noelene tore Hogan to shreds for deserting her—but I explained she had steadfastly refused to do so. The strongest piece I could write was along the lies of '... the public might expect her to be furious, but Noelene refused to be drawn ...' It was an old journalistic trick to put up all the negatives and then use quotes that could be closely associated with them, without actually confirming all the bad things.

The magazine wanted more. They wanted the knife stuck in, metaphorically speaking. But despite going back to Noelene several times, and getting her back up, she refused to attack her former husband. I wondered how the story was going to be treated. But one thing I could be certain about: they would use that picture of Noelene with the gun and perhaps turn it to their advantage with a heading that said something like 'Noelene comes out gunning for deserter Hoges', even though the story would not have supported it.

My story ran word for word, which I was happy enough about. But, as if in a revenge attack for failing to come up with the goods, for the cover the magazine had chosen what was probably the worst picture in the entire batch. In order to cover every angle on what was a very important assignment, I had taken pictures of Noelene sitting by a fountain, standing in a square, laughing with that policeman, sitting on ancient steps, grinning at a statue, wandering across a bridge, drinking coffee in a square—just about everything I could think of and from every angle. Because the rolls of film had been sent off to London without my seeing the results of the photoshoot, I had not been in a position to edit out the disagreeable ones. And it was the most disagreeable picture of Noelene that had been used.

It was a close-up of just her face and because she had been sitting on some steps, the shot had been from the ground up towards her. By a trick of the light and because of the angle, it looked like Noelene, a plumpish woman in the first place, had an enormously fat neck. In fact, it looked like she was suffering from a very serious goitre.

I didn't see the magazine until several weeks later—but Noelene did. Friends in London despatched a copy to her post-haste and the fury I had wanted her to aim against Paul was instead directed at me. She was on the phone complaining bitterly about the picture and asking why I had put it on the front cover. I tried to explain that it wasn't my choice, that there were literally hundreds of fabulous pictures of her. But she would hear nothing of it.

Weeks later the magazine returned all the slides to me and what I had told her was true. Virtually every shot showed her in a flattering light and I was left in no doubt that the worst one of all had been singled out for use. I knew perfectly well why that was. A comparison had to be made between the glamorous Linda Kozlowski and the frumpy wife Paul Hogan had left behind. Of course, I couldn't tell Noelene that but I think the implication was quite clear to her.

I tried to placate her by picking out 200 of the very best and very flattering pictures of her and having them printed, one by one, at a specialist printers—not the local chemist—and at my own expense. The bill shocked me because they had all been individually and carefully processed but I felt it had to be done. I learned later that Noelene hardly glanced at them. And she never spoke to me again.

◆

Inevitably, my job involved looking into the affairs of families from all walks of life, but few sagas could match the one that was to be played out, first in the United States and then in Tahiti, surrounding the children and grandchildren of movie giant Marlon Brando. Tahiti was in my 'patch', although it is thousands of miles east of Australia, and inevitably I was drawn into the saga. It was more real-life—filled with high drama—than the famously reclusive Marlon and his family wanted.

One of his daughters was Cheyenne, born after a fling in Tahiti with local woman Tarita, whom he met when he was starring in the 1962 movie *Mutiny on the Bounty*. (Isobelle's Uncle Jim, who came to stay with us for a while in that overcrowded house of ours, was a mouth-organ playing wanderer who had worked as an extra on the film. He'd drunk beer with Marlon Brando and while Marlon was falling for Tarita, Uncle Jim had his eye on another grass-skirted beauty. He could never work out why she didn't smile until one day he playfully pinched her bum which made her giggle—and he saw that she had no teeth. Too much sugar cane. That was the end of his romantic intentions.)

Marlon's daughter Cheyenne grew up in the main town of Papeete with her elder brother Teihotu, and spent a lot of time on Marlon's private island, Tetiaroa. Cheyenne and her father had never got on well together—she claimed he had deserted her and her mother—but even so she agreed to fly to the US to spend some time with him and her half-brother, Christian. She took her boyfriend, a Tahitian man, 26-year-old Dag Drollet, to Hollywood with her. At the time Cheyenne was pregnant with Dag's child.

On the night of 16 May 1990, during a fierce argument, Christian produced a gun and shot Dag through the head. The story made world headlines and Christian was charged with murder. But there was much more of the story to run—circumstances that were equally dramatic.

When Cheyenne gave birth to Dag's son, the child was immediately disowned by Dag's family. The Brandos had taken a beloved son from them. The fact that Dag was the child's father made no difference to the hatred the family had for the baby Cheyenne had given birth to. The Drollet family revealed these feelings when I talked to them in Tahiti. I hadn't known what to expect. It was a sensitive story and I wouldn't have been surprised to have the door closed in my face. There was no-one at the Drollets' modest seaside home and a neighbour thought perhaps that Mr Drollet—Dag's father—might be found at the cemetery, visiting his son's grave.

I found 66-year-old Jacques-Denis Drollet there, kneeling quietly at a freshly dug grave. I waited until he stood up and then introduced myself. 'I have Marlon Brando to thank for this,' he said, nodding towards the grave. 'I hold him personally responsible. My family is now at war with the Brandos and their celluloid cinema world. Unfortunately my son fell for a girl who had been brought up in that pseudo world. He loved her with all his heart and in the end it was that love which killed him.'

His face was cold, concealing the anger he expressed.

'As for Cheyenne's son, let him carry the name of Brando because I will never allow him to carry mine, even though my poor son is the father. I see that child as Cheyenne Brando's child, not my son's. And I warn Cheyenne to stay away from this hallowed grave. I don't want her here. Her presence would desecrate this ground.'

They were harsh words, but it was obvious that Jacques-Denis was hurting badly. He talked about the immense power of the Brandos and how their influence and riches had brought death and misery to his family.

Cheyenne was still in hospital with her baby Tuki, who lay in an incubator suffering from jaundice. While the baby was recovering, yet another child—a four-year-old girl—was to play a prominent role in Marlon Brando's life in the coming months. The dark-haired child, Tiairani, was Dag Drollet's first child by another Tahitian woman, and the baby's name, in the ancient Polynesian language, meant: 'Waiting for the sun to come from behind the cloud'.

Jacques-Denis led me to the child's mother, a beautiful 23-year-old islander called Titaua. She told me that a $100 million lawsuit had been started against the Brando estate to ensure that Tiairani was well provided for. Even though Dag Drollet had run off with Cheyenne shortly after her little girl was born, he had promised he would provide for her.

'My family and I don't want the Brando money just because he's a rich man,' Titaua said. 'We will need the money to ensure that she is cared for throughout the rest of her life. She might not have a father to care for her, but her life will be filled with love.'

I watched as the little girl ran along the beach. Titaua told me how she and Dag had gone everywhere together and then she had found she was pregnant. It was about that time that he met Cheyenne in a discotheque—and a new romance began. In the Tahitian islands, once a man has gone off with another woman, he has gone forever. Titaua believed that had it not been for Cheyenne they would still be together—and that Dag would still be alive.

When Dag's body, with a .45 bullet wound under his left eye, was returned to Tahiti for burial, Cheyenne's elder brother Teihotu was the only Brando to attend. He sat beside Dag's mother at the funeral and did his best to comfort her. Conspicuous by their absence were Marlon Brando, pregnant Cheyenne and her mother Tarita.

I tracked Teihotu down, not expecting him to talk to me, but he paused beside his Mercedes and told of his deep concerns for his younger sister.

'Cheyenne's in a mess,' he said. 'In LA everyone was at her, the police, lawyers, the press. It was all too much. She's lying up there in that hospital now with her sick baby and she's not well herself.

'Nobody knows what she's going through. Psychologically, she's really screwed up. She comes from two extremes. She comes from here, from Tahiti, where everything is slow and quiet, and suddenly she finds herself in the middle of a Hollywood murder—a real murder with everybody looking in. She has had a baby whose father died in the home of a world-famous film star and she's being torn apart by two cultures.'

My story, with pictures that I took of Jacques-Denis and Titaua and her daughter, ran as a centre-page spread in the *Daily Mail*. But feelings were running so high I felt I had not heard the end of the melodrama.

There was, of course, more to come in California, with Christian Brando's murder charge to be heard. But I believed that Tahiti would be the setting for another story involving the Brando family.

Four months after my visit to Tahiti, Cheyenne Brando was on a life support machine after a suicide attempt made on the day the islands celebrate the Festival of the Dead. She had taken a drug overdose after Dag Drollet's family repeated to her that she would not be allowed to visit his grave.

Marlon Brando flew from Los Angeles to be with Cheyenne, who was beginning to come out of her coma.

Alberto Vivien, a friend, of the Brando family, told me that, 'For days she's been saying, "I want to be with Dag, I want to be with Dag." It's been impossible to shake her out of it. We've all been worried that she might do something like this.'

But Dag Drollet's father, Jacques-Denis, refused to be blamed for Cheyenne's overdose. 'She is, and always has been, responsible for her own actions,' he said

The drama was still far from over.

Back in America, Christian was sentenced to ten years in prison for voluntary manslaughter, serving six before being released in 1996. But when he walked free he knew he would never see Cheyenne again—a year earlier she had hanged herself at her home in Tahiti. Whether a car crash much earlier had left her mentally unstable or whether the crazy mixed-up world she lived in had disturbed her has never been established. After Cheyenne's suicide, her mother Tarita took Tuki into her home.

Christian was to die of pneumonia in 2008. He was just 49 years old. Marlon had died four years earlier at the age of 80. It has never been revealed whether Dag Drollet's former girlfriend Titaua succeeded in any claim against his estate.

CHAPTER 17

The High-class Escort with Friends in High Places

'Rich, get to Bali as fast as you can! They've found Pamela Bordes!' It was the end of February 1989. The caller was Gerry Hunt, the *Mail*'s foreign editor, and Pamela Bordes—well, I didn't need to be told who she was.

The 27-year-old former Miss India had caused a sensation in London when it was revealed she had taken up a new career as a high-class escort and had wormed her way into the House of Commons as a researcher. She had friends in very high places and a few low ones, a reminder of the days of John Profumo and Christine Keeler. In 1963 Profumo, then secretary of state for war, was at the centre of a major scandal when it was revealed he was having an affair with Christine Keeler, the mistress of an alleged Russian spy, and there were concerns that Britain's security had been compromised. Any woman of questionable repute who ends up getting close to gentlemen of authority—particularly anyone working for, or a member of government—can be deemed a security risk.

When the Bordes scandal broke in March 1989, with claims that Pamela had not only been working as a researcher at the House of Commons but was a 'close friend' of Colin Moynihan, then the minister for sport in Margaret Thatcher's government, and of *Sunday Times* editor Andrew Neil and *Observer* editor Donald Trelford, she got out of town—fast. Every newspaper in the country sent its reporters out searching for her … the cities of Europe … the nightspots of New York. She was reported to have been seen everywhere, and reporters' expense accounts soared. Nothing like a good hunt for a touch of the grand life away from the office.

Pamela was not to be found. Nowhere in the world. She had made good her getaway. But as somebody once said, you can run but you can't hide. It was due to a freak of circumstance that Pamela's hideaway was discovered.

She had flown to Bali and made her way to the hilltop village of Ubud, once a hippie retreat, where, months later, Mick Jagger and Jerry Hall were to go through a Balinese marriage ceremony. (Turned out it wasn't a real marriage, more a ceremonial one, but it was colourful enough with a black chicken being sacrificed and its blood dabbed onto the heads of the rock star and the model.)

The fiery-eyed Pamela Bordes believed she was safe from the media in Ubud, staying in a private residence in the company of a couple of very close women friends, including a 32-year-old American who was to identify herself only as Rachael. The only way she'd be discovered would be if she ventured out and a reporter, or a British newspaper employee, came across her by sheer chance. And that's exactly what happened.

One evening Pamela and her friends decided it was safe to go out to the Lotus Café, a popular dining-out place located beside a fabulous lotus pond. An employee of *The Sun*'s advertising department was also having a meal there during a holiday with his wife.

It didn't take much more than a second glance for him to realize that he was in the presence of the most hunted woman in the UK. Later, when Pamela and her friend Rachael left on a small motorbike, the advertising man followed in a car. It turned into a chase, a camera flash went off and Pamela and Rachael crashed. Pamela was left with cut lips, another cut under her left eye, grazing and a broken front tooth.

'I'm dying! I'm dying!' she cried out into the darkness as help was summoned. She was treated by a local doctor before going into 'deep hiding' in what was believed to be a thatched-roof bungalow in the middle of a rice paddy. When *The Sun* ran photos of Pamela riding off into the night, the game was up. She'd been found—hence the call from Gerry for me to 'get up there immediately'.

I arrived with freelance photographer Brendan Beirne, as other journalists and photographers flew in to the Indonesian island from London. Again, no expense was to be spared. We all wanted to find Pamela and hear her entire story—if she was well enough to talk. Those of us who waded through knee-deep water in rice paddies to the cottage she was now thought to be in and knocked on the big wooden door were greeted by silence. Was she in there at all, silently lurking behind the shuttered windows? Had we all been fed a 'bum steer'?

Lines of journalists' rental cars lined a nearby road, long lenses trained on the bungalow for signs of life. We took it in turns to watch the place day and night—although night-time, of course, made it difficult to see if anyone was escaping. But with a thick, seemingly impenetrable forest at the rear of the house, we suspected that any getaway would be through the front or to the sides—and we had those areas covered.

We did not foresee the incredible James Bond-style, one-man mission carried out by a handsome London solicitor called Tim Taylor. He had been contacted by friends of Pamela to fly to Bali and take care of her affairs—meaning her dealings with the press, not any other kind of affairs. The first thing Tim decided was to get Pamela out of the bungalow without her being seen, a task that seemed impossible. But from what I was able to ascertain, he negotiated the forest at the rear of the bungalow late at night, scrambled through the undergrowth, then stealthily waded though the rice paddies. The story went that he climbed onto the bungalow roof and lowered himself through a hole in the thatch—although I was never able to confirm that particular detail.

There was, however, evidence he had been up to some kind of daredevil stunt. When he summoned us to a brief press conference in the Bali Beach Hotel later, his once-immaculate grey suit and black shoes were spattered with mud. And when he pulled at the once-sharp crease of his trousers, it was revealed he was wearing no socks. Hot and bothered, he had turned up three hours late and said he was now Miss Bordes' legal representative and would be reading a statement on her behalf. After that, his role with her was over. It came as no surprise that Pamela was prepared to sell her story. Unfolding three crumpled sheets of paper, on which the statement had been handwritten, Tim said that press coverage had suggested that Miss Bordes' activities had had ramifications for national security.

'When the true facts are made known—as Miss Bordes intends—that inference will be shown to be wholly without foundation,' he said, adding that in order to allow her to return to a normal life and lay to rest, she would allow only one news organization to publish what she had to say. Oh, yes, she was also looking for money, which would be a matter for lawyers in London, but she planned to make a substantial donation to a charity.

Much to the *Daily Mail*'s horror, in virtually no time a deal had been struck—with the opposition *Daily Express* newspaper. A senior executive was already on his way out to Bali to seal the arrangements with Pamela. The word was that she would be moved in secret out of Bali to a safe place where she could receive further medical treatment—and tell her story without having to look over her shoulder all the time. With the *Express* now very much in the picture, those of us from other papers left on the 'outside' realized we had to pull out all stops to discover where she was going to be taken. No deals were struck among us. We just decided to spread out, watching the airport, and all possible exits by sea and whoever found her, well, it was good luck to them.

I sat with Brendan in our hotel, the Bali Hyatt, and tried to work something out. Why, I wondered, had Tim called the meeting at the Bali Beach Hotel? We didn't think he was staying there, so why choose that location? Could it be that Pamela had been put up there? That didn't make much sense either because surely Tim would have checked into the same hotel she was at. I told Brendan we had nothing to lose by driving back to the Bali Beach and hanging about. You never knew …

We drank endless cups of coffee in the coffee shop, wandered around the lobby and began to wonder if we shouldn't be doing something else, such as joining a handful of others at a ferry terminal on the north of the island. It would break the monotony. I was on the point of suggesting it when I almost choked on my words.

Walking through the lobby was a man I recognized from some 20 years earlier: Alan Frame, who had sat with me on the *Daily Sketch* Foreign Desk in the late 1960s, where he was working as a subeditor and I was the deputy foreign editor for a short time. Alan had gone on to greater things and was now either number two or number three on the *Daily Express*. Anyway, a big number.

'I don't believe it!' I exclaimed 'There's the *Express* man!'

Pamela had to be staying in the hotel because Alan wouldn't be there otherwise. It was not exactly the best hotel on the island and perhaps that was deliberate—the *Express* might have assumed that journalists would be looking for the former Miss India in a more salubrious establishment.

'He'll recognize me, Brendan,' I said. 'You follow him!'

Leaving his camera bag with me—we couldn't afford to drop any clues—Brendan hurried across the lobby and just managed to get into the lift with Alan. As the doors closed, I made my way to the coffee shop for yet more coffee and to await developments. An hour went by and still Brendan hadn't returned. What was going on up there? Had Alan called security, which had thrown Brendan out of the hotel? But when he finally returned after 90 minutes he was triumphant.

'We're going to Hong Kong in the morning,' he said.

'How did you manage that?' I asked.

'It was just like in the movies. When we got out of the lift I hung back in the corridor and watched what room he went into. I hovered about a bit and then went to his door. I could hear him talking on the phone but couldn't hear him well enough. I saw a trolley in the corridor with a glass on it, so I put it against my ear and then against his door and I could hear much clearer. He was talking to his wife and telling her that they would be leaving first thing in the morning for Hong Kong.'

When Alan had said 'they', we could only assume he was referring to the Pamela Bordes party of the lady herself, Tim and Alan.

I didn't like doing this to an old friend like Alan. But this was business and when it came to competition between the *Mail* and the *Express* it was fair to spill blood, metaphorically speaking. As my late pal James Oram, from Sydney's *Daily Mirror*, once told a tearful journalist he had scooped and who had come after him for not sharing his story when she thought he was her friend, 'None of us is in this business to make friends. Remember that and you'll get on.'

I had to apply this principle to the man from the *Express*. It looked like I was on the cusp of at least what we referred to as a 'spoiler'. A picture of Pamela flying to Hong Kong would be the first photo of her since the London scandal had broken.

Now I need to explain something else, following on from the 'friends aren't really friends when it comes to journalistic competition' statement. Sometimes personal loyalties are so strong and sometimes favours given in the past are so binding that the 'never share stuff with the opposition' rules have to be broken.

Brendan owed one of the photographers in the London gang a huge favour from the past. Such a huge favour, in fact, that he wondered how he would ever be able to repay it. Until now. It wouldn't hurt just to mention the Hong Kong flight to that photographer, whose paper was so small that it wouldn't matter if he got a picture of Pamela anyway. And that is where the kindest of thoughts went horribly wrong. Brendan mentioned Hong Kong to his colleague, assured that the word in his ear would cause no problems. However, just as Brendan owed a favour to that photographer, so he owed a favour to another. And so on it went down the line until by the following morning every newspaper team was at the airport.

'How the hell did they find out?' I asked Brendan.

'Dunno,' he said, but he shamefacedly admitted later that he was the cause. If there was ever a time when I wanted to murder a photographer, it was then. But

I eventually forgave him because it was his initiative with the old glass trick that had turned up the Hong Kong connection.

The start of the flight to Hong Kong was only part of the extraordinary Pamela Bordes story.

Pamela arrived at the airport with Alan and Tim, both of whose faces dropped when they saw us all. She had a scarf wrapped around her face, but it failed to muffle a barrage of words aimed at us that weren't very nice.

There were several flights they could have been booked on, because the connection to Hong Kong had to be made in Jakarta, 45 minutes away.

We had no idea what local flight they were taking and only when they went to the check-in counter could we be sure. That meant that some 20 reporters and photographers all had to fight one another at a tiny opening in a glass window to buy tickets. Wads of money were thrust at the astonished sales clerks.

'Doesn't matter how much it costs, give me a seat!' came the shrieking chorus. 'I'll pay double, triple, four times—just give me a fucking seat!'

In the end we all managed to get tickets and ran across the tarmac just as Pamela and Alan reached the aircraft steps (this was before the days of covered walkways). At the top of the steps, a throng of photographers made it impossible for Alan and his charge to get to their business-class seats. In the nasty melee that ensued, Pamela's scarf fell away to expose very bad cuts and bruises to her face. She took her seat and gave up trying to hide her features as the cameras fired away.

Alan was exasperated. This was his story but he had no control over what was happening. Other business-class passengers could not believe what they were seeing—a mob of photographers and reporters, shouting, shoving, flashguns going off, questions being fired. Finally the captain ordered everyone to sit down, which everyone did because they had their pictures.

There was, of course, much more that was needed from Pamela. She'd sold her story—yet to be told—to the *Express* but that didn't prevent me and other reporters from deciding to pursue her, me in particular because this was a case of the *Daily Mail* against the fierce opposition that was the *Daily Express*.

Hong Kong photographers, tipped off by the London papers that Pamela was on the way—because they could not be sure that any of their people in Bali had been successful—were waiting as the hapless woman hurried through the airport. More cameras were fired at her. Alan was lost in the throng.

And suddenly I was hit by the kind of luck that could only be dreamed of. My backpack was one of the first off the carousel and Pamela's luggage came along right beside it. Alan was left behind with the other reporters waiting for his baggage. I slung my backpack over my shoulder and grabbed Pamela's two bags.

'Come on,' I said, 'I'll carry this for you. You'll be mobbed if you don't come now.'

She followed me, because I had her bags, out to the taxi rank where she said she had to wait for Alan and Tim.

'You'll never get out of here alive,' I told her. 'Look, here they come!'

Sure enough a large pack of Chinese and British photographers were racing through the airport doors towards us. I threw Pamela's bags and mine into the back of a taxi, told her to jump in and I followed.

'I've got to go to hospital,' she said. 'I've been checked in.'

'OK,' I said. 'Let's get you there. You're in safe hands with me.'

I was telling porkies, of course. What I'd done was stolen the *Daily Express*'s super-scoop. She didn't know who I was and I realized I'd probably have to hand her back once a furious *Express* editor had got onto the *Daily Mail*'s editor and made his demands for her return.

We had the most extraordinary conversation as we sped to the hospital. Pamela, who had been in a daze up to now, suddenly decided to ask who on earth I was. She had obviously not seen me among the mob on the plane and might have thought that I was just a good Samaritan getting her away from the hands of a mob of photographers and reporters.

'Well, actually, Pamela …' I began.

She interrupted me. 'You know who I am! You're one of them!'

'Don't get out! Don't get out!' I cried as she reached for the door handle. 'We're still moving and in any case I'm only doing this to help you.'

'Where's Alan? Alan's supposed to be here with me, not you.'

I carefully introduced myself and explained that Alan was an old friend from way back, which was true, and that she would be safely delivered back into his hands. Wasn't I making sure she got to the hospital?

And then she said something which, as it turned out, was to stun both of us.

'Now I know how poor Phoolan felt.'

I felt the hair on the back of my neck rising. 'Phoolan … you don't mean Phoolan Devi?'

'Yes, why, have you heard of her?'

'Heard of her! I wrote a book about her.'

'You! You wrote that book about her? You're lying!'

'*Devi: The Bandit Queen*—that's what it's called.'

'You're lying, you're lying! How low will you people stoop! You found out that I've been reading it and you're saying this to get on my side. Very clever but it's not going to work.'

'You've just read *Devi: The Bandit Queen*?' I asked, not believing this. Phoolan Devi was a young Indian woman who, after being raped by a number of men in a village, went off into the ravines and formed her own gang. Then she led the gang back to the village with them and gunned down her attackers. She went on the run with her gang for two years before eventually surrendering. She served a term of imprisonment, became an MP—but was gunned down by an unknown assassin one night in Delhi.

'I've just finished it,' said Pamela, referring to my book. 'Somebody must have told you that.'

'No, no, I can tell you how it begins, how it ends, what photos are in it. I can tell you about her lover Man Singh, and her terrible father and all of that. I wrote it with my wife Isobelle'—we had by now married—'who comes from Vanuatu and when she's dressed up she can make herself look kind of Indian-ish. Isobelle got into the jail in Gwalior where Phoolan was being held, dressed up in a sari and talked to her at length.'

'That was your wife, that woman you wrote the book with?'

'Yes, yes!'

'Well, you know how Phoolan was persecuted, how everybody lied about her and the press wrote terrible things about her.'

'Yes, I knew the pain she felt and I can imagine how you're going through the same thing. I learned a lot about persecution researching the book on Phoolan,' I said.

Pamela turned to look at me. I couldn't help but stare at her injuries before turning my eyes to hers. Looking at her, I believed I had won her over, journalistically speaking.

It was extraordinary that of all the books Pamela, a former Indian beauty queen, had read recently was the one I'd written about an Indian bandit queen. And we were sitting side by side in a taxi together.

By an equally amazing stroke of luck, Brendan, who was travelling light, had managed to jump in a taxi immediately behind ours and was following. By the time we reached the hospital things had changed. Pamela agree to 'reconsider' her arrangement with the *Daily Express*, partly because of the strange events in the cab, but also because I had assured her that any figure the *Express* had offered the *Mail* would top.

She had already begun to open up on the way. She talked of 'this terrible nightmare', of her love for her fiancé Nick Adam in London, and expressed fears that she would be scarred for life. 'I'm going to need plastic surgery and a lot of dental surgery. Several of my teeth have been loosened in the crash and one was broken.'

At the Adventist Hospital, which she had been booked into, I had to fib to a doctor that the people following us were a pack of mad journalists from London and at all costs they must be kept away from Pamela. He agreed and security guards were placed in the lobby to keep everyone back—including Alan. Pamela was helped into a wheelchair and taken to a private ward. Later *Mail* reporter Paul Henderson met up with us there, having been despatched from London when I reported from Bali we were heading to Hong Kong. Henderson's job was to draw up contracts and ensure that enough security was in place to keep other reporters from reaching the room.

The *Mail*'s editor, David English, took personal charge of the story from London. And because he wanted absolute security he insisted that he receive copy directly into his hands—and he wanted the gist of Pamela's entire story within the hour of her arrival at the hospital. Speaking to him from a phone beside Pamela's bed, I tried to explain that at that very moment a doctor was hooking her up to an intravenous drip and pushing tubes up her nose.

David English was a good-humoured man, a brilliant 'on the road' journalist in his time—with, by coincidence, the *Daily Express*—and I heard his chuckle at the ludicrousness of it all. Nevertheless, he wanted the copy and he said he was putting me through at that very minute to his PA, Ina, who would take it down.

I was about to protest that I had nothing for her to take down but thought better of it. Never tell an editor, especially David English, that 'it can't be done'. I turned to Pamela and told her that I had to interview her there and then. She shook her head and said she wasn't well enough. A precious ten minutes were lost as I tried everything to persuade her to talk just a little. Meanwhile Ina was calling down the phone: 'Are you ready, are you ready?'

Finally Pamela agreed to answer some questions. It was one of the most bizarre interviews I'd conducted.

I began by dictating to Ina a 'stock' intro just to get the ball rolling and, straight off the top of my head, began with the words I hoped Pamela couldn't hear: 'The woman at the centre of the "call girl in the Commons" scandal spoke for the first time last night—and revealed how she learned British secrets through her sexual encounters.'

I hoped she would describe events that supported the intro I'd just sent over. Questions and answers turned into a new paragraph which I would dictate to Ina. It was painstakingly slow, but the story was coming together. Pamela mentioned people in very high places who she had been 'acquainted' with, from royalty to Libya's Colonel Gadaffi. After two hours, the editor had close to 3000 words of copy—more than enough for the front-page lead the following day.

But the amazing events surrounding Pamela were far from over. The instruction from David English was to get her out of that hospital and put her in a safe place where none of the other papers could reach her. I was well aware of the urgency—Brendan had seen Tim Miles, chief reporter for the now-defunct *Today* newspaper, in the corridor and he had been ushered away at the last minute by a security guard.

As I continued to interview Pamela, who was by now very groggy and falling under the influence of relaxants, Paul Henderson returned with two private detectives, British men who had set up a business in Hong Kong. We worked out a plan. It was going to be too difficult to get Pamela out of the hospital and drive her through the streets of Hong Kong, which were clogged even late at night, without the rest of the press catching up with us—so we agreed to keep her where she was. Or rather, right next door. The detectives had found a luxury flat in a block beside the hospital. Pamela would need to travel less than 100 yards (90 metres).

But first we had to get her out of the room, down to a car and around to the apartment block.

It was now close to two o'clock in the morning and there were no doctors present—and the fewer people who knew what we were about to do the better. However, journalists were still loitering around the hospital lobby. I was wondering what Alan was thinking—he would have known by now that the *Mail* had snatched Pamela away and had more than likely persuaded her to 'defect'.

I looked at the drip attached to Pamela's hand and the tube that was in her nose. 'Pamela,' I asked, 'is that tube in your nose attached to anything in particular?'

She shrugged. I removed the needle from her hand and tugged at the nose tube, which came away easily. The two private detectives, Paul Henderson, Brendan and I helped a very groggy Pamela into a wheelchair. With one of the detectives hurrying ahead to make sure the coast was clear, we got her into a lift and rode down to the basement. We manhandled her into a car and drove around the corner and into the basement of the neighbouring apartment block.

There we remained for the next week as the rest of the British pack hunted all over Hong Kong for Pamela. Because this was such a major story, the *Mail* also sent out assistant editor Len Gould and respected columnist Linda Lee-Potter. After all, Pamela had no female company.

A doctor—not from the hospital, because we felt the staff there would be furious at the way their patient had been whisked away in the night when she was under sedation—was brought in to check Pamela over. Apart from the scarring and a loss of weight, he saw no immediate signs of danger to her health, but said her injuries would need to be tended daily and she would need to go back into hospital. Hong Kong was out and in any case Pamela was by now declaring that she wanted to be treated back in London.

Food was brought in to us. We paced the large apartment as Linda interviewed Pamela for a three-part series. Cabin fever was setting in. We all wanted to get out, but the British papers had kept their reporters in Hong Kong, watching the airport and keeping their eyes peeled for anyone from the *Mail* they might recognize.

On one occasion I was sitting in the kitchen drinking coffee, not feeling tired enough to go to bed, even though it was close to 3AM, when Pamela strolled in wearing a long dress and shawl. She couldn't sleep either. She just wanted to talk about … anything. She sat on the corner of the table and began chatting about the arrogance of people in high places.

'They are so right and proper in the eyes of the public but behind the scenes they are just like pigs,' she said. Was there someone she was referring to in particular? She told me about how a very public person I cannot name had taken the opportunity of being alone with her and had had his wicked way with her. It was not so much who he was, she said, but what he did as he thrust her up against a radiator. It was clear Pamela had a lot of scandal to reveal.

Eventually those of us who had become her guardians decided the coast was clear enough for Brendan and I to venture out with Pamela so we could get pictures of her in Hong Kong settings. She specifically asked that I go with her. The Bandit

Queen connection was still strong. It was risky, but the pictures were needed—and we got away with it.

Although working as a foreign correspondent has its advantages—you don't have to report to an office every day and you are basically the master of your time as long as you get the job done—you are also out of touch with the internal politics on the editorial floor.

I was to hear from several trusted sources that a colleague who was on the peripheral end of the story had claimed all the glory and had dined out on it for months. Being far away in Australia, I was not able to immediately object to his claims. Fortunately, Gerry on the Foreign Desk and editor David English knew the truth. In the newspaper world, they say dog doesn't bite dog, but on this one, I felt justified in biting hard and making sure that everyone knew it was me, and not my boastful colleague, who won the story for the *Daily Mail*.

CHAPTER 18

Captain Mark Phillips and the New Zealand Love Child

Sometimes reporters find themselves on the other side of the cameras—staring into the lens, the subject of the news.

When I returned home from yet another assignment—for the stories were flowing thick and fast and I was constantly rushing to the airport—Isobelle was in a tizz. Her elderly Maltese terriers, Rolly and Sassy, had got lost while Isobelle's sister was walking them and it was suspected they were in the nearby bush … somewhere.

They were not allowed in there anyway because the council rangers were worried that dogs would kill the wildlife, of which there were shrews, snakes, spiders and birds, to name a few. There were also rabbits and a few foxes, which the rangers did not like because they were considered pests, introduced by the early arrivals from Britain, and from time to time poison would be laid in the hope of reducing the pest population.

I decided to try the bush anyway. It was four in the afternoon. I followed a number of tracks calling the dogs' names, but the only response was the twittering of birds. I climbed up slopes, slithered down the other sides and forced my way through the thicket, but there was no sign of the missing terriers.

On my way back to the house, I jumped onto a large rock, one of a cluster of boulders in a clearing, and called the dogs' names one last time, hoping my voice would carry down over the hillside that ran down to one of the harbour inlets, Taylor's Bay.

Was that a bark I heard? I called again and now I could make out the sound—it was definitely a bark. But I could not work out where it was coming from. It was very faint and muffled. I strained my ears, thinking at first the barks were coming from the south, then the west. I jumped off the rock and scrambled southwards but now I couldn't hear anything. So I went in another direction with the same negative result. Climbing back on the rock I could hear the barking again … hardly discernable and mystifying. I sat down and tried to solve the puzzle—and heard the barking more clearly this time. It suddenly hit me. The dogs were right under my feet.

I scrambled down to the base of the rock and found a narrow opening. Now I could hear them clearly. They were in a tunnel, deep under the rock and certainly out of sight. Perhaps they'd chased a rabbit in there. But, whatever the reason, they obviously couldn't get out.

When I led Isobelle back to the rock, she realized the situation was hopeless and went off to call for help. A ranger from the zoo came. A vet arrived. Then the police and finally the fire brigade. As if that wasn't a big enough circus, a TV cameraman turned up.

The rocks were hard granite. It was obvious Rolly and Sassy couldn't get themselves out. The firemen, aware of Isobelle's distress, said they would do all they could. The best angle of attack, they believed, was not through the narrow tunnel which seemed to twist and turn, but down through the granite from the top. Out came drills, jack hammers, mallets. Up went arc lights. 'Operation Terriers' was under way. It was after midnight when the cry went up from one of the firemen: 'I'm through! I've got them!'

From out of the bowels of the earth came two very dusty dogs, yelping with delight as Isobelle took them in her arms and the TV camera recorded it all. How on earth had I found them, the reporter wanted to know. 'Strange forces,' I replied.

The story made the evening news, but Isobelle and I wondered about the mysterious events behind the story. Of all the clusters of rocks in that vast area of coastal bushland, why had I chosen that particular group to stand on while calling for the dogs? What had led me there? The bushland stretched for several miles in each direction and there were many, many granite clusters I could have clambered on to. And how on earth had I managed to hear that faint barking from so far below the ground? It was so faint it could have easily been missed.

Strange forces. Do I believe in the paranormal? When seemingly impossible stories worked out for me, I'd often wondered: are we born lucky or do we make our own luck? Or is there something else that is just inexplicable?

◆

Rumours were persisting in the early 1990s that singer Olivia Newton-John's marriage to Matt Lattanzi was on shaky ground and that he had formed a 'friendship' with a young Australian student, Cindy Jessup. The *Mail* wanted me to find Cindy and ask her about the gossip. My colourful, and sadly late pal, Peter Carrette, a freelance photographer based in Bondi—who had become famous in 1969 when he had taken an exclusive picture of Marianne Faithful, who at the time was Mick Jagger's girlfriend and muse, in a Sydney hospital after she suffered a drugs overdose—said he'd heard that Cindy was living 'somewhere on the north coast of New South Wales'.

This was one of those occasions when I got in behind the wheel of my old Ford and headed north, having no idea where I was heading but believing that I should place myself in the area to at least give myself something of a chance of finding Cindy.

Some 400 miles (650 kilometres) north of Sydney I decided on a whim to turn off the main highway onto a dirt road towards the town of Armidale. Darkness had descended as I bumped along the road that soon became a track, with a steep cliff rising up on the right and a sheer drop on the left. My headlights lit up the trees as I drove very carefully, aware of the potential disaster that lurked on my left.

As I rounded a bend, my foot slammed down on the brake pedal. Illuminated in the headlights was a figure, its head covered in a hood, standing on the very edge of the steep drop. I had a glimpse of a thin face—it was impossible to tell if it was male or female—before the apparition turned its back on me, slowly raised its right arm and raised a finger in the direction I was heading. I felt my blood run cold. This person—if it were a person—should not have been there, miles from anywhere, wearing a hood on a warm summer's night, perched on the edge of a cliff. I started to edge past and as I did so the figure kept its back to me. Once I was past I touched my brakes and looked in the mirror. The brake lights illuminated the area behind the car—but the figure had gone. I was certain that apparition was not a hitch-hiker and, let me make this clear, I hadn't knocked it off the road!

An hour or so later I checked into a motel. It was late but I'd managed to get the owner to come to the door. I mentioned my experience but he shrugged. Never heard anything like it before, he said.

But what was extraordinary about this story is that a few inquiries around the town led me to an address where Cindy was staying. We went out to dinner and she told me of her friendship with Matt Lattanzi but insisted they were just friends who had met when he was taking part in a marathon cycling event. Despite my elation at finding Cindy on what had seemed like an impossible task, what remained was the memory of that figure. Something about it just didn't seem right. And that pointed finger directing me to continue on the way … should I dare to think that 'something' was telling me to carry on and I'd reach my goal and find Cindy?

As events turned out, Olivia and Matt divorced and Matt and Cindy set up home together.

◆

But in London, the attention of the British press was taken up with a much bigger story—claims that Captain Mark Phillips, the estranged husband of Princess Anne, had fathered a child in New Zealand while they were still together. It was my old friends on the opposition *Daily Express* who had broken the story after striking a substantial financial deal with the mother of the child, New Zealand horsewoman Heather Tonkin. Miss Tonkin and the man from the *Express* were bunkered down at her farm on the outskirts of Auckland after the explosive claims had been made public. The *Express* planned to run more revelations surrounding the birth of the child, Felicity who had been born five years earlier. I was given the task of trying to come up with a 'spoiler'.

What Heather Tonkin was claiming was that she and Mark Phillips had spent a night together in an Auckland hotel room after she met him during a horse-riding clinic in 1983. She later found she was pregnant.

This was a curious affair—not just for them, but for me, because I'd written that dramatic story when Mark and Anne had been attacked by a crazed gunman in London many years earlier. Now I was about to become heavily involved in another saga that was to spell the official end of that marriage.

On 21 March 1991, as I was flying to Auckland, solicitors for 37-year-old Heather Tonkin filed a paternity claim in the Otahuhu District Court. Just how long Princess Anne had known of the affair was an intriguing question, but my colleague and long-time friend, Richard Kay, the *Mail*'s royal reporter in London, had no doubts that she would now be allowed to divorce Mark and start a new independent life, particularly as the couple had been separated for two years.

Although trying to find out more about the birth of Felicity when the *Express* man was continuing to talk to Tonkin on a one-to-one basis was going to be difficult, I rented a car and drove to her home. The curtains at the gabled farmhouse, standing in 50 acres (20 hectares) of rolling meadows at Whitford, south of central Auckland, were tightly drawn. Outside, peacocks strutted on the lawns. Horses grazed nearby. Burly security men sat huddled in a car at the main gate and more men could be seen in the driveway. The *Express* was making absolutely sure that no-one was going to get within a peacock screech of Miss Tonkin.

I spoke to a neighbour who said that in a way Miss Tonkin had built a prison for herself, for how could she go out now without everyone in New Zealand knowing of her affair with Mark? If the paternity suit was pursued, it seemed certain that she would seek both maintenance and a lump sum. As the claims continued to flow from Heather Tonkins' lips and were fed to *Daily Express* readers, Captain Phillips announced he would contest the paternity claim.

It was revealed that she had originally tried to sell her story to British newspapers for £5 million, but eventually reached an agreement with the *Express* for a much lower amount. Among the sordid details the *Express* released were claims that Miss Tonkin had told Captain Phillips that doctors had informed her she could not have children and it was safe for them to have unprotected sex.

Could this be my way into the story, a way of finding that 'spoiler' the *Mail* was so anxious for? Numerous inquiries later, I was heading north out of Auckland to meet former jockey Ray Mathers, who had lived with Heather Tonkin for five years. What he told me was sensational—and resulted in a front-page story in the *Daily Mail* and severe embarrassment for the *Express* and Miss Tonkin.

Ray said he was astonished at Heather Tonkin's claim she was infertile and therefore did not use contraception when she slept with Mark. 'That's a very strange claim,' he said 'because she fell pregnant with my own baby before she met Mark Phillips and insisted on having a termination. To say she was infertile is just nonsense.'

Foreign editor Gerry Hunt was delighted when I told him what Ray had said. 'Bloody hell!' said Gerry. 'Give us everything you've got!'

And it was a lot—revelations that the *Express* had failed to reveal to its readers.

'I'd lived with Heather for five years and having to drive her to the abortion clinic to terminate my child was the worst experience of my life,' Ray told me. 'I really wanted her to have my baby, but she was determined to get rid of it. I'm also surprised that, after living with me for so long, she should go against my wishes, then later decided to give birth to a child she says she conceived in a one-night stand.'

Referring to Heather's claim that doctors had told her she could not have children as a result of an infection, Ray said the infection was before she became pregnant with his own child. According to her claims, Captain Phillips urged her not to have the child when she told him she was pregnant by him. But she said that at the age of 32 she had never had a chance of motherhood and might never have it again. She is said to have questioned her right to destroy the 'young life inside her'. She was also reported to have thanked God for helping her do what she called 'the right thing' and go ahead and have Mark's baby.

Ray, who by now was working as a horse trainer and was married with two children, recalled that Heather had become pregnant by him in late 1983 or early 1984. After the abortion they had used contraception. They broke up later in 1984, before she claimed to have slept with Captain Phillips.

Ray said he realized people would suspect he was Felicity's father now that Captain Phillips had announced he would fight the case—but he was confident that if he took DNA tests they would show he was not the father.

The story was sensational enough and I wondered what the *Express* would be making of it. Confirmation of Ray's claims were needed—they came from a couple who knew Heather well. Yes, they said, adding that they were speaking out in fairness to Captain Phillips, Ray had lived with Heather for several years and after he had moved out another man had moved in. 'Everyone knew baby Felicity wasn't Ray's because she'd let that slip out,' said the couple.

Ray's revelations had a disastrous effect on the *Daily Express* buy-up. Word around the Auckland press was that the *Express* journalist had confronted Heather about the *Mail's* story and a fierce argument had broken out, resulting, it was claimed, in the horsewoman hitting the *Express* man over the head with a frying pan. He moved out of the house where he had been spending many hours each day putting her story together.

With the *Express* out of the way and the security men removed from the gate, I thought I would take my chances and call on Heather. She would have been aware that I was the scoundrel who had destroyed her relationship with the *Express*—but nothing ventured, nothing gained. To my amazement, she invited me into the kitchen. She offered me a cup of tea and said she wouldn't be able to talk for long. But even a few words would have made me happy.

'Things are in turmoil,' she said, without explaining what she meant by 'things'.

'It has all got way out of control but I will be pursuing my paternity claim. I know what the truth is, that Mark is the father of my child.'

I asked her about the claims of Ray, who had suggested to me that when she had allegedly spent the night with Mark Phillips she knew she was not infertile.

'That's something I can't go into,' she said and soon she was showing me the door.

But then a curious thing happened. On a whim I asked if she wanted to meet me for dinner that night to help her get over the pressure of recent days. She agreed. We went to a harbourside fish restaurant, where she ordered a Black Russian cocktail. Although she remained hesitant about many of the fine details of her alleged one-night stand, she said the affair had taken place in the Town House Hotel in Auckland after a polo event. Mark had told her she would be able to find his room because he would leave his boots outside the door. Wow—that struck me as an astonishing scenario … a man who was still married to the Queen's daughter leaving his boots outside his hotel room door so a woman he had just met would know where he was. I wondered why he didn't just say 'I'm in room such and such …'

I dined with Heather several times in the same restaurant, during which she sipped numerous Black Russians and continued to insist that she knew 'perfectly well' who Felicity's father was and would be pursuing Mark for paternity payments.

Two months later I returned to New Zealand to find out, if I could, what was happening in the extraordinary affair. Legal papers had by now been served on Captain Phillips claiming he was Felicity's father. Heather welcomed me into her home, where her daughter (known as 'Bunny') was watching TV.

'I have no intention of giving up my fight,' she said in an exclusive interview—I knew those Black Russians would win her over. 'Just as I would fight to the death to keep my lovely daughter, I'll also fight until Mark faces up to his responsibilities and legally admits he is Bunny's father. There is no way I am going to give up. I started this business for the sake of Bunny and I'm going to see it right through.

What kind of father he is when he refuses to accept her as his? He hasn't set eyes on Bunny in the flesh since the day she was born.'

She poured tea as we stood in her kitchen. 'There is no-one else. They can turn New Zealand upside down looking for someone but they won't find anyone.'

We went out for dinner again that evening. More Black Russians. I had a glass of white wine.

The next day I flew home to Sydney. My job of spoiling the *Express*'s exclusive was over. I doubt whether I had any friends left at that paper.

◆

What has made the *Daily Mail* such a great paper is that it refuses to view the world through rose-coloured spectacles. Over the many years I've worked for it, I have learned never to accept everything at face value. Of course, that should be the role of every journalist: to ask all the penetrating questions and be a hundred per cent satisfied that the story he or she is about to write is totally accurate. I've got things wrong from time to time. And without doubt I have upset some people. But those I have upset, I hope, have in the main been those who deserve to be exposed for wrongdoings. It would be a rare journalist who could know absolutely everything about a subject he was writing about. But, as Princess Margaret said to me all those years ago, 'One does one's best.'

Speaking of royalty, I should refer back briefly to that royal couple of show business, Mick Jagger and Jerry Hall, and their Indonesian wedding, which happened when they were staying in the home of an old friend of Mick's, a wealthy furniture-maker called Amir.

After the blood of that sacrificial black chicken was sprinkled on their foreheads, the meat of five different coloured chickens was offered to keep away evil. The hills must have been alive with the clucking of hens, for the meat of a white-feathered chicken was offered to protect the couple from evil from the east, a yellow-feathered bird to cover the west, black for the north, red for the south and a mixed-coloured bird for the centre. Then it was time for Mick and Jerry to cleanse their bodies. Usually couples go to the river where the wife stands downstream of her husband and washes his clothes as a symbol of her devotion for the years to come. Jerry was spared this. Instead, the couple went to the bath in Amir's house, where they shared a scented tub.

The aroma of sandalwood incense filled the evening air and candles emitted a soft glow. Mick and Jerry were given balls of coloured rice with which they touched the sides of their heads and shoulders in the sign of the cross. Jerry then had to lay a small raffia mat on the ground which Mick, now wearing a kris—a sword—approached. He produced the sword and pierced the mat, another symbolic act to signify the union of man and woman.

What Gerry, the foreign editor, wanted to know was whether this was recognized as a legal marriage. He was known around the office for his loyalty to his staff. If he thought a story should get into the paper, he'd fight for it, push hard to get it in, no matter what the editor might think of it. But Gerry never left any stone unturned. I've lost count of the number of times he's called me in the dead of night with a justifiable query. There were times when the entire editorial floor would look up when Gerry, reading copy that he felt a reporter had not done justice to, would yell out in his Birmingham dialect: 'Bloody hell—what the fuck is this? I've told him what I bloody well want and ...' Well, you get the idea.

Now I was on the phone to Gerry trying to explain Indonesia's complex marriage system.

'It was a Hindu ceremony, Gerry. I spoke to a bloke called Widjaya Idabagus.'

'What?'

'Widjaya Idabagus.'

'Who the bloody hell is he?'

'Mr Widjaya Idabagus works at the office of births, deaths and marriages and, by coincidence, happens to be a fan of the Rolling Stones.'

'I don't care if he's a fan of the bloody Beatles—are Mick and Jerry married?'

'OK, Mr Widjaya Idabagus says it's not easy for foreigners to go through a real marriage ceremony on Bali—only a traditional one. First, they have to change their religion to the Hindu faith and after the wedding they have to present to Mr Widjaya Idabagus a document proving they've switched faiths, along with a letter from officials of the temple where the ceremony took place.'

'Christ, let's forget this bloke Iddy or whatever his name is. Tell me simply, are Mick and Jerry married?'

'Well Mr Widjaya Idabagus says he hasn't seen any of the paperwork and so they're not considered married in the eyes of the law. No paperwork, no legal marriage.'

'Great, that's all I wanted to know. They're not married.'

'Well, they're only "partially" not married because if they can show they've converted to the Hindu faith, that gets them a bit farther along.'

'What the bloody—'

'It's very complex, Gerry. They haven't put in the paperwork that they have to put in.'

'So they've got to be Hindus.'

'Right.'

'And they're not Hindus?'

'Well, they are according to the ceremony they went through. They just have to put in the paperwork saying they are Hindus.'

'Bloody hell!'

This conversation went on for some time but I finally got the story into the paper with a couple of simple paragraphs explaining the inexplicable.

Whatever the status of Mick and Jerry's marriage, it didn't last. It ended in 1999 after he fathered a child, Lucas, with Brazilian model Luciana Morad. In 2010, in a book detailing her relationship with the Rolling Stones front man who had by then become Sir Mick Jagger, Jerry referred to him as a 'sexual predator'.

CHAPTER 19

Lord Maxwell and the Israeli Arms Dealer

His name was Ari Ben-Menashe and he was perhaps the most extraordinary person I have met. I have been introduced to a number of spies, both real and pretenders, over the years, but none was more real, more informative, more travelled, better read, more politically astute, more daring, more controversial than Mr Ben-Menashe. He was an enigma, a man so mysterious, his claims so astonishing, that you had to take a deep breath before absorbing all that he had to say. Some of it was unprovable—but the facts that could be proved left me shaking my head in astonishment.

I met the Iranian-born former Israeli intelligence officer (now there's a contradiction in terms) in a luxurious Sydney apartment where he had been ensconced by a solicitor who was handling his affairs. Mr Menashe had arrived in Australia in mid-1991 after being released from prison in the United States, where he had spent 11 months for attempting to steal three Hercules aircraft to sell to the Iranians. He was acquitted by a New York jury in November 1990. Accompanied by his solicitor, he had approached a Sydney book publisher and said he had a story to tell. And what a story it was, as I soon found out because Isobelle and I were hired to 'ghost write' it.

He was being pursued by a number of major newspapers and magazines in the US, with no less a journalist than Pulitzer Prize-winning reporter Seymour Hersh after him for his story. *Time* and *Newsweek* had already run big pieces about him, along the lines of the spy who had come in from the cold. Now he was about to spill the beans on the dirty tricks played by Israel, the United States, Iran, Iraq and a number of other countries, including Britain.

This all seemed too good to be true. My mind flashed back to Charles Evans, the spy who never was. Certainly, there were curious elements to Ari's story that did not add up and his incredible claims were far too numerous to enter into here when a 100,000 word book, which I later ghosted for him, could not contain them all.

The revelations from this burly, dark-haired man, were, in the main, about America's role in supplying Israel with weapons, which were in turn provided to the armies of Iran and Iraq during their war fought between 1980 and 1988. Israel and the US shared the profits, although the Americans vigorously denied any knowledge of such a trade. It was eventually revealed that the US had illegally supplied Iran with arms in a 'swap' for the release of seven American hostages.

But Israel was supplying weapons to a number of other countries and many of the orders passed through the offices of London's *Daily Mirror* and its owner Robert Maxwell—something I simply did not believe but eventually conceded was fact. Ari claimed to be a close associate of Maxwell and was able to describe his office, and that of his foreign editor at the time Nick Davies, down to a tiniest detail. Ari also claimed to be a friend of CIA chief Robert Gates and said he had often visited his home. Such claims were extraordinary but after weeks of interviewing Ari, I was left believing that to a large extent they were true because, when I asked contacts of both Mr Gates and Mr Maxwell if they knew of Ari, the flustered answers I received appeared to confirm the question. Seymour Hersh had also backed up most of the claims.

'Let me tell you this,' said Ari. 'Robert Maxwell has upset the Israelis for a number of reasons, including an attempt by him to blackmail Mossad, and he has treated them with contempt. Do not be surprised if you hear of something big in the not-too-distant future.'

He would not elaborate but went on to speak about his travels around the world on Israel's behalf, working hard in talks with characters ranging from presidents to drug barons, to change the balance of power in countries that would ultimately be of benefit to Israel and the Americans. He told of negotiating with both sides in the Sri Lankan conflict and of travelling to South America where he stayed in the home of Shining Path leader Abimael Guzman. He travelled to North Korea where he was asked to pay his respects to the waxworks model of Great Leader

Kim Il Sung—just as I was to many years later—before getting down to top-secret talks with military officials.

I did not have to wait long to find out what Ari meant when he said something big would happen involving Robert Maxwell. In a mystery that remains to this day, in early November 1991 the media mogul disappeared from his luxury yacht off the Canary Islands. His body was found floating in the ocean. At the time there were reports that Mossad agents had climbed aboard under cover of darkness, pushed Maxwell into the sea and held him down until he drowned. When I asked Ari about this later, he smiled softly and shrugged. 'You might as well ask me what he was doing out on the deck of his yacht at five o'clock in the morning.'

Well, I said, I was asking. Ari grinned and, then, as if he couldn't hold back any more, he said he wanted to tell me a story and I could draw my own conclusions.

What he told me was to result in my writing a feature for the *Daily Mail* which was run on Saturday 9 November 1991, under the heading: 'Maxwell, Mossad and the Strange Catalogue of Death'.

Since 1986, I learned, dozens of people connected in one way or another with arms deals between Israel and Iran had been sent to their graves and six of those deaths, at least, involved mysteries just as deep as the one surrounding the last hours of Robert Maxwell.

There was Dr Cyrus Hashemi, a multimillionaire arms dealer who died in a London hospital at the age of 47 after succumbing to what was officially described as leukaemia. Prompted by the American government, Hashemi had set up a trap for a number of other arms dealers, among them a well-liked Israeli general who was funnelling weapons to Iran from Israeli stockpiles. Hashemi was suddenly taken ill in July 1986, rushed to a London hospital and died there three days later.

Although leukaemia was the official cause of death, Hashemi's brother came forward to say that 'certain Middle East intelligence services' could kill by introducing toxic substances into the body using sprays, drinks or injections. The results of tests on Mr Hashemi's tissue at Britain's Porton Down government laboratory have never been made public.

Then there was Amiram Nir, one-time terrorism adviser to former Israeli prime minister Shimon Peres. He had been scheduled to be a key witness in the trial of Lieutenant Oliver North over the Iran-Contra scandal, but died in 1988 when the light plane he was travelling in crashed in Mexico.

Nir had briefed George H.W. Bush, then US vice-president, in 1986 about Israel's secret sales of weapons to Iran and it was said by sections in the Israeli intelligence community that he knew too much and had to be killed. 'Mind you,' said Ari, 'there is another story, which I cannot confirm—that it was not Nir's body which was pulled from the wreckage, and he went on to have his face surgically altered in Geneva where the clinics are very discreet.'

While this sounded like the imaginings of a fiction writer, Ari went on to talk about Dr Gerald Bull. And he was someone I knew something about, but only 'what I'd read in the papers'. A Canadian artillery scientist, Dr Bull refused to listen to Israel's constant pleas to stop working on a supergun he was building for Iraq. It was a weapon with an enormous barrel that would easily be able to fire missiles into Israel. After several warnings, he was shot dead outside his Brussels flat in March 1990. Designs for his supergun were in his pocket. Dr Bull had told associates earlier that he had heard Iraq planned to murder him as soon as his work was complete. But an unnamed Mossad intelligence official was quoted as admitting that Israel had killed him for helping the enemy.

'Were you that unnamed intelligence official, Ari?' I asked.

'Hmm, an interesting question,' he replied—and would not elaborate. 'But I'll confirm it now, if you like and tell you that, yes, Israel did have him killed.'

Ari said that the deaths did not stop there. A number of German scientists believed to have been secretly working for chemical-weapons manufacturer Carlos Cardoen in his Chilean and Paraguayan operations were also systematically murdered by the bullet or died in car crashes. Israel did not mourn their losses because the chemicals were to be shipped to Saddam Hussein.

Among Cardoen's associates was an Iraqi called Dr Ihsen Barbouti, who was sending cyanide to Saddam Hussein for use against his enemies. Barbouti died in London in the early 1990s and, like so many others in the murky world of arms dealing, there is a question mark over his death. Business associates in the US believed he had been assassinated by Mossad. Others said he had faked his death to escape Israel's wrath. That was not such a fanciful suggestion—21 years earlier he had 'killed himself' to cover his tracks, said Ari, although details of this are uncertain. Barbouti's death certificate stated merely that he had died of heart ailments.

The incredible list, as described by Ari over the days we spent discussing it in his Sydney hide-away, went on.

Former Senator John Tower, one of President George H.W. Bush's closest friends and whose nomination for US defence secretary in 1989 was rejected because of his drinking and womanising, met his death in a plane crash, which claimed the lives of 18 others as his commuter aircraft tried to land in Georgia in April 1991. In 1986 Tower had been appointed by President Ronald Reagan to head a three-man team to investigate the Iran-Contra scandal. When he died, he was said to have taken to the grave a number of unpublished secrets concerning arms sales to Iran.

Chillingly, even journalists who had stepped into the murky shadows of espionage and dirty politics to probe the covert operations of the Israeli and US governments have died in questionable circumstances.

Ari reminded me of the deaths of two writers who had set out to get to the bottom of arms dealings and the movement of weapons. They had never got around to writing their stories.

The first to die was 28-year-old British journalist Jonathan Moyle, who was found in March 1990 hanged from a sheet in a cupboard in a hotel room in Santiago, Chile, where he had been inquiring into the arms trade and Iraq's involvement. At first, police said his death was suicide, but then a judge concluded he had been murdered. The case was eventually closed because of lack of evidence.

Then, in August 1991—just three months before I was holding this enlightening, if not frightening conversation with Ari—a 44-year-old American freelance journalist, Joseph 'Danny' Casolaro, was found dead in a motel bathtub in Martinsburg, West Virginia. He was said to have been on the point of receiving 'explosive' documents that threw light on the arms trade to Iran. It was also said that he was about to receive evidence of a computer software programme used by the US and Israel to spy on the military might of other nations. Casolaro was found with multiple slash wounds to both wrists. Despite a suicide note, his family insisted he was not suicidal—and they asked why his body was embalmed without permission before an autopsy could be performed.

'Is that enough to convince you that things go on behind the scenes while everyone else goes about their daily business?' Ari asked.

I had to agree that the list he had given me was worrying. As I continued to interview him for the book, which was to be published under his own name, it was evident that Ari Ben-Menashe's knowledge of international political affairs was detailed. He was, however, a worried man. He was concerned that word would get out that he was writing a book. I always had to call him and say that

I was on my way—with or without Isobelle, who often accompanied me to these meetings.

When the rough manuscript was finished the three of us flew to Isobelle's birth country, Vanuatu, where we checked in under assumed names so we could go over the whole thing, correcting, tidying up. But all the time Ari was worried about shadows. He was always on the phone talking in Yiddish or Arabic and eventually he announced that he would have to fly to Europe. Our work with him was finished in any case. When I asked what he would be doing in Europe he replied, tantalisingly, 'Time will tell. I might have to go to Moscow.'

We drove him to the airport, promised, as you always do, to 'keep in touch' and off he flew. It was 18 August 1991. Eight hours later he phoned from Singapore.

'Has anything happened while I've been in the air?' he asked.

'Happened …? Like what?'

'Oh, just anything. You would know about it if it had.'

And then he was gone, leaving me to wonder what on earth he was talking about. A few hours later the news broke that there had been a coup in Moscow overthrowing Mikhail Gorbechev, although his government was reinstated after three days. This was either an astonishing coincidence, coming in the wake of Ari's question as he was flying to Moscow, or he knew that the attempted coup was to be mounted.

The explosive book came out in the US, Britain and Australia under the title *The Profits of War* and proved to be a bestseller, although, of course the profits of the book quite rightly went to Ari. We lost touch with him. Years later he was making news in Zimbabwe. Then in 2008 we saw him on TV. He had put on weight, but the voice of authority, discussing Zimbabwe's politics this time, was still there. What he had told me for his book was just a small insight into the secret workings of governments.

◆

In June 1992 concerns were raised about the whereabouts of two British girls, 21-year-old Caroline Clarke and Joanne Walters, aged 22, who were backpacking in Australia. Their families had heard nothing from them for two months after they had left a hostel in Sydney's notorious redlight district, King's Cross, to travel to Melbourne. Police began investigating possible links between their disappearance and that of German backpackers Gabor Neugebauer, 21, and his 20-year-old girlfriend Anja Habschied. They, too, had set out to hitchhike to Melbourne. None of the four had touched their bank accounts for weeks—and, with no phone calls from Australia either, their families began to fear the worst.

In September of that year two men running along trails through the Belanglo State Forest, south-west of Sydney, on an orienteering exercise, investigated a foul smell coming from near a rock. They thought it might be a dead animal—and were shocked to find a decaying body covered with sticks and leaves. Police rushed to the area and soon found the remains of another person some 50 yards (45 metres) away, in a shallow grave near a fallen tree trunk. Clothing gave them a clue as to the identities—and on 20 September the parents of Caroline and Joanne were told that the bodies were almost certainly those of their missing daughters.

What was then an unmade road leading into the depths of the Belanglo State Forest ran past acres of pine trees before giving way to native plants and trees. The sky was heavy with dark threatening clouds when I started along another rough track that broke away from the pine trees. And that was as far as I could go because police had blocked the road with a vehicle as the forensic investigators conducted their grim work. A handful of other journalists had also stopped at the roadblock and we all agreed that the area would have been a fabulous place to go bush-walking—but the knowledge of what had happened there had changed all perceptions. A place of beauty had become a place of evil.

It wasn't long before we learned that the two friends had been executed in cold blood. Joanne had been gagged and stabbed several times in the back with a knife, a forensic pathologist revealed. Caroline had been shot 'more than once' in the head. 'These young women,' said one of the detectives I spoke to, 'were claimed by wickedness.'

Late in September, as sheets of rain swept across the Southern Highlands, a priest walked across the sodden undergrowth and paused by the log where Caroline had been found. 'So much evil,' he whispered through clenched teeth. Someone had draped a Union Jack over the log in readiness for the service that Father Gray would be conducting for the murdered friends. The Welsh flag, the Red Dragon, had been laid on the rock where Joanne had been found and flowers placed in the shallow grave. Then Joanne's parents, Ray and Gill Walters arrived.

As Father Gray began his short service, the rain stopped and a shaft of sunlight lit him. It was an extraordinary sight and those of us in the small group could not help but be moved. Father Gray said: 'We have come here today, where something wicked happened, so that this place can be peaceful again and its memories put to rest. Where evil is very strong, and it has been in this place, it does not have the last word … no-one is beyond the reach of God.'

He closed his prayer book. The sun was still shining through the gum trees. The cleansing, it seemed, had been completed. But neither the priest nor anyone else who had prayed there that afternoon could have known the horror that remained.

As the months rolled by, the forest yielded up more victims: the bodies of Gabor and Anja, another German backpacker—Simone Schidl—and two young hitchhikers from Victoria, Deborah Everist and James Gibson.

I frequently travelled to the forest and watched as police teams made their way through the bush and climbed down over treacherous cliff faces searching for other victims, for it was evident that the Belanglo Forest was a killer's dumping ground.

The vicious killer might never have been found out except that an earlier would-be victim had escaped. The attempt to abduct the man had been made two years before the British women were killed.

On 25 January 1990, Paul Onions, another British backpacker, was befriended by a dark-haired, moustachioed man when he called at a shop on the outer reaches of western Sydney. He was offered a lift and happily accepted. But an hour or so later, as they travelled south-west along the Hume Highway the driver pulled over and reached under his seat to find a cassette tape to play—or so he said. Instead he drew out a revolver and a length of rope. As Onions recalled later, 'It wasn't the gun that frightened me so much as the rope. The rope was really sinister.'

The backpacker flung open the door and ran up the road, hearing what he thought was a shot as the driver pursued him. Onions waved down a woman motorist, who was terrified to be stopped by a frantic young man but eventually drove him to the nearest police station. Incredibly, the police report he filed was not followed up on until Onions, back in England and reading of the gruesome discoveries in the forest, phoned police to remind them of his ordeal.

Suspicion began to fall on particular members of the Milat family. Members of the public had been contacting police suggesting the sons, who were known to have weapons and to have gone on pig-hunting excursions, be checked out in relation to the Belanglo murders. Onions' description of his assailant matched that of one of the Milat brothers, Ivan.

Eventually police raided the home of Ivan Milat and found a treasure trove of incriminating evidence: parts of a rifle hidden in the roof and in a wall cavity, and property that had belonged to some of the young victims. A raid on another house owned by Milat's brother Richard led to the discovery of more gun parts. At the home of Milat's mother detectives found sleeping bags and more clothing that had belonged to the murdered hitchhikers. Ivan was charged with all the murders. But I could not help feeling that he had not acted alone.

As well as keeping *Daily Mail* readers up to date with the progress of the investigation, I began researching the whole terrible story for a book, which was published under the title *Highway to Nowhere*—for that was what the road the young backpackers had set out on turned out to be. On one occasion I went to a remote farmhouse, located in a clearing among towering eucalyptus trees, where one of Ivan's younger brothers, George, was living. An iron gate at the end of a track prevented my driving up to the run-down weatherboard farmhouse and a sign warned me to beware of the dog. The dog, whose breed I could not identify, came running to the gate, snarling, so I returned to the car and tooted the horn, hoping someone would come out. A short, stocky figure walked to the gate, said he was George, told the dog to 'geddown ya mongrel' and led me to the old house. George lived alone. I felt curiously uneasy as I sat in the gloom at the kitchen table and began asking my host about his arrested brother.

He told me how he and Ivan had often gone pig shooting together and that Ivan was 'into cars', trading tyres and spare parts, and was always driving up and down the highway. He and his brothers had even set up a shooting gallery, building up an embankment so they could practise their skills with rifles and handguns.

'If Ivan did this, they should string him up and hang him,' said George as he paced around the kitchen. 'I don't know if he did it or not. It would be easy to say that just because someone has guns and knives they are responsible for murder. You could use a gun or a knife for all sorts of purposes and it might look like you've killed someone when in fact you haven't.'

And without warning, as he stood behind me, George brought a huge kitchen knife down over my shoulder and plunged it into the table, where it remained quivering beside my hand—which in turn started to quiver. 'It's as easy as that—or not as easy as that,' he said.

The extraordinary interview was over. George and the dog, now so docile it seemed you could give it a pat, accompanied me to the gate. 'Only time will tell,'

George said. As I closed the door of my car, I heard him call out again, 'Only time will tell.'

There was one other person I wanted to talk to: Ivan Milat's former wife Karen. I'd learned that the police were trying to track her down. Although I thought that if they had already found her, they would have told her to make no comment, I was compelled to start a search. If she agreed to talk to me, I hoped to be able to use it at a later stage when Ivan's trial was over, one way or another. I had learned that she had left him because, as she had told a neighbour, 'he treated me like a cavewoman.' From her friends and neighbours I established that Karen was terrified that Ivan might find her before the police arrested him. She had gone deep into hiding and there was no way anyone would be able to track her down. And, I was told, she had changed her surname.

Nevertheless, I decided to give it a try. But where do you start when you don't know a person's name? The only clue I had was information that Karen had kept her first and middle names. Without any official help, the only records I had to go on were the electoral rolls. There was no guarantee that she would even be on the rolls and there were thousands of Karens in the electoral rolls for New South Wales alone. I knew I would have to find a woman whose first name matched what was an unusual middle name. It meant ploughing through every name in the New South Wales electoral rolls—over one million people.

Over the course of a week, from morning until close of business at the State Library of New South Wales, where the electoral rolls were kept on microfiche, I ran my finger down thousands upon thousands of names. And then I hit on Karen and that unusual middle name. The address was a caravan park on the New South Wales central coast.

There was no guarantee this was the right Karen, but instinct told me it was. The caravan she was living in, I assumed, was a permanent fixture, otherwise she wouldn't have been registered at that address.

When I walked towards the caravan the following day, I saw three women sitting in fold-up chairs. As I approached a burly woman jumped up and hurried towards me.

'Who are you?' she demanded.

I told her I was looking for Karen. The moment I uttered the name, one of the other women scrambled from her chair and hurried into the caravan. The woman who had blocked my path told me in no uncertain terms to leave immediately or

Left: With tribesmen in Irian Jaya during my search for a group of young British scientists kidnapped by 'stone-age warriors' in 1996.
Below: In 1989 Martin Popplewell and Helen Freeman lived out his *Blue Lagoon* dream on a deserted Pacific island. Helen told me, before fleeing, that Martin had 'gone troppo'.

Left: Christopher Roberts with his double bass, which was a prop in the movie *Some Like It Hot.* He used it to play Bach to people in Papua New Guinea. I tracked him down in the jungle and spent a bizarre day, with villagers, listening to him making music. *Below:* From jungle to ocean: my front-page story on the rescue of 'lost' round-the-world yachtsman Tony Bullimore. I witnessed the rescue from the air in the Southern Ocean in January 1997.

FRIDAY, JANUARY 10, 1997   NEWSPAPER OF THE YEAR 35p

WIN UP TO £50,000 INSTANT CASH EXTRA
PLAY TODAY ON PAGE 68

The truth about Diana and the mysterious Dr Khan PAGES 28-29

 Exclusive: Mail man Richard Shears witnesses that amazing rescue from a floating tomb

MIRACLE

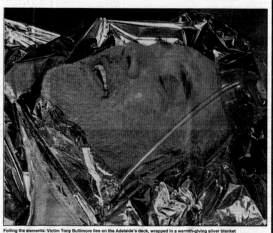

FROM just 100ft — so close, it seemed, I could reach out and help him — I watched a 'dead man' emerge from a watery grave yesterday.

At first, the shock of tangled grey hair that bobbed to the surface could have been another part of a yacht slowly breaking up.

Then the shape became a man as Briton Tony Bullimore started swimming a frantic crawl, his arms sweeping in big wide arcs, towards the rubber dinghy and its open-mouthed crew.

As I gazed down at the breathtaking scene from a Royal Australian Air Force Orion, the plane's crew were repeating the message they had just heard over the radio.

'He's alive! He's alive! It's a bloody miracle!'

I was the only newspaperman on the aircraft for the astonishing drama in the rainy half-light of the southern Indian Ocean.

It was a sight none of us expected. We had set off from Perth on a mission to look for a dead man.

No one said it in so many words, but there were huge doubts that anyone could have the willpower or the endurance to survive in a submerged yacht in below-freezing temperatures for nearly four days.

But 56-year-old Bullimore was there all right, waiting patiently even after his fresh water ran out.

He will never forget the vivid picture that greeted him as he broke the surface — the Orion roaring overhead, the Australian frigate Adelaide with her crew in their bright lifejackets and the bobbing, inflatable dinghy with its astonished sailors.

'A miracle, an absolute miracle,' he said as he was whisked on board, wrapped in a foil blanket.

His rescuers had smiles of joy all Turn to Page 2, Col. 4

Foiling the elements: Victim Tony Bullimore lies on the Adelaide's deck, wrapped in a warmth-giving silver blanket

INSIDE: Andrew Alexander 10, Ephraim Hardcastle 11, Diary 39, TV & Radio 54-56, Letters 59-60, Coffee Break 66-68, City 69-71, Sport 72-80

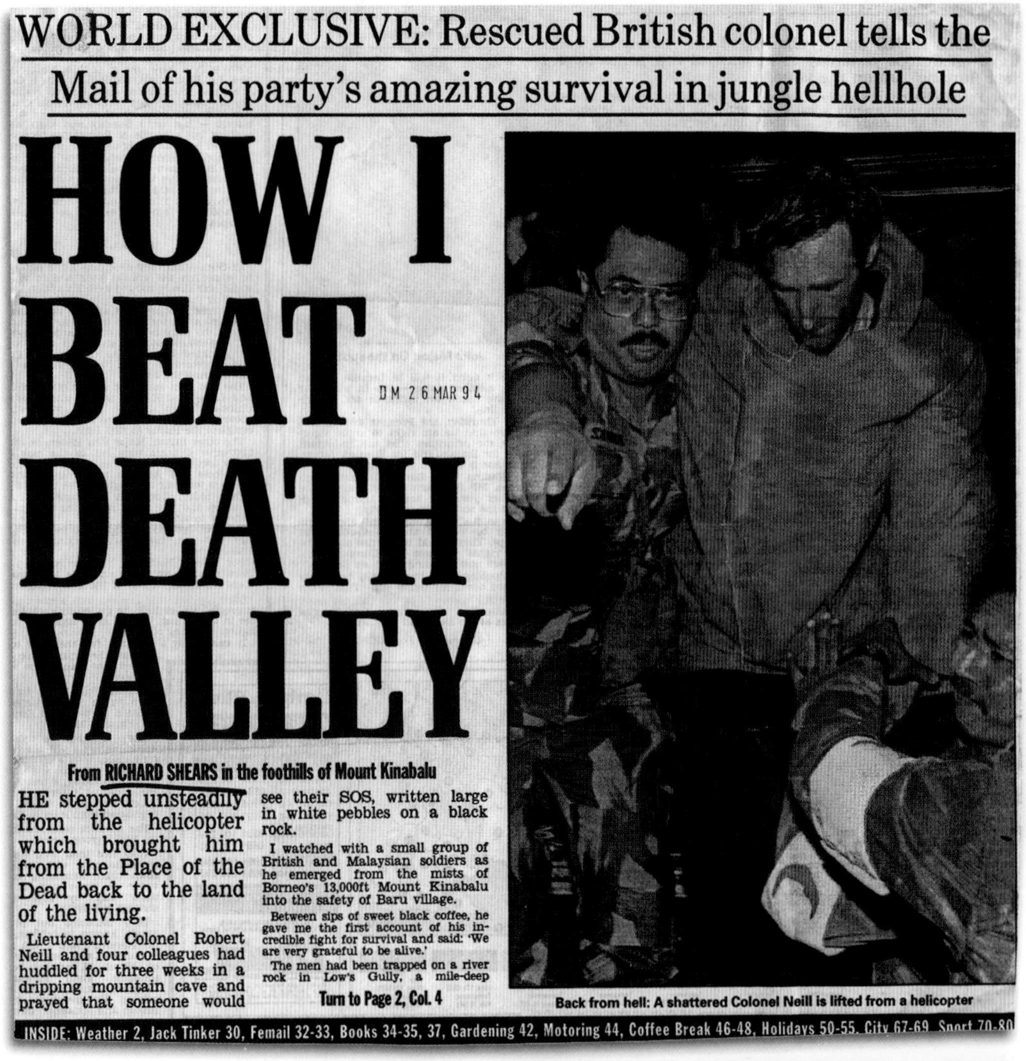

WORLD EXCLUSIVE: Rescued British colonel tells the Mail of his party's amazing survival in jungle hellhole

HOW I BEAT DEATH VALLEY

DM 26 MAR 94

From RICHARD SHEARS in the foothills of Mount Kinabalu

HE stepped unsteadily from the helicopter which brought him from the Place of the Dead back to the land of the living.

Lieutenant Colonel Robert Neill and four colleagues had huddled for three weeks in a dripping mountain cave and prayed that someone would see their SOS, written large in white pebbles on a black rock.

I watched with a small group of British and Malaysian soldiers as he emerged from the mists of Borneo's 13,000ft Mount Kinabalu into the safety of Baru village.

Between sips of sweet black coffee, he gave me the first account of his incredible fight for survival and said: 'We are very grateful to be alive.'

The men had been trapped on a river rock in Low's Gully, a mile-deep

Turn to Page 2, Col. 4

Back from hell: A shattered Colonel Neill is lifted from a helicopter

INSIDE: Weather 2, Jack Tinker 30, Femail 32-33, Books 34-35, 37, Gardening 42, Motoring 44, Coffee Break 46-48, Holidays 50-55, City 67-69, Sport 70-80

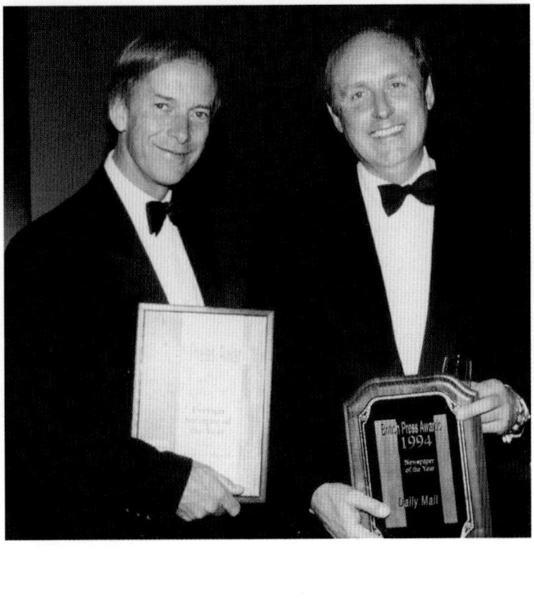

Above: My exclusive story, which ran for seven pages in the *Daily Mail*, of the remarkable rescue of a group of British soldiers given up for dead on a mountain in Borneo in March 1994. I won a British press award for foreign reporting for the story.
Right: Tuxedo time—the awards night with *Daily Mail* editor Paul Dacre (on the right).

Above: My golfing companions hole out in Borneo.

Left: The victorious orang-utans grin as they pose with me, the vanquished, after the match. No wonder half of Britain laughed when they saw this picture on TV!

Opposite top: Golf on Mars in 2004. Actually, it was outback Australia—the landscape was strikingly similar to pictures sent back from the Mars rover. (Photo: Cameron Laird)

Opposite bottom: I got into North Korea in 2011 to play golf—the only way a journalist could enter the secret country—but also managed to have a good look around. These young army girls were learning their goose steps.

Above: I've tried to hit a golf ball in unusual places and the Kabul course in 2002 was perhaps the most unusual—it was covered in abandoned guns and unexploded bombs. (Photo: Mark Large)

Left: My Afghan visa.

Opposite top: One of my stories from Afghanistan, telling of the capture of some of Osama Bin Laden's men in early 2001.

Opposite bottom: A sad victim of war, this lion was so unwell that its keeper allowed me to enter its den and sit with it for a while. A team of US vets arrived later and gave it vitamin injections but it was too much for its frail body and it died soon after. (Photo: Mark Large)

END OF THE TALIBAN / Prime Minister insists we must not 'walk away' from

Faces of defeat: Captured Al Qaeda men yesterday

The humiliation of Bin Laden's broken army

By **Richard Shears**
near Jalalabad

THEY were herded down the mountain on foot and on the backs of mules, hands tied behind their backs, crude bandages on their wounds – and humiliation on their faces.

Once they were proud members of Osama Bin Laden's army. Now, as captives, they were little more than wrecks, tired, hungry, thirsty and shell-shocked.

'They are suffering from what we call "rag order",' said a former British Royal Marine who is advising on security. 'It's what you get when you are bombed day after day after day.'

And if the Eastern Alliance fighters who put their prisoners on display yesterday were to have any satisfaction after failing to find Bin Laden himself, it was in the knowledge that he would be going through hell if he was still in the freezing mountains.

'If he is up there, trying to go through to Pakistan, he will be suffering,' said one soldier. 'You only have to look at these men to know what is happening to him.'

The uncertainty over Bin Laden was echoed at the Pentagon. Rear Admiral John Stufflebeem was asked where he might be hiding. He replied: 'Anybody's guess is the latest thinking.' He said little radio traffic was coming out of the Tora Bora caves, which are still being scoured by British and U.S. special forces.

'I am not sure how close we ever have been,' Admiral Stufflebeem said. 'Maybe he is still there, maybe he has been killed, maybe he has fled.'

Whatever Bin Laden's fate, the destruction of his army was all too apparent in a dusty village square near Jalalabad yesterday.

After three weeks of crouching in caves as U.S. bombs rained down, the 19 Al Qaeda captives who were ordered to show their faces to the world's cameras appeared to have lost even the spirit to live.

'I would rather be killed than be humiliated,' said one – but they put him on display in any case.

'When they were fighting us, they were very proud men,' said Manoghul, 23, who cradled a Kalashnikov. 'Now they are weak, they cannot even look at us.'

First to appear was a tall bearded man in a long striped robe, his head heavily bandaged. When someone asked where he was from, one of Commander Haji Zahir's men replied: 'They are all Arabs.' He forbade further questions.

An older man, limping badly, was brought into the square, confusion on his face. Others followed, the shame of defeat keeping their heads to their chests.

One was barefoot; another nursed an injured arm.

At Tora Bora, searchers have found the bodies of women and children - tragic confirmation that reports of how Bin Laden's men had taken their families with them into the mountains were true.

U.S. Defence Secretary Donald Rumsfeld yesterday said that the war was not over although 'Al Qaeda are running and hiding'.

In apparent contradiction to his colleague Colin Powell's remark that 'we have destroyed the Al Qaeda in Afghanistan', Mr Rumsfeld said: 'The first rule of war is that it is presidents that decide when something conclusive has been achieved.'

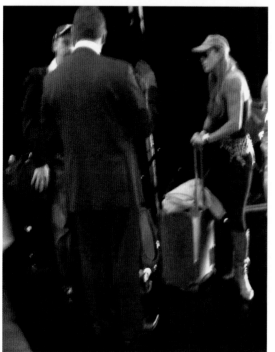

Above: A family of 'hobbits' in eastern Indonesia, living close to a cave where the skeleton of a tiny woman who died about 15,000 years ago had been found. (Photo: Cameron Laird)

Left: My blurry picture of Rachel Uchitel in the foyer of Melbourne's Crown Casino in 2009—a grabbed shot which exposed Tiger Woods' affairs with her and with numerous other women.

she would call the police. I had no doubt that I had tracked Karen down. I also had no doubt that she wouldn't be talking to me that day or any other day.

She eventually gave evidence at Ivan's trial. The public just knew her as Karen. In a soft voice, she told of trips into the Belanglo Forest with her former husband and said he was 'gun crazy'. On one trip with him and other members of the family he had worn a revolver in a holster, called himself 'Tex' and was 'mucking around like a cowboy'.

The evidence against Ivan Milat produced at his committal hearing and trial was overwhelming. A relative was shown in a photograph wearing a sweater belonging to one of the victims. Paul Onions—who had left his backpack in his assailant's car when he fled—identified 'my favourite shirt'. Rifle parts matched the weapon that had been used on some of the victims. Plastic ties used as handcuffs were matched with those issued to Ivan Milat by the roads department where he worked. Sleeping bags, a water bottle—they were all clearly identified as belonging to the victims.

There was no way out for Milat and on 27 July 1996 he was found guilty of murder and sent to prison for life. To this day he continues to protest his innocence from his maximum security jail, but former prisoners say that he has started to go mad. Then again, to have done what he did, Ivan Milat must always have been mad—and very, very bad.

◆

While the Milat investigations were running, I was despatched to Bangkok where Michael Jackson was preparing to perform as part of a world tour. But it had suddenly been interrupted by sensational claims that he had been sexually abusing children who had shared his bed.

Jackson immediately cancelled his first two performances, his aides saying he was suffering from dehydration. Then reports emerged claiming that Jackson had tried to commit suicide. They were immediately denied. But movie producer Tony Pastor, a friend of the Jackson family, said: 'There is deep concern within the family. Michael has never had to handle anything like this before. He has never faced revulsion and hate.' And Jackson's brother-in-law Jack Gordon expressed concerns that the star could be driven to suicide over the allegations. LaToya Jackson added to the concerns. 'I really think he will kill himself,' she said. 'I truly believe that is how it will end. Michael is not very strong.'

But I was there in a humid auditorium in Bangkok to hear Michael declare, defiantly, as he stepped onto the stage for the third concert scheduled, 'I'm back!' And police in Los Angeles said videotapes and photographs seized during raids on the star's two homes in California showed nothing incriminating.

Not surprisingly, the *Mail* asked me to 'stick with him' as he continued his tour, so I travelled to Singapore on the next leg of his tour—and missed out on what would have been one of the most amazing show business photographs of all time. I cursed my bad luck for days.

Elizabeth Taylor, Michael's long-time friend, had flown to Singapore to lend him moral support and moved into his hotel, the famous Raffles, an atmosphere-soaked reminder of the days of British colonialism. 'Michael would rather cut his wrists than harm a child,' the veteran actress said to an aide as her jet flew across the Pacific.

Unknown to me and the dozens of other journalists who were following the controversial star around Asia, Michael arranged with Liz to hold a special tea party beside the swimming pool. I learned this from one of the hotel staff who had been asked to attend the couple.

Michael, it transpired, had wanted to visit the Singapore Zoo, but to avoid mob hysteria at his presence he had requested the entire place be closed down, which the staff refused to do. Michael had wanted to visit the ape pen because he was missing his friend Bubbles the chimp, who he had left back at home in California. As a compromise, the zoo offered to bring some of its most popular orang-utans to him at the hotel. When Michael's aides mentioned to the hotel management that he wanted to entertain apes in his suite there was a collective intake of breath. He might be paying £2500 a night, but this was taking things a little too far.

'They might pee on our Persian carpets,' said one executive.

A compromise was reached. The orang-utans could enter the grounds of the hotel as long as they remained in the pool area, which would be closed off from other guests during their visit. So just after 3PM Michael and Elizabeth Taylor made their way to the terrace beside the pool. Their special hairy guests were waiting for them at two marble-topped tables, sitting in cast-iron chairs with cushions.

At the centre of the ape group was the matriarchal Ah Meng, aged 28, whose portrait once appeared on a Singapore postage stamp. Once Michael and Liz were seated, a white-jacketed butler arrived with a tray of Coca Cola. Liz sipped hers demurely from an ice-filled glass. The apes slurped theirs straight from the bottle.

As they do. Michael preferred to sit and watch the action. Wearing dark glasses, a purple shirt and black trousers, he was said to have looked happier than he had in days.

'I just love them,' he told the butler. 'They are so happy and they make me feel so happy.'

But Liz, who was wearing a white trouser suit, appeared lost for words. As one hotel staff member said, 'Her expression suggested she was asking herself, "What does one say to a big ape?" '

The younger orang-utans soon grew tired of drinking Coke and left the table to do a spot of sunbathing on the poolside recliners.

Liz seemed relieved when it was over and the apes were returned to the zoo's trucks. Michael, however, was clearly upset at having to say goodbye to his new friends. The hotel had once been the haunt of Rudyard Kipling and Somerset Maugham and I have to wonder how they would have described the astonishing tea party.

I had been left cursing when I learned the details of the orang-utans' tea party.

Hundreds of thousands of Michael Jackson fans from neighbouring Malaysia had flown in for his concerts and every hotel in Singapore was booked out. I had searched high and low for a room and found one that was around the corner from Raffles. I could have the room for only one day and night—the same day that the tea party was held. My room, high up, looked straight down onto the Raffles swimming pool and even a relatively short telephoto lens would have picked up the mind-boggling scene of Michael Jackson and Elizabeth Taylor having 'afternoon tea' with a bunch of apes. Instead I had been at the front of Raffles in case anything was going on from a news point of view.

If I had remained in my room and looked out of the window I would have been able to capture everything on film. It was the best viewpoint in town and I had missed it.

CHAPTER 20

'I've Found Them! They're All Alive!'

Mist, like white ash clouds from an angry volcano, tumbled down the hillside as I watched a crack RAF rescue team armed with guns and machetes plunge into the jungle on the lower slopes of Borneo's Mount Kinabalu—the 'Revered Place of the Dead'. They were searching for two British commandos and a team of Hong Kong soldiers who had been missing on the mountain for a fortnight.

With its treacherous precipices, rain-swamped slopes as slippery as ice, raging waterfalls, malarial mosquitoes and poisonous snakes, the mountain had claimed many lives in the past. And the missing men, all highly trained survival experts, had gone on to half rations of 1500 calories a day when last seen. At the search headquarters in a village at the foot of the mountain, a Malaysian rescuer conceded that, 'Their chances of getting out of there alive are probably zero after all this time. To be perfectly honest, we need a miracle.'

It was 17 March 1994. Lieutenant-Colonel Robert Neill of the Royal Logistics Corps and Major Ron Foster were part of the 20th Commando Airborne Unit based in Hong Kong. On 22 February Neill had set out at the head of a hand-picked ten-strong RLC party to climb the 13,455-foot (4100-metre) mountain after six months of planning.

Their mission was to attempt to climb down the extremely difficult and dangerous Lowes Gully. At the summit of the mountain, they split into two groups and after 18 days the second group—Captain Peter Shearer, Sergeant Robert Mann, Corporals Richard Mayfield and Hugh Brittan and another soldier, Steve Bank—

stumbled from the jungle into a village, so malnourished and exhausted they could barely speak. They had no information about Lieutenant-Colonel Neill's party.

On 23 March, 24-year-old Corporal Brittan was well enough to describe something of the horror he had been through to a group of British journalists. We had gathered in Kota Kinabalu, four hours' drive from the base of the mountain. They had gone to a place, 'where no human should ever go,' he told us.

'When you are confronted with thundering waterfalls, giant leering rocks and your stomach is empty, you need all your willpower to keep on going. Despite being taught to live off the land if necessary, all we saw were three ant-covered strawberries, two snakes as small as pencils and fish no bigger than tadpoles. There's nothing there ... nothing there.'

Towards the end of the descent he and his companions were reduced to eating curry powder in cold water, and then nothing at all for the last three days. There were times, he said, when he might easily have died. On several occasions he led the others through a narrow river channel by swimming underwater and coming up further downstream. He was the guinea pig for these ventures and on one desperate venture he was swept underwater and came up in a cave gasping for air. The others, thinking he had swum through a rock channel safely, followed and had an equally terrifying experience. It was his belief that the second party led by Lieutenant-Colonel Neill and Major Foster had run into extreme difficulties because of rain that had fallen on the mountain, making the descent treacherous.

For days I drove with other journalists up to the base of the mountain, where British and Malaysian military officials had set up a base camp on a soccer field in the village of Baru. They were using a school hall as shelter from the rain squalls that swept across the mountain. The soccer field was also a useful landing point for a Malaysian helicopter that was making hourly flights around the mountain in the hope the missing men would be seen. But each day the helicopter came back with the pilot shaking his head. It seemed by now, after three weeks, that there was no hope. One by one journalists who had hopefully made the eight-hour return journey to the foot of the mountain each day decided they would wait it out in Kota Kinabalu.

I have always believed in sticking to a job, no matter how tedious, and over the years I had devised seven golden rules—if all or some could be applied while on an assignment, it would usually end in success. Those 'commandments' were: be logical, observant, relentless, patient, generous, don't panic and never assume.

I pause here for a moment for an illustration of pursuing what seemed like an impossible task.

I was once asked to find the father of a man who had been accused of a hideous murder. The convicted killer was Robert Napper, who had murdered young mother Rachel Nickell on London's Wimbledon Common. All that was known about his father, Brian Napper, was that he had migrated to Australia many years earlier. I went through the electoral rolls and found a Brian Napper living in Inverloch, east of Melbourne. But after flying to Melbourne, all I found was a deserted house with a vastly overgrown garden that had pointed chunks of coloured concrete sticking up through the grass. I spoke to neighbours but no-one knew where Brian Napper was these days—he'd left the rented house at least a year earlier and no-one else had moved in.

'Where do I go from here?' I asked myself. I went for a coffee and began wandering around the area, my mind ticking over, thinking, thinking. Then I stopped—and walked back a few paces to look up an alleyway. Something had caught my attention. At the end of the short alley was what looked like a small Buddhist temple with the traditional pointed dome. I stared at the dome. Surely my imagination was running amok. I went into the temple and found a lady cleaning the floor.

'This is crazy,' I said to her after introducing myself, 'but I'm looking for a gentleman who's moved out of the area, but there are pieces of concrete in the overgrown garden of the house where he lived—and they are the same shape and colour as parts of your roof.'

'Oh, you're talking about Brian Napper,' she said. 'Yes, he used to come here and loved it so much that he built a small Buddhist shrine in his garden. I think he broke it up when he left the area and that's what you've probably seen lying about in his garden.'

She didn't know where he was these days, but directed me to a haberdashery shop down the street. The woman there was a friend of Brian's and had his address in her little black book. He had moved to Ulladulla, about three hours south of Sydney. I couldn't believe my good fortune. When I eventually knocked on Brian's door, he told me all he could about his convicted son, although he hadn't seen him for years—he had split from his family many years earlier.

But the experience had taught me that even when all seems lost, keeping your eyes open and following up the most tenuous of leads can sometimes pay off.

Back in Kota Kinabalu I was applying my 'be relentless' code. Along with one other reporter, I continued to go back to Baru village every day. When I got back to the city, it was always close to 11PM, which meant I'd end up eating in a small café in a backstreet somewhere. On 25 March, I headed back up to the mountain. Several of the other reporters had already been pulled off the story, their news and foreign desks convinced that there was no hope for the missing men. Even the Malaysian military, who knew the mountain well, said that by now there would be no survivors.

'No hope, no hope,' said one of the Malaysian officers as I sat on the edge of the soccer field sipping a soft drink and the lightweight Alouette IIB helicopter was landing. It was expected to be the last day of searching.

The pilot, Michael Izhar, to whom I'd chatted several times in recent days, was running across the field towards me and the British officers who were grouped around the hut.

'What's happened?' I asked.

'I've found them! I've found them!' he cried. 'They're all alive!'

No-one could believe it. He and his co-pilot, Sergeant Mohammed Salleh, had not been able to radio back the news because the mountain had blocked the signal. But now he was practically dancing on his feet—along with everybody else.

'There was just a second or two to look into a narrow part of the gully because of the dangerous updraughts and then we were past it. But in that second, we saw two figures and then a third and beside them, on a black rock spelled out in white stones, were the letters "SOS". We turned around, went back, looked down and we saw that sign again and the men. I tell you, my heart missed a beat.'

Sergeant Salleh jumped from the helicopter and told me, 'It was difficult to make out who was who, but as we got lower we could see three men. They were wearing dark clothing and they were waving. One of them held up two fingers to indicate two more men, pointed into the jungle behind them and then patted their stomachs. We realized they were telling us that the other two who were out of sight were still alive but they had stomach problems. We thought the best thing was to get back here to the landing area as quickly as possible and relay the wonderful news.'

I rushed to the village store to use a landline to phone the news to London. Even though there would be no-one manning the desks in the early hours of the morning in the UK, I was hoping to leave a message with the switchboard to relay the news that the men had been found and that I was on the spot. But infuriatingly, the store's phone was broken and all military equipment was in use. It was a huge story—and I had no contact with the outside world.

Ration packs were loaded into the helicopter. They contained porridge oats, an oatmeal block, milk chocolate biscuits, fruit biscuits, mulligatawny soup, cheese spread, three boil-in-a-bag meals of lamb stew and potatoes, sausages and beans, dumplings in butterscotch sauce and a packet of Rolo chocolates. Captain Izhar took the helicopter back up towards the mountains, now increasingly shrouded in cloud, and Sergeant Salleh lowered the food, wrapped in a yellow waterproof plastic bag, towards the rock about 30 yards (25 metres) below. He let go of the rope and the helicopter, still at the mercy of updraughts, swept away. Sergeant Salleh had seen a figure walk out of the treeline and pick up the bag.

The lost men had food, but their ordeal was far from over. The tiny helicopter was simply not powerful enough to defy the updraughts and remain steady to winch them out.

As it roared back to Baru, RAF Flight-Lieutenant Richard Mowbray, a 37-year-old jungle training expert in charge of the base camp movements, frantically tried to get a bigger Sea King helicopter in. But it was also vital to get medical aid to the trapped men—and for a third time the Alouette lifted off, carrying a British medic. With ice-cool nerves, Captain Izhar held his aircraft steady against the fierce buffeting as he lowered the medic and an emergency first aid pack.

Meanwhile, Flight-Lieutenant Mowbray saw that the weather was closing in. It was extremely urgent that a bigger helicopter be brought in. Finally at 1.20PM a Sea King touched down at Baru. The rotors kept whirring as Mowbray, other British officers, Captain Izhar and a Malaysian doctor climbed aboard to brief the crew on the location of the survivors.

At Low's Gully, the big aircraft was also battered by updraughts and there was a very serious chance that the rotors could strike the rock in a space no wider than a London underground tube tunnel. Frustrated, the crew decided to return to Baru. But by 2.55PM they were back in the air, determined that this time they would not be beaten. When they got back to Bari they described how they had hovered over the gully and pinpointed the rock, where all five men were now waiting. Lieutenant-Colonel Neill and Private Lam Ywai Ki from Hong Kong were lying down and on the medic's advice they were the first two out. As the Sea King pilot fought to hold steady, they were winched up. But there could be no more risk-taking. As visibility worsened, the Sea King made its way back to Baru, leaving the remaining three to be rescued later.

I watched the helicopter touch down on the football field. I was elated, not only for the missing men, but in the knowledge that I was present as a major story was being played out. So often I've had to pull dramatic stories together from eye-witness accounts simply because they happened in places miles from where I was. I was thankful, too, that I'd persevered and had made the tiresome journey back to the mountain again. But then there had been no chance of not returning because I'd always believed that no matter what the story, you cover it in its entirety, no matter how boring the event—just in case 'something' happened.

The moment the rotors stopped whirring I was at the door, watching as Lieutenant-Colonel Neill, with three weeks growth of beard and dressed in a red jacket and black slacks, was helped out. A group of men were ready to carry him to the hut but he held up a shaky hand and said, 'No, I'm determined to walk.'

In a scene that reminded me of the moment when Alec Guinness's character, Colonel Nicholson, stepped from a tin hut in the film *Bridge Over the River Kwai*, Lieutenant-Colonel Neill started his unsteady walk across the soccer field. Curiously—and was this an omen?—the other main character in the film, played by William Holden, was my namesake, Commander Shears, who had been presumed dead when he fell into a river but eventually stumbled into a village. But, in the foothills of Mount Kinabalu, this was real life. As Lieutenant-Colonel Neill began his walk across the field I decided this was my moment.

'Welcome back to civilisation, Colonel,' I said.

And as he turned to stare at me, bewildered—after so many days of hanging about in frustration I was now dressed in a T-shirt and shorts—I added, 'It's OK, I'm from the *Daily Mail*.'

'Thank you,' he said, his voice low and hoarse. I still don't know whether he was thanking me for my welcome or the fact that a reporter from a paper he was familiar with was there to greet him. 'It's great to be back.'

'I know you're suffering, but do you feel up to having a word with me … please?'

'Let me have a sip of coffee first.'

So I let him walk, taking photos of this momentous occasion as he made his way, close to stumbling at times, towards the wooden hut. Minutes later, between sips of sweet black coffee, brewed in a tin mug army-style over a fire in a ring of stones, the man who had come back from the dead told me how they had reached a ledge in a dry waterfall gully—then the rains had come and a torrent of water had made their descent impossible.

'We listened with growing despair to the sound of the helicopters flying overhead repeatedly but their crews obviously couldn't see us because we were in a narrow crevice,' he said. With remarkable composure he told how they had finally run out of their ruthlessly rationed food a week earlier.

'We were trapped on that rock for three weeks,' he went on, shaking his head. 'It was meant to be a ten-day expedition. This is day 30. We had food for ten days but we realized on day six that we might be in a survival situation. We made the final bit of our food—a single biscuit—last until last Sunday and then we had nothing but a couple of Polo mints between us. We've been surviving on water since then. … I knew we would be found one way or the other. We wrote out our wills in case one of those other options came into play.' Then, with typical British understatement, he added, 'It is not an experience I would wish to repeat.'

They'd spelled out the SOS hoping the searchers would see it. It was doubtful, he admitted, that they would have been found if they hadn't made the sign.

I was told the other Briton, Major Ron Foster, and the two other Hong Kong privates had been left in the care of an army doctor who had been winched down to them. He gave them emergency injections of glucose and vitamins and wrapped them in blankets for their last night on the mountain before their rescue the next day.

As I sped back to Kota Kinabalu with the sensational story, for which I had recorded every single detail I could think of gathering, dramas were being played out in the *Daily Mail* office. News of the soldiers' discovery had hit the wires, with scant details, and suddenly the world was ringing Kota Kinabalu. The *Mail*'s foreign editor, Gerry Hunt, told me later of the agony he had gone through trying to reach me, only to be told I was not answering the phone in my hotel room.

The editor Paul Dacre, he said, had called him into his office on hearing the news of the rescue.

'Sit down Gerry,' was the way Gerry told it later. 'Make yourself comfortable. Now, I want to ask you this … are you a religious man?'

'Well, boss, I'm a Catholic, if that's what you mean … er, what do you mean, exactly?'

Then came a quote which should go down as one of the classics: 'Because, Gerry, whatever religion you are, you had better get back to your desk and get down on your knees and pray that the reason you can't get hold of Shears is because he is working on this astounding story and hasn't pulled himself off it and got on a fucking plane and is on his way back to Australia!'

I got through to the office three-and-a-half hours later, having first frantically dashed around Kota Kinabalu trying to find a film-processing place that was still open so I could load my pictures onto a scanner and transmit them to London. When Gerry picked up the phone, his first words were:

'Where are you?'

If a sigh can carry 9000 miles (14,000 kilometres) across a phone line, I heard a gasp of relief when I said, 'I've just got back from the mountain. I've got it all, including a chat with Colonel Neill and the pictures are on the way.'

As Neill and the others recovered in hospital, some of the British team who had been working with the Malaysians on the rescue gathered in a bar to celebrate a successful mission. I shouted them a round of champagne. The *Mail*, I correctly assumed on this one, would be more than happy to sign off the expense.

Paul Dacre loved 'boys' own' stories, those grand adventures of derring-do in far-flung corners of the world. This one had it all. So much so that the story ran across seven pages in the *Mail*, including the front page, under the headline, referring to Lieutenant-Colonel Neill: 'How I beat Death Valley'. Later I was invited to London to receive a foreign reporters' award for the story, but somehow it seemed inconsequential against the enormity of the story.

◆

From time to time I worked for the *Mail*'s weekly paper, the *Mail on Sunday*. Despite being intent on finding big exclusives that the dailies had either missed or had failed to get their teeth into, there was one area that could never be ignored: the world of entertainment. I've never been successful as a celebrity spotter because in many cases I've never heard of them—unless they are big-time stars. But I didn't have to run to the internet to check on the background of Pierce Brosnan, who had just been announced as the next James Bond, replacing Timothy Dalton.

British newspaper editors were, and continue to be, fascinated by the Bond movies. Whenever a new 007, or the next Bond girl, is announced the rush is on to gather every piece of available information—and then some.

Pierce Brosnan, the *Mail on Sunday* informed me in 1995, was starring in *Robinson Crusoe*, which was being filmed somewhere in Papua New Guinea. The

MOS news editor Jon Ryan and picture editor Gary Woodhouse were already imagining a centre-page spread showing Pierce with a flowing beard and a ragged loin cloth walking along a deserted tropical beach followed by his Man Friday.

'That's the picture and story we want,' said Jon. This was a typical case of 'writing the headline and finding the facts to match it later'. Sometimes it worked, sometimes it didn't. It was up to me to make it work, but first I had to find out where the film was being shot. Movie companies tend not to broadcast where their sets are in order to avoid unofficial photos leaking out, but on my arrival in the capital, Port Moresby, a call to a reporter on *The National* newspaper put me in the right direction. He had learned the film was being shot in Madang, a small town on the north coast which was a popular spot for divers with a fascination for World War II shipwrecks.

The next available flight from Port Moresby was in the very early hours of the morning, so that when I arrived, unannounced, at the recommended Madang Resort Hotel it was 3AM. With any luck, I thought, the film crew might be staying there too—and I was immediately informed by the sleepy receptionist that that was indeed the case. I was also very lucky, she added: the hotel was fully booked, but just an hour earlier one of the film crew had checked out, presumably to catch the flight I had arrived on, so there was a room available. What was also fortunate, she said, was that one of the day cleaning staff, who had worked a double shift, had already tidied up the room and changed the sheets so I would be able to move straight in.

It had been a long day, so after a shower I was soon asleep.

Something woke me. A rumbling like the deep roar of a volcano. It was still dark. I fumbled for the bedside lamp, turned it on—and let out a loud screech. Just as the man with lipstick-red lips in the bed beside me and whose snoring had woken me also filled the room with a loud yell. I jumped out of bed on my side—and he jumped out on his. He was big and black and totally naked. I was skinny and white and also totally naked.

'What the …' I began.

'Oh, oh, oh …' he mumbled sheepishly.

We eventually worked it out. My sleeping companion was the self-same employee who had cleaned the room an hour earlier and, having finished his double shift, had decided to sleep for a few hours in what he expected to be an unoccupied room. Then he was going to tidy it up again so it would be ready for the next guest. He had not expected anyone to be checking in at 3AM. And he was so dog tired—and a little stoned—that he'd just got into bed on the nearest side without realising the other side was occupied. And he wasn't wearing lipstick— his mouth was stained with the bright red of the narcotic betel nut that virtually everyone in the country chews.

When the sun rose over the adjacent lagoon on what was to be another hot and steamy day in Papua New Guinea I searched out the film company's public relations person before she set off for the film set. She turned out to be a feisty blonde who demanded to know what I was doing there—'in our hotel'—and insisted I leave immediately. I politely explained that it was a hotel and I had as much right to stay there as anyone else, but in the meantime I'd be grateful if she could grant me access to Pierce Brosnan. I didn't think it would work—and it didn't. That meant I had to try to complete the assignment the hard way, as they say.

I had to assume that I was not the only journalist despatched to this corner of the world, but I suspected I might be the first. Aside from time being against me, I could not afford to slip up and find that another paper had achieved what I had failed to do. Failure was not a popular word at 2 Derry Street, Kensington, where the *Daily Mail* and the *Mail on Sunday* were located.

It was now Thursday and the story and pictures needed to be filed by Saturday— which meant I would have to fly back to Sydney on Friday or early Saturday morning in order to get the pictures processed and sent, this still being the days of film. Pictures? What pictures? My only hope of getting shots of the new James Bond in character as Robinson Crusoe was to find a vantage point from where I could use a long lens. There were enough crew cars leaving the hotel heading for the film location so I was able to follow one discreetly.

But first I thought there was nothing to lose by contacting the star himself, bypassing the difficult PR lady. I wrote a short note explaining who I was and requesting either an interview, the chance to take a picture of him as Robinson Crusoe or, better still, both. I asked one of the hotel staff to deliver it to his room.

Fat chance, I thought, and started up my rental car.

I followed a crew vehicle for several miles, passing along a narrow road lined with sugar cane plantations and sweeping through villages, then it turned down a small track leading to a cove through a forest of coconut trees. Two security guards stood at the entrance to the trail and I could see others in among the trees. Getting close in that area was obviously out. I drove up and down the road looking for a way down to the water but when I did get through the thick undergrowth I realized it was impossible to see the beach where the film was being shot because it was in an inlet.

I pulled off the road and parked in a clearing near a cluster of huts close to the start of the heavily guarded track. I was frustrated. As I stood leaning against the side of the car I watched village children playing in the clearing with hoops and sticks. Some were riding up and down the road on bicycles and scooters—and one rode out of the track leading down to the film set. I idly watched him ride past me—and a thunderbolt hit me. What was I doing? The boy had come from the film set! He had not been stopped by the security guards!

I ran after him, calling out for him to stop. At first he was alarmed when he realized a foreigner was chasing him, but he eventually braked. I told him my name was Richard and he told me he was David. He was the son of the village chief from whom the film company had rented the use of the beach, which was on tribal land. And, yes, he went down to the film set every day to watch Mr Pierce Brosnan acting and he was allowed to do it because of his status as the son of the chief—as long as he kept out of view of the camera. This was my chance. If I gave the boy a small camera—an Olympus Ixus—and showed him how to use it, would he take some photos for me? Oh yes, he grinned, he would love to do that, especially as I said I would send him some prints. I cautioned him against interfering with anything the film people were doing and instructed him on how to take horizontal and vertical pictures of Pierce.

It was agreed I would return that afternoon at around 4PM and would meet David in the village clearing. I spent an anxious few hours driving back to the small town and wandering around, attracting stares from everyone. They all seemed to be chewing betel nut. The pavements were red with blotches of spittle, as if someone had gone berserk with a paint gun. I drank Coca Cola and ate a greasy hamburger in a small café, took some touristy pictures around the lagoon with my Nikon FA and got back to the village clearing at four o'clock.

There was no sign of David. My heart sank. I waited for half an hour, three-quarters of an hour—then down the road he came from the direction of the track.

He stopped his bike beside me, a wide grin on his face, which sent my spirits soaring. But then, I looked at his pockets, where he had stuffed the Olympus previously. There were no bulges. Warning bells began to clang in my head. The conversation went like this:

'How did you get on, David?'

Long pause. Head down. Awkward shuffling of feet.

'There was a bit of trouble.'

'Oh yes? What happened?'

Pause.

'I did what you told me. I stood by the trees and took some pictures.'

'Yes …?'

'I took them this way'—and he pretended to take a horizontal shot—'and then this way'—as if taking a vertical picture.

'And?'

'Mr Brosnan was in all of them.'

'That's very good, David. And then?'

'And then a woman came and put her hand on my shoulder.'

'A woman with blonde, light-coloured hair?'

'Yes.'

'And …?'

'And she said, "Where did you get that camera?" I didn't tell her that you gave it to me because you told me not to tell anyone.'

'Very, very good indeed, David. And what happened next?'

'She kept asking and asking. Then I said a man called Richard gave it to me.'

'Oh.'

'Then she said, "Give me that camera".'

'And did you give it to her?'

'She took it from me.'

'And then …?'

'And then she opened up the back and she got the film and she pulled it out and held it up to the sun.'

'I see. So where is the camera now?'

'She's still got it.'

'Well, thank you for trying, David. You've been a good boy. Here's ten kina for your help.'

'Thank you, Richard.'

'Thanks, David. Now I'm just going to drive back to my hotel. I expect she'll give me the camera later. Goodbye.'

'Goodbye.'

I cursed all the way back to the Madang Resort Hotel, replaying the conversation with David over and over and envisaging that scene as the PR lady ripped the film from the camera. There were going to be fireworks when she saw me at the hotel later.

As I walked into my room I stepped on a large brown envelope. There was no name on the front but I assumed it was for me. I opened it—and couldn't believe my eyes. There were four eight-by-ten inch black-and-white photos of Pierce Brosnan as Robinson Crusoe, long hair, long beard. There was a single piece of paper with them with a simple message: 'Best, PB.'

I sat on the bed, stunned. Pierce had obviously received my earlier request and had arranged, unknown to the PR woman, to have the photos taken by the on-set photographer, Bob Greene, to be sent to my room. They were fantastic pictures— but then my thoughts turned to horror. At that very moment, Pierce might be learning that I had tried to use a young village kid to take sneaky pictures on the set. At that very moment, a security man might be speeding towards the hotel to snatch back the photos. I had to get out of there!

My bag was still packed, so I hurriedly checked out and took a taxi to a nondescript lodgings on the edge of town where I hoped no-one would find me. The next morning I was on the first flight out of Madang, again praying that no-one would be at the airport to grab me, and was just able to make the connection in Port Moresby to fly back to Sydney. Later, after I had sent the pictures back to London, I called Jon Ryan on the News Desk to check that all was well.

Jon put it this way: 'The picture editor has just wet himself with joy.' What they envisaged had came off—the picture and my story about the next James Bond playing Robinson Crusoe was the centre-page spread. I never did get my Olympus back—I decided it was a worthy sacrifice.

◆

In February 1995 Barings Bank, the oldest merchant bank in London, collapsed after a rogue employee, Nick Leeson, lost more than £800 million speculating mostly on futures contracts. Nick was to join the list of heroes and villains I had flown back to London with over the years to round off stories that might need just a little bit more than I might be able to extract during the long flight across the world.

I had rushed from Sydney to Singapore when news of the bank collapse began to race around the world naming Leeson as the cause. It was close to 1AM when I reached my Singapore hotel after a delayed flight. Surely, I thought, there wouldn't be anyone at the bank at that hour—but I decided to go there anyway. I caught a taxi around to the towering office block where Barings' was located and, on a whim, told the block's security guard that I was 'going up to the bank'. He kindly pressed the lift button for me. He must have thought I was an employee. That told me that something was going on. I could see that all the lights were on in Barings' offices. I walked into the unlocked entrance where, understandably, no-one was manning the reception desk. But I could see into the main office and went to stand at the doorway.

It was an amazing scene. Men in shirt sleeves were staring at computer screens, shaking their heads, women were running around with arms full of files. Phones were ringing but no-one was picking them up. Documents were being stuffed into briefcases. Papers were being shredded. There was panic in the air. And then, as one, they saw me standing there, a silent observer. And as one, everyone froze—until a woman came running over to me.

'Who are you? What do you want?'

'I'm from the *Daily Mail*,' I said.

Aghast, she shrieked: 'Get out!' Then a man came over and told me in no uncertain terms that I had to leave immediately. But I had my story: as far as I could take it at that stage, a description of the scene at the bank as news of the collapse was reverberating around the world. It was a story that no-one else would ever have.

I made my exit, but not as fast as Nick Leeson had made his. He had left a confessional note for the bank's chairman, Peter Baring, and had fled to Kuala Lumpur. I followed his trail to Borneo, but by then he had flown to Frankfurt, where he was arrested.

Four years later, when he was released from Changhi prison in Singapore—I had been there when he was sentenced in a Singapore court after pleading guilty to fraud—I got on the plane with him and flew with him to London. There he was delivered into the hands of the *Daily Mail*, which had bought his exclusive story.

Arriving back in the UK gave me the chance to catch up on journalist friends and to visit Cyril, my childhood guardian, in Torquay where he and his wife Midge were still living. He was in his 70s by then and getting frail; having trouble with his balance, he said. I took him and Midge out for afternoon tea beside Torquay harbourside and we talked a little about old times, but I felt he didn't want to dwell long on those dark days of poverty.

I returned to Devon three years later for Cyril's funeral and couldn't stop the tears as I took the opportunity of telling the congregation of the sacrifices he had made for me when I was a kid. At the funeral I met one of my half-sisters, Linda, who was now a grandmother, for the first time in heaven knows how many years. I went for dinner with her and her husband Colin and she told me a little about my background—information that I had not been able to glean from our mother before her death some years earlier.

It seems my father might have been a US airman stationed in Devon during the war. Well, there you go. Linda had no idea who he was—our mother had never told her. And no, I don't have a trace of an American accent. It's pure Devonian.

I took the opportunity of visiting my old haunts from my days on the *Herald Express*. This time, instead of driving around on a Lambretta motor scooter, I decided to walk. Everywhere seemed so … small. I returned to the original council house from where the pram I was in had run away down the hill. The garden was neatly kept but when I knocked on the door to say hello to the occupants no-one was home. But I could see that the air raid shelter in the back garden had been removed.

I walked along Torquay seafront and wandered around to the next town, Paignton, just a few miles away, and then continued on to Brixham. As I neared the small fishing town I recalled the first big story I'd covered for the *Herald Express*: the death of the matron of Dartmouth Hospital. She'd parked her car on a wharf beside the River Dart but when she had attempted to drive away she put the vehicle into reverse by mistake—and it plunged into the river. The car remained afloat for perhaps ten minutes and the woman had managed to wind down her window, reach out an arm and grab a metal ladder attached to the wall. As people tried to reach her, she had managed to keep the car afloat through an enormous surge of strength by hanging onto the ladder. But the car had filled with water and it sank. By the time rescuers got to her it was too late.

◆

What makes one story better than another? I've often tried to answer the question in cases where there are similar instances of no hope but end in dramatic rescues.

Was the rescue of the men on the mountain a 'better story' than that of 56-year-old British yachtsman Tony Bullimore, who was lost in the freezing waters of the Southern Ocean in January 1997 as he was taking part in a round-the-world yacht race? Their stories of survival were examples of human determination to take on the elements. Man against nature. When man wins, others want to read about it because they like to think that if something should ever happen to them there is always a chance of winning through. I became personally involved in the story, the only newspaperman to witness his minute-by-minute rescue.

Bullimore's 60-foot (18.25-metre) yacht *Global Exide Challenger* was 63 days into the race when its keel was ripped away by fierce seas. A satellite distress signal was set off but all that it indicated was that Bullimore was in trouble in the world's most dangerous waters. What no-one knew was that the yacht had immediately turned turtle.

A Royal Australian Air Force Orion flew down to the search area daily from Perth but all that the crew had been able to see was the upturned hull, battered by the waves. An Australian Navy frigate, HMAS *Adelaide*, set sail, but it would take several days to reach the yacht. I phoned the Air Force to ask what my chances were of flying to the area on the Orion but was told that Australian reporters had precedence. I would have to wait for at least four days. The *Adelaide* had already sailed, so there was no chance of getting on board.

I flew to Perth and patiently waited my turn as the Orion flew down and back each day, disgorging its group of reporters and photographers who had seen nothing more than part of a white hull bobbing around.

'OK,' said the Air Force PR man on 9 January, 'your turn'. A reporter with an Australian TV network and I were the only journalists on board—all that really mattered to me was that I was the only British journalist. It was probably going to be a wasted trip anyway. But as we flew south, the plane hitting rough turbulence at times, we learned that the *Adelaide* was close to the upturned hull—close enough to see it with the naked eye whenever the big swell allowed. It was another three hours or so before we came within view of the *Adelaide*. From our height it looked like a toy ship in a bath, a curious sight I will always remember. Then I saw the white hull bobbing about in the waves, the number 33 and the name *Exide Challenger* clearly visible.

'There's no way he can be alive in there,' I said. The crew of the Orion agreed. We had set out from Perth on a mission to find a dead man, or at least be around while frogmen from the *Adelaide* checked out the capsized vessel, the Orion crew acting as observers from above. As we began circling above the *Adelaide* I was allowed onto the flight deck for a better view. Before we had to make another circuit I saw a rubber dinghy being launched from the *Adelaide* and frogmen huddling in it. That was the difference between being in a plane and not a helicopter—we had to keep moving!

Flying Officer Sean Corkill banked the Orion over at such a steep angle I thought the wing tip might strike the water. Then he was up and flying over the dinghy, which was half way between the Orion and the upturned yacht. Again we had to circle and this time I saw the dinghy was beside the yacht. Once more we circled and now the frogmen were in the water, banging on the yacht's hull. Then an incredible thing happened.

'He's alive! He's in there and he's alive!'

The frogmen had heard tapping from inside the hull in response to their banging. They radioed the information back to the ship, which had then passed the astounding message to the aircraft.

'Go around! Go around!' I yelled at the flight crew, as if they weren't already doing that—and as if they were going to take any notice of a newspaperman's excited orders. They completed another circuit and then, unbelievably, there was an orange figure in the water at the yacht's bow. It was Tony Bullimore! He had swum out from under the stricken vessel and bobbed up to wave at the frogmen who were at the stern. I fired off as many pictures as possible in the fleeting moment before we had to make yet another circuit.

It was like watching an old movie being played out before my eyes, with cuts in the frames … there were the frogmen heading towards the yacht, then they were tapping, then there was Bullimore … and now as we flew over the scene again I watched as he was being hauled into the dinghy. A couple more circuits and the dinghy reached the *Adelaide*. Tony Bullimore, the man everyone had give up for dead, was in safe hands.

'Satisfied?' asked Flying Officer Corkill.

'You could say that,' I said, rewinding my film.

As we were making our way back to Perth, Tony Bullimore was talking to reporters on the *Adelaide*. Their stories hit the wires as I was still in the air so I had to rely on the quotes that Bullimore had given to them to add to my own copy. But what I had seen was extraordinary, a historic episode that no-one on the

Adelaide had witnessed—the moment a 'dead man' rose up from a watery grave. That became the introduction to my exclusive story, which was splashed across the front page of the *Daily Mail* the next day.

We learned from Bullimore that he had been in his sleeping quarters when disaster struck. With the yacht bowled over after losing its keel and then upside down, he managed to scramble to a position of comparative safety. But he faced further peril when a window broke, creating a vacuum that sucked equipment away and drew in a water spout 'like an upside-down Niagara Falls,' he said.

As he described what had happened, we all realized what remarkable luck he had had. In order to keep out of the icy water that was pouring in, he managed to fix up a hammock and he remained there keeping out of the water. He knew that if he got wet the freezing water would be the death of him. He dangled in the hammock for three days, inches above the water.

'It was sheer determination, a little freshwater and a little chocolate,' he said. 'When I heard the frogmen banging on the side, I picked up anything I could, used my fist, anything, to bang the side. I went through three cabins to get to the other end screaming as I went "I'm coming out! I'm coming out!" I took a few deep breaths and came out straight through the hole and the ship was there and I thought, "I'm saved, I'm all right!" If God had been standing there in front of me, I could not have been more delighted.'

Bullimore had taken an enormous risk. Before he plunged into the water to swim under the yacht, he asked himself whether he had imagined the tapping on the side. If he had got it wrong and found no-one there when he bobbed up, that would have been the end of him. It would have been impossible to get back into the yacht. Even if he had, his soaked clothing from those chilling waters would have brought on hypothermia very quickly and he would have passed out and died.

Adelaide's commander Raymond Gates said that, 'When he got on board he was acting like a schoolboy. He said he felt like kissing one of the sailors—except the guy had a beard. Then he asked for a cup of tea.'

CHAPTER 21

'He Wants to Put You in Jail, He Says You Are a Spy'

The rescue stories just kept coming in the late 1990s. And of course no rescue can really be said to be a 'better story' than any other. The circumstances are different, the difficulties of the rescue vary, but at the end of it all lives are saved and that is all that matters. Even so, each event has its dramas and often associated tragedy—none more so than 30 July 1997 when an avalanche of earth, rock and trees swept down through the New South Wales mountain village of Thredbo, burying 60 people as two ski lodges were engulfed.

Thredbo was crowded at that time of the year. It was the middle of winter when skiers make their way to the Snowy Mountains, which has Thredbo at their heart. For many people in other parts of the world, Australia is seen as a dry parched land with a vast desert in the centre and a fringe of green mostly around its southern and eastern coasts. But in the winter the mountain chain that spreads from New South Wales into Victoria is covered in snow and the ski slopes range from 'easy' to 'expert'.

I drove the five hours to Thredbo, arriving in the evening as rescuers were tearing at the wreckage. They dared not use heavy machinery in case another landslide occurred. They pulled some 40 people out alive but another 18 were presumed dead. A 165-foot (50-metre) wide strip of land, believed to have been weakened by water infiltration, had fallen away, carrying with it the two-storey Carinya Lodge. It tumbled down the hillside like a rolling box and was stopped only when it smashed into the Bimbadeen Lodge. Both buildings were crushed and then buried in the following rush of earth, rocks, trees and cars carried from a road that had been sliced in two. Those I spoke to who were staying nearby and escaped told of scenes of terror. A 22-year-old British woman, Deirdre Leitch, said that, 'There were people lying injured and there were screams all around. My friend and I tried to help but all we could see was mangled bits of building.' Police probed the debris with listening devices for hours, but believed that all those still alive had been rescued.

And yet someone remained alive down there under the rubble. Stuart Diver, a 27-year-old ski instructor, was trapped under a massive slab of concrete as water continued to gush down over the hill and then welled up from below his feet to cover his entire body—except for his face. Underneath him was another huge concrete slab. He was a human sandwich, unable to move anything but his fingers. And those fingers clutched the hand of his wife Sally, lying trapped beside him, for the next incredible 66 hours. I watched as they pulled him free and carried him on a stretcher down over the rubble and the water. Sally was dead. He, too, had been a hair's breadth from drowning.

'Water swelled up from beneath my feet and covered my body,' he recalled from his hospital bed. 'I had to keep bringing my head up, but I could only raise it a couple of inches before I hit the slab above me. Sometimes the water came up over my mouth and only my nose was clear. I sucked in whatever air I could, not knowing if it would be my last.'

His story was one that claustrophobics would have had trouble listening to. He and Sally had been sleeping when the avalanche struck, hurling them down the slope in their bed amid the disintegrating lodge, its carpark and half a dozen vehicles.

When it all stopped, Stuart reached over and tried to hold Sally's head above the water with his one free hand, but there was no space above her face and he realized that even if she had escaped without injury she was going to drown. She slid further away, her body shifted by the water, until all he could touch was her hand. He knew that she was beyond hope but realized he had to keep alert if he was to survive—and he took himself, in his mind, around the world, to romantic places where he and Sally had stayed, reliving their happiest moments together. Then, as the freezing water began to rise over his body and face, he desperately lifted his head until his forehead touched the upper slab. Time and again the water receded, then built up again.

'I was going to give up,' he said. 'There comes a point when the effort of staying alive becomes too hard. But then I found another bit of willpower and once again lifted my head.'

He lost all sense of time, passing in and out of consciousness. More than two days later, when he heard a voice calling out, 'Can you hear me?' he thought he was dreaming. He was going to be safe.

His amazing story made headlines around the world. I was just happy to have been there to witness what everyone was describing as a 'true miracle of survival.'

Three months after Threadbo I moved to another tragedy that made world headlines. Michael Hutchence, lead singer of the band INXS, was found hanging in his room at the Ritz-Carlton Hotel in the wealthy eastern Sydney suburb of Double Bay in November 1997. Had he deliberately killed himself over rows with his lover and former TV presenter Paula Yates—the ex-wife of musician Bob Geldof—with whom Hutchence had a daughter? Or was his death a terrible accident, a result of an act of auto-eroticism gone wrong? I spoke to his father, Kel Hutchence, many times, reminding him that I'd interviewed his son on two previous occasions. Kel, who had had dinner with Michael hours before his death, was at a loss to come up with an explanation. He didn't want to believe either scenario as we talked from time to time in a park near his home, which was less than a mile from the hotel where Michael had died. Finally a coroner came up with what he believed was the answer—that Michael had killed himself in a state of depression, partly over his child custody dispute with Geldof.

Hours before Hutchence's suicide he had two phone conversations with Geldof in London in which he begged him to allow Paula's children to come to Australia with her. Later Paula called Hutchence to say the children would not be coming. She said the singer sounded 'desperate'. Before he died, he made numerous phone calls to friends and acquaintances. He left a voicemail for his personal manager in New York, Martha Troup: 'Martha, Michael here, I've fucking had enough.' The tragedy was not over there—on 17 September 2000, Paula, at the age of 41, was found dead at her London home after a drugs overdose.

Many years later, in 2009, I called on Michael's mother, Pamela Glassop, who had become tangled in legal battles over Michael's estate, but the main thing on her mind was that she wanted to see the child that her son had fathered with Paula, Heavenly Hirani Tiger Lily. Following Paula's death, Bob Geldof had won custody of her so she could be raised with the children he'd had with Paula—

and he reluctantly allowed Mrs Glassop to see her granddaughter on only a few occasions.

'I'm getting on now,' she told me in her apartment on Queensland's Gold Coast. 'I can only beg Bob Geldof one last time to let me see Tiger Lily.' She died just a few months later. When I left her with her memories—photos of Michael on the wall and his platinum records from his days as lead singer with INXS—she was holding back tears. I had no doubt they would start to flow as soon as she closed the door on me.

◆

The *Mail* could never get enough stories about people who had been given up for dead and then miraculously reappeared—and I have had more than my share of them. Perhaps because of where I lived: the unforgiving deserts of Australia, the swamps of the tropical north, the vast oceans around the continent, and then, to the north of Australia, the jungles of south-east Asia. Such landscapes attracted young travellers from Europe and America. Clive Sutton was one of them. In 1993, as a young soldier, he ploughed his Ford Fiesta into a taxi queue in Bristol when he was twice the legal alcohol limit and a mother and a young man died. When his four-year jail sentence was over, he could not bear to go home to constant reminders of the tragedy and took to travelling in search of adventure. He almost lost his own life in the process.

In December 1998, he set out on the famous Kokoda Track in Papua New Guinea. When his young guide deserted him for unexplained reasons, Sutton became hopelessly lost and for 21 days he stumbled through the jungle, cutting his body badly on thorns, being bitten by malaria-carrying mosquitos and suffering severe dehydration. He was close to death when two tribesmen—the *Mail* insisted they had to be described as 'stone-age' tribesmen—found him lying on a dried-up river bed. They made their way to a Salvation Army outpost north of Port Moresby and raised the alarm. 'Me fella findem wun White Masta. He sleep long stone blong river,' said one, meaning: 'We've found a white man sleeping on the river stones.' They added: 'All same, he dead': 'He looks almost dead.'

An Australian Army team mounted a rescue, and soldiers and medical supplies were flown by helicopter to a clearing four miles (six kilometres) from where 30-year-old Sutton lay. The rest of the team hacked their way through the rainforest to his side. It was touch and go whether he would survive.

He was British and the *Mail* wanted his story. I caught the first plane to Cairns, the North Queensland city he had been airlifted to, and then ran into a snag. Despite his weak state, he had appointed a solicitor to take charge of his affairs and he wanted payment for his story. Other reporters were on their way to Cairns from Sydney. The last thing I wanted was to get caught up in a bidding war when I was the first on the scene. The problem was, it was too early in the morning in London to get hold of anyone, so I did what is usually frowned upon by the higher-ups of British papers: I made an executive decision and offered £15,000 on the *Mail's* behalf, after learning that the *Daily Express* had gone to £12,000 and was likely to offer more. I signed the documents with the lawyer, hoping to God that I was doing the right thing because I didn't know just how good Sutton's story was going to be. The only stipulations I made were that I had to conduct the interview right then, before anyone else arrived—and that he must not talk to any other reporters who might find their way to his room.

Sutton's story was everything I could have wished for. He told me how, after his guide had decided he did not want to continue walking, he was left alone in what was one of the world's most dangerous jungles. He had become totally lost, injured, and towards the end, before his lucky rescue, had started hallucinating. In his fevered mind logs turned into crocodiles and fireflies became people with torches.

'For 19 days no-one saw me and I saw no-one. The loneliness and hunger drove me to delirium. As the end drew close, I would lie beside the river with rain pouring down on me and I'd hear voices. Sometimes I heard singing. I'd call out into the darkness: "Hello, can you hear me! I'm here! I'm here!" But of course there was never anyone there. Just the mosquitos biting all through the night before the sandflies started in the morning, tearing out pieces of my skin. It seemed the only part of my body that didn't hurt was my head. I knew I was close to death. I tasted what it was like.'

I pieced together a diary of his daily terror and the story ran the following day as the *Daily Mail's* front-page lead, along with a picture I took of him in the hospital. There was a further spread detailing his story on the inside pages. But what of the £15,000 I'd committed the *Mail* to paying?

'It had a great show in the paper,' said Gerry, the foreign editor. 'Don't worry about it.'

'And if it hadn't had a good show …?'

'That,' he said, 'is when you do worry about it.'

◆

From the day I arrived, keen and excited, in Fleet Street back in the 1960s I was aware of the fierce competition between the national newspapers. 'Scoop' is such a dated word these days, but that's what it was all about. If word was out that a paper was working on a great exclusive, or had already published one, the others had to work at finding a 'spoiler' that would ruin the impact of the story they had missed out on. My involvement with the call girl in the Commons, Pamela Bordes, and with New Zealand horsewoman Heather Tonkin—who actually did laugh at the sobriquet of 'Bonkin Tonkin' that some cruel journalists had given her—demonstrated yet again the *Mail*'s delight at being able to insert barbs into the sides of its opponents.

So I could almost hear the whoops of joy from faraway Australia when I was able to tell them 'It's all a load of codswallop' about a Balinese prince who had married a very pretty and naïve English woman. Setting aside what I'd already learned about Balinese marriages from my investigations into the Mick Jagger–Jerry Hall wedding, the groom turned out to be anything but the princely lord that the broadsheet and very correct *Daily Telegraph* had made him out to be. The *Telegraph*'s story, for which they had reportedly paid a four-figure sum, was picked up by magazines and newspapers around the world.

But the *Mail* wondered if there was anything odd about the marriage of 23-year-old tall, beautiful British model Marianne Roy who, said the *Telegraph*, had become one of the highest ranking members of the Bali royal hierarchy and was now to be known as Princess Maitre Vairokani Dewi of Pandji. She would, we were told, have the choice of eight magnificent palaces to live in, where bowing servants would attend her every whim, while in the streets and temples her subjects would throw themselves at her feet. Which was fair enough for a woman who had married a demi-god known as The Precious One, Prince Sri Acarya Vajra Kumara Pandki Pandita, a 12th-generation descendant of the enlightened King Pandji Sakti of Singhaaraja. Or, as his friends knew him, Ratu.

The Precious One made it known that he would not take up his constitutional role, but would instead act as a spiritual adviser to his people. However, I was able to reveal that the man Marianne married was not a prince. There were no palaces, no bowing servants and she had not even been crowned. The couple, as they claimed, could not have received the blessing of the old king of Bali because he died in 1978. Far from prostrating themselves at the approach of 'Prince' Ratu in Bali, most people in the street ignored him. And as the most cursory of checks would have revealed, Ratu could never have assumed any constitutional role on the island because it had been a republic for the past 48 years.

But the best evidence of Ratu being a mere pretender to the throne came from the real prince, the man whose title he had assumed. 'I'm afraid he is not who he says he is,' I was told when I tracked down Dr Anak Agum Udayana, the first son of the last living king of Bali, who would be the only true claimant to the throne—if there were one.

'He certainly doesn't own eight palaces. Not even I live in a palace because most of them have fallen into disrepair,' said Dr Anak at his modest home on the north coast of Bali. 'In fact, my father's palace is now used as the town library and to house government departments.'

I showed Dr Udayana photographs of the wedding ceremony and he shook his head. 'That crown the young lady is wearing is what dancers wear when they put on a show. I can assure you that despite what she has been told, it is not a princess's crown and it is not made of solid gold. I am sorry to have to disappoint this young lady, but she has absolutely no standing as a Balinese princess.'

Marianne's rapidly evaporating fairytale began two years earlier, in 1996, during an educational trip to the US, when she went into a club in Santa Fe, New Mexico, where Ratu, a 42-year-old divorcee, was propping up the bar with a group of friends. She told the *Daily Mirror*, which reportedly paid her for her story, that it was 'love at first sight'. Mind you, pretty women who talk of romance to British tabloids are always quoted as saying that. But even so she was obviously smitten by his exotic looks.

'We all ended up at a friend's house and we just got talking,' she told the paper. 'We talked for most of the night about Buddha, and Ratu told me that, as the lotus flower grows from the mud but remains unstained, so does compassion, love and kindness grow from understanding suffering, rather than cursing it.'

Marianne was clearly anxious to tell the world of the incredible man in her life. She told the *People* newspaper in an interview, for which she was said to have been paid around £10,000, that at 16 she had been raped but because she was 'too young and too embarrassed to do anything about it', the attacker escaped prosecution. All her English boyfriends, she told the paper, 'just used and abused me—sex always seemed dirty to me.'

That was followed by a six-year struggle against anorexia and bulimia, during which her 5 foot 9 inch (175 centimetres) frame shrivelled to just 7 stone 6 pounds (47 kilos), she revealed in an interview with the *Daily Mirror*. But she sailed through her A-levels and was offered a place studying for a fine arts degree in London. It was during an exchange trip to study Native American art that she met Ratu. She promptly abandoned her studies and moved to Melbourne, where Ratu was teaching Buddhism. She put her name down with a local modelling agency.

As romance blossomed and the couple began discussing marriage, Ratu said that first she had to receive the blessing of 'his uncle, the king' before the ceremony could go ahead. She told of the wedding at the Orchid Palace at which 'everyone who was anyone was present. The king and queen were there, the high priest, Ratu's father and all his friends. There was incense and flowers and I was drenched in holy water. The ceremony went on for six hours but I'll remember it for the rest of my life.'

Days later the *Daily Telegraph* stumped up big money for access to Marianne and Ratu, before gushing in a report: 'She looked a template of nuptial loveliness; bare-shouldered and carrying white roses. He with his slipper black, Disraeli-like curls and Victorian wing collar, seemed to have strayed from the sub-plot of a Dickensian novel.' The paper added that for someone so recently translated from student to royal personage, 'Princess Marianne maintains a remarkably cool demeanour. This may, of course, be because she was a princess all along. The old king of Bali clearly thought so; after their blessing, their union, he turned to Marianne and said: "Welcome home".'

Back in Australia a magazine paid the couple an estimated £20,000 for an interview and photographs. This time the former Marianne Roy said she was a direct descendant of Rob Roy, despite that being the Gaelic nickname of an 18th-century Highland outlaw called Robert MacGregor. There's nothing like being the descendant of a nickname. There was more to come from the 'royal' couple. Marianne and Ratu told the *People* newspaper 'the amazing details of their insatiable sex life' and how they made love for six hours a night 'in 21 positions'.

I felt sorry for Marianne. She'd fallen under the spell of a dreamer, but for her it all turned into a nightmare.

Bali, which lies to the east of the Indonesian capital Jakarta, was often the destination for my assignments, usually chasing up stories involving British people who ran into problems of some kind—south-east Asian correspondents referred to such events as 'Brits in the Shit'. But on a few occasions I'd ventured farther east to Irian Jaya (now known as Papua). Because it was a sensitive area, bordering on Papua New Guinea, it was a prohibited region for journalists unless a special pass could be obtained from the Ministry of Information and requests were almost always turned down.

However, the government had turned a blind eye to reporters like myself who flew to the miserable, poverty-stricken Irian Jaya capital of Jayapura in 1996 to cover—or at least try to cover—the story of a group of British and Dutch scientists who had been held captive in the jungle by tribal members of the Free Papua Movement. They were eventually rescued when Indonesian troops raided the jungle hideout where they were being held.

But a request to return to Irian Jaya in 1999 set me wondering about the wisdom of venturing into the region again without proper authorisation. I knew, however, that putting in a request for a journalist's pass and then waiting for a response could take weeks—and the *Mail* wanted my story for the following weekend's paper. I had been on a job in Thailand, tracking down the tumbledown shack that a poor village girl had grown up in before she 'married' one of the richest men in Britain and ended up living in a mansion in the UK. And no, there weren't shades of the Balinese prince in that story: the village girl really did marry a millionaire.

Having filed the pictures and an interview with the girl's parents, I was preparing to fly back to Sydney when Gerry on the Foreign Desk asked me to go to Irian Jaya instead. The Boss (as editor Paul Dacre was referred to in the office) wanted a feature on two tribes who had met in the jungle and, because they could not understand each other's tongue, had created their own language. It was a sort of 'Esperanto of the Jungle'.

All I had as a clue to their whereabouts were a few lines from an Indonesian wire service stating that the tribes lived in the jungle a day's travel along the Mamberamo River, west of Jayapura. This was not on any travel company's itinerary (although an adventurous company was to offer limited tours to the region years later). I had to make my own arrangements. The quickest way, it seemed, was to fly to the small island of Pulau Yapen, off the northern coast of Irian Jaya, and then find a boat crew who were willing to take me on a short voyage across the Yapen Strait and then down the river. This was typical of the rush arrangements that foreign correspondents, who have no back-up researchers working with them, have to make—just find out where you have to go and then get there as best you can. I knew this one was going to be difficult. Aside from my seven rules—be logical, observant, relentless, patient, generous, don't panic, never assume—there was another rule that I would apply on 'must get' stories: no matter how hard it is, no matter how long it takes, no matter how much it costs, just do it.

From Bangkok I flew to Jakarta, then across the Indonesian archipelago to Jayapura. After a night in a grim hotel room that did not even have a window, I was on a light plane to Biak. From Biak I had to take yet another short flight to Pulau Yapen. At the tiny airport a kindly old man, who with his crooked grin reminded me of an Indonesian version of the actor Alastair Sim, offered his services as a guide. I was there to dive down to the World War II shipwrecks, was I not? Er no, I told him on our way into the tiny town, not exactly.

Because I was there as a journalist without a permit I treated my new friend, whose name was Charles, with some caution. I didn't know whether he would ask for credentials. On the other hand, it wasn't as if I was there to write political stories, which is why journalists are deterred from visiting the region. Tourists were always welcome and the story I was after was sort of touristy, so I thought I would be safe in explaining my mission. In any case, there was no chance of my writing anything political because a) the *Daily Mail* would not have been interested, and b) there was nothing political to write about. Right?

Wrong. The main town of Serui was a mess. I had landed on the island in the hours after supporters of the Free Papua Movement had rioted, smashing shop windows, beating up and killing people and raising their illegal flag. There had been an exchange of fire with troops before the perpetrators were gunned down or arrested, but the movements of everyone in the town were restricted. I could not have chosen a more sensitive time to have arrived if I'd spent months planning it.

'Don't worry about all the wreckage,' said Charles after I checked into the Hotel Merpati where I was destined to share my dark room with swarms of mosquitos, 'there's been a bit of trouble here, but as you're a tourist you'll be quite safe.'

Over a hamburger in a small café across the road I explained my mission to Charles, describing myself as a photographer who wanted to meet these two unusual tribes. I thought the word 'journalist' might start alarm bells ringing. What Charles told me about the Mamberamo River, though, would have been music to the editor's ears. The river was a kind of Amazon of Asia and there were tribes deep in the interior who had never had contact with the outside world. They still used stone weapons and hunted with bows and arrows and spears. What started to dawn on me, and which obviously had not been considered by the *Mail*'s editorial department, was that even if I found the two 'Esperanto tribes' how on earth I was going to be able to interview them if they could only understand each other? Well, it would have to be sign language—and, hey, the pictures would be great anyway.

Charles went off to arrange for a boat to be on standby the next morning. Two hours later, having found a crew of two and a motorboat to take me on the adventure down the river, we went shopping. On Charles's instructions—because the tribes would expect this—I bought a sack of rice, two big sacks of potatoes, three gallons of water, matches, mosquito repellent and several containers of noodle soup to which hot water had to be added, which meant purchasing a small pan and a packet of firelighters. We'd decided that a gas tank and a little cooking top was just too much to carry and, anyway, Charles assured me, the natives were 'probably' friendly and would provide me with food.

'Are you coming, too, Charles?'

'No, but the boatmen can speak a little English and they will make sure it all will go well for you.'

That night I lay in the gloomy light of my room looking at the pile of food purchased for the natives stacked in the corner. I had visions of the boat sinking with all the weight and crocodiles moving in to consume me as I struggled to the river bank. But a story was a story. I had to make it work.

Charles knocked on the door at 7AM as arranged.

'All set then, Charles? We go to the harbour now?'

He hung his head. I didn't like the look of that.

'Is there a bit of a problem, Charles?'

'No, no problem, but first we have to go somewhere else.'

'To get more food?'

'No, to go to the police station.'

My heart sank. 'Why do we have to go to the police station?'

'Because I have to tell the police when a foreigner arrives and they wanted to know where you were going and when I told them you were going to go down the river to look for two tribes who can only speak to one another they all shook their heads as if they did not believe me.'

His explanation did not surprise me one bit. I had arrived, out of the blue, on the morning after a big political riot and now I was telling everyone what, in the minds of the police, was a cock and bull story. I knew it was going to be futile trying to explain that I was 'just a photographer' not interested in politics.

The senior police officer, who had a bristling moustache—in fact he looked rather like Saddam Hussein—and was dressed in civvies, could hardly speak a word of English, so poor Charles, humbled in his presence yet seemingly not wanting to let me down, had to do the interpreting. I repeated the purpose of my mission, being careful not to mention editors or newspapers. The policeman stared stony-faced at me. For the next five hours I sat in his sweltering office answering question after question about the 'true' purpose of my visit. I kept to the truth about my planned trip down the river.

At the end of my grilling, he stood up.

And Charles said, 'He wants to put you in the jail. He says you are a spy.'

That didn't sound too good, so I struck a deal. I was willing to turn over my two cameras, a small notebook (with empty pages and no shorthand in them, thank goodness) and my pen until such time as I could receive permission to go down the river. There would be no permission to go down the river, he quickly snapped through Charles.

But he agreed in the end not to throw me into jail. However, I had to leave Pulau Yapen on the next available flight. That would be the next morning. In the meantime, the officer added as he reached into a drawer and placed a dirty great big revolver on his desk, I would remain under house arrest at the hotel. Not only did he take my cameras, but he also confiscated my passport. I was thankful that he didn't go through my wallet, for in there was a Scotland Yard press card containing the words *Daily Mail* in large black letters.

The hotel did not serve food, so I was given permission to extend my house arrest to the small café across the road. The following morning, accompanied by a sheepish Charles, who had become my official keeper, I went to the airport to be told that the flight in the light plane to Biak was full. I should return the following day. Could I make a booking? No, I should just turn up. Interestingly, my interrogator, the policeman, was loitering around the terminal, watching me. I smiled at him and gave him a short wave, neither of which was returned.

For the next six days, with no means of making an international call to the *Mail*—which would have been a foolish move in any case—I waited for a flight to be available, although it was Charles who had to try to arrange it. Each day he came back to the hotel and said there were no seats. I was left with the distinct impression that this was deliberate. How long did they intend to keep me there, I wondered?

I lay in my room looking at the sacks of potatoes; I sat on the hotel steps and I walked to and from the café across the road each day with absolutely nothing to do. I asked Charles to find me a book, as I had finished reading the one in my bag, but he could only find ones written in Indonesian. No such thing as an e-book reader with hundreds of stored titles in those days! It was the dreariest time I could remember. Finally Charles turned up with my equipment and my passport and told me that because the flight situation was not improving, the police said I should leave by ship.

At the dock, where the ferry to Biak was waiting, Charles shook my hand and said he was sorry I had not been able to go down the river. I didn't blame him for telling the police about me—if he had failed to do so he would have ended up in jail himself. He had very little money and I paid him well for his assistance and suggested he took his family out for a nice meal that evening.

'Oh no,' he said. 'We always eat at home. This money will help us for the next few months.'

'And what will you have for dinner tonight, Charles?'

'My wife, she is cooking us some potatoes.'

'Nothing else?'

'No, we like potatoes.'

Potatoes. I suddenly remembered. 'You'll be able to eat for several more months, Charles,' I said. He looked confused.

'In my room, remember …? There's two huge sacks of potatoes—and they're all yours.'

He broke into that big Alastair Sim smile. He was still grinning when I waved goodbye to him from the crowded deck of the ferry. A nice, humble man and even though I had failed on my mission I felt that personally I had gained a great deal by meeting him.

As I'd been out of touch for so long, I called the office as soon as I could and explained what had happened. There was no grief and we were to learn much later that the two Esperanto tribes had had a falling out and had gone their separate ways—before I had even set out to find them.

CHAPTER 22

A Senseless Death in the Jungle

Dili, East Timor, 20 September 1999. I stood in the back of an old farm truck as it rumbled into the deserted streets of this tiny capital of an eastern Indonesian province. There were people there, all right, but you couldn't see them. They were hiding—in the bush, behind buildings, in the dark rooms of bullet-blasted homes. The rumble of my truck had sent a new wave of fear through the residents. They had no way of knowing whether or not it was another Indonesian army vehicle filled with soldiers ready to shoot anything that moved.

East Timor had been struggling for independence for years and now the people had virtually won it—but at the cost of hundreds of lives. And the killing was still going on as Indonesian soldiers took their last revenge after being ordered by Jakarta to pull out. Smoke from an orgy of arson hung over the city and some buildings were still ablaze in the last gasp of a scorched-earth policy by violent pro-Indonesian militias. They had left their mark on every building—windows smashed, doors broken down, rooms gutted by fire. Dili had the eeriness of a ghost town and, not surprisingly, because hundreds of decapitated heads of those who had voted for independence had been jammed onto sticks which were then rammed into the roadsides. It was a bloody signal from the rag-tag army of militiamen that they were intent on punishing everyone they could find who had voted to break away from Jakarta rule.

With Roger Maynard, a colleague from *The Times*, I checked into the Hotel Turismo, which had been trashed, and set up base in a room taken over by rats. I had to clear up clothes that had been thrown across the floor during the previous guest's desperate escape. As I did so John, the manager, returned. It was the first time he had been back since the violence began more than two weeks earlier after the UN referendum in which people had voted overwhelmingly for independence. Then, he had cowered behind a desk as militiamen, with machetes and guns, went from room to room, looking, he said, for westerners and pro-independence supporters.

'Believe me, anyone here from the West remains in grave danger. The militia are still out there, prowling, looking for westerners because you have been seen to support the push for independence,' he said.

It was a warning that was to prove horrifyingly true within 48 hours. In the meantime I made my 'bed'—throwing a sheet of three-ply over the bare bedsprings. We had brought food with us and a small cooking stove and later shared a generator with a reporter and photographer from the *Daily Mirror* so we could charge our computers and satellite phones. Among the other journalists who arrived two days later was Sander Thoenes, a British-Dutch citizen who wrote for the *Financial Times*, and Jon Swain, an old friend of mine from the *Sunday Times*. Jon had been based in Paris when I was the deputy foreign editor on the *Daily Sketch* and he used to call into the office from time to time. I'd run into him now and then on jobs in south-east Asia.

Hardly had Sander and Jon dumped their belongings into the smashed-up rooms of the Turismo when they declared, independently, that they were going for a tour around. To this day, I can clearly remember saying to both of them, 'It's not a good idea to go outside the town area. There are still bad men out there and they're looking to kill people like us.'

But they decided to leave anyway, Jon in a vehicle with a Timorese driver and a photographer, and Sander on a small motorbike. By nightfall they had not returned. I had a bad feeling about it. In the morning my fears were confirmed. A local man arrived at the hotel crying, 'They've found a body. A white man.'

I was compelled to go and, if nothing else, try to identify the body. Was it Jon Swain? Sander? Or someone else entirely? I borrowed a motorbike and, accompanied by a convoy of locals also on motorbikes, headed along the seafront, then turned north. We rode along dirt tracks, through small villages where I worried that a shot might ring out at any moment, and finally stopped at the gates of a cemetery. The locals led the way up a small hill to a body, a man sprawled on his back beside a grave, a large bullet hole in the centre of his bare chest. But it was neither Jon nor Sander. The victim was a local man. I'd been taken to the wrong body—but I was soon on my way again to a second body.

We stopped beside a path leading to another village and there, in a clearing, Sander's body lay sprawled. He was on his stomach, his head twisted sideways, revealing savage injuries to his face. His lips had been cut off and so had his ears—a message, said one of the locals, that he would no longer hear, speak or communicate with the outside world. But there was no chance of that. He was clearly dead. The enduring image that remains with me to this day was that Sander had died courageously with his notebook in his hand. As police roped off the body I returned to the hotel, even more worried about Jon Swain.

He returned later that day, shaken, after a terrifying ordeal. He would be writing a full account for the *Sunday Times*, but he agreed to share a little of it with me, aware that I would be writing a piece for the *Daily Mail* about the man who lived and the man who died, a death that seemed so unnecessary when the worst of the violence seemed to have been over.

Jon said he had set off with US photographer Chip Hires and the driver to go to a place called Bekora. But after a few miles the car started belching black fumes, so the driver tried to return to Dili.

'We were suddenly surrounded by guys on bikes,' Jon told me as we sat in his smoke-blackened room. 'They forced the driver to stop and he was pulled out and roughed up. The back window was stoved in and there were a lot of shots. An Indonesian army officer came along, but seemed powerless to intervene. The driver was hit on the side of the head with a rifle butt with such force that his eye was left hanging out.

'We were pushed about and more shots were fired. We were told to turn the car around. Our driver managed to turn the car but we were made to stop and then they shot out the radiator and the tyres. We got out very quickly because we thought we might be shot while still inside. I edged along to the side of the road and said to Chip, "We're going to have to leg it very fast because they're going to kill us."

'One guy shouted, "Go! Go! Go!" and, as we ran, he fired. We disappeared into the bushes. We were very isolated there. There were burned-out houses everywhere and we didn't know whether we were in a safe area. All I can say is "Thank God for cell phones." Hiding in the bushes, I was able to get a call through to my office and they were able to arrange to start getting help to us.'

But it was five anxious hours before help came—in the form of an Indonesian army armoured car.

Jon, one of the last journalists to leave Phnom Penh when the Khmer Rouge entered the Cambodian capital in 1975—and who was featured in the movie *The Killing Fields*—likened the two experiences. 'It was the same hysteria, the same anger. I am very lucky to be alive. The only issue was not that I was a journalist, but that I was white.' He believed the attack against him and the murder of Sander were carried out by the same gang. Sander's body had been found just half a mile from where Jon had run into trouble.

Later I learned from Florindo Araujo, a local man, what had happened to Sander. 'He asked me to take him around Dili on the motorbike. He asked me to take him to Bekora. When we got there some motorbikes showed up being ridden by guys in Indonesian military uniforms with an Indonesian flag tied to the back. They ordered me to stop but I did not want to because I wanted to save the journalist. I wanted to turn around and come back to Dili. As soon as I turned around, they started shooting bursts of automatic fire. I tried to speed away but they kept firing.

'Then they sped past and got ahead and blocked the road. I shouted back to the journalist to hold on tight to me. I went fast and bullets were flying all around. Suddenly I lost control and we crashed down and were dragged along about 50 yards with the bike. I looked over my shoulder and saw the journalist lying next to me. He appeared to be unconscious. Then I saw those men running towards us and I knew my only hope was to run. As I ran into the bushes, I heard shouts of "Kill him! Kill him!"'

An investigation by British and UN military officials suggested that Sander had regained consciousness after the crash and had then been forced to march along a track before being attacked with machetes. Blood on a log near his body and heavy bloodstains on the front of his mud-splattered white shirt suggested he had been stabbed or shot in the chest.

Jon Swain returned to Bekora later with a safe military escort to search for his injured driver. He found him almost blinded, cowering under a bridge where he had hidden in terror for nearly a day. He was taken to a Dili hospital.

There was more violence, but slowly it moved westwards as the military thugs began to withdraw to the border, leaving behind what had been Indonesian territory. But they had left their mark. It was to be years before Dili recovered and even today, with an assassination attempt on President Jose Ramos-Horta on 11 February 2008, bad memories and a sense of unease remain.

◆

As the new millennium loomed, reporters in Australia began looking for locations from where they would be able to report on the first sunrise of the 21st century. They hired boats to perch on the international dateline or selected the Chatham Islands, south-east of New Zealand. I pored over a detailed ordnance survey map and saw that the dateline cut right through the island of Teveuni in the Fijian group.

I checked into a small hotel there and as I wandered around I came across some wonderful curiosities. The dateline cut across the middle of a soccer pitch, where a match was being played between two groups of schoolboys. The odd thing was that one side was in 'today' and the other in 'yesterday', depending on which half of the pitch they were playing in. Farther along the street, which was also divided by the imaginary line, an engaged couple were saying goodbye to one another. I heard him say to her, 'See you tomorrow' and I jokingly said to the girl that if she walked forward a few steps (crossing the line) she'd be able to see him tomorrow today.

As the magical hour of midnight approached, with the clock ticking towards the last few minutes of the old century, I took a photo of a beautiful Fijian girl, holding an intricately carved bowl of kava towards the camera, as if greeting people into the new world. The picture was taken in the middle of a coconut plantation near my hotel, but this time I did not have to dash off to the bathroom and start developing film, as I had done so often in the past when unaccompanied by a photographer. I had with me one of the world's first consumer 'advanced' digital cameras, a Ricoh with just three megapixels, but it more than did the trick. I set up the three panels of a satellite phone, ensuring there was gap in the coconut tree fronds for a signal, and beamed the picture across the world to London as, from the distant hotel restaurant, I heard a group of German tourists shout in English: 'Happy New Year! Happy New Millennium!'

The picture arrived at the *Mail* at one minute past midnight and it was without doubt one of the first photos to land on a picture desk anywhere in the world to mark the start of the new millenium.

Encouraged by the use of the photo as a spread in the *Mail*, the following day I thought I would try something new—with disastrous results. The hotel kept a number of fibreglass canoes in a boatshed and I asked to borrow one so I could paddle out 100 yards (90 metres) or so and take a photo towards the west of the last sunset of the old century—as viewed from the 'old' side of the dateline. I thought the rays of the dying sun shining through the trees on a small hillside might make a picture for illustration purposes, rather than being anything sensational, so out I started to paddle.

The canoe was one of those crafts that you sit on, rather than in. There was a depressed area as a seat and another part to put your feet. My problem was, I couldn't work out which end was which—and got it all wrong. As I started to paddle away from the shore I realized I was in a bit of trouble because the front started to rise up. I kept going though, thinking I could work my way forward towards the middle of the canoe and even up the balance. But then it twisted sideways and threw me into the water.

I'm a lousy swimmer at the best of times and the next thing I realized I had my head in the sand—underwater. But the shock of that was nothing compared with the second shock I received. The digital camera had been in my pocket and when the seawater reached the battery it emitted such an electric charge that I thought my leg had exploded. I hauled myself to the surface and struggled back to the beach. The canoe continued drifting out to sea. I checked my leg. There was a big red scorch mark on the thigh. The camera, of course, was dead.

Too embarrassed to admit my stupidity, I mumbled to the hotel owner that someone would need to sail out and recover the canoe and the paddle because it had got away from me as I was launching it. He grinned at me and said, 'A boat's already on the way. I hope you've recovered from your ducking.'

Someone had witnessed the entire episode. It was then that I confessed my ineptitude as a sailor. There were to be no more photos from me from Teveuni.

◆

At home, things hadn't changed much on the madness front. There were rescued dogs and cats that Isobelle had taken in 'temporarily' everywhere. Fortunately, Dennis had long gone and Rover the kangaroo was now happily ensconced in the zoo, although I wondered whether Rover couldn't have just stayed on anyway because the house had become a kind of miniature animal sanctuary. On one extraordinary occasion I returned home from a prolonged assignment to find a woman waiting at the front door. She'd come to collect her dogs, which were being shampooed and trimmed.

'What?' I exclaimed.

'It's arranged I can pick them up at 3PM and it's 3PM now.'

I opened the door. There was no sign of life. But then down the stairs came Jackie, a friend of Isobelle's, dressed in a wet apron, her hands covered in soap suds.

'Oh, I didn't realize you were coming back,' she said. 'Isobelle's gone to Vanuatu and she's asked me to look after all the animals while she's away.'

'And this lady here?' I said, turning to the woman at the door.

'Oh yes,' said Jackie, 'I, er, um, … I'll get her dogs.'

It turned out that in Isobelle's and my absence Jackie had set up a dog washing business in the house, using the bath to wash the animals before blow-drying and scenting them. There was a dog bed in the bedroom and large bags of dog biscuits in the kitchen. It was, I learned, quite a flourishing business. There comes a time when you just have to put a stop to such things.

◆

A foreign correspondent never works to a set 'day off'—he or she grabs whatever time there is to, perhaps, fit in a game of golf, do work around the house or just enjoy a movie. But it is always a case of having to keep an eye on the ball, read the wire service stories, check the news pages on the internet, listen to the hourly news reports on the radio, watch the TV news.

And to be successful, a devout reporter has to be ready to drop everything and hit the road when a story breaks.

In early June 2001 I was asked by the *Mail*'s deputy editor Veronica Wadley (later to become editor of the *Evening Standard*) to get to Nepal as soon as possible. Nepal was half a world away, but on the map in London it looked like half a finger's length from Sydney. The story was huge—the entire Nepalese royal family had been massacred.

The story was a day old by the time I reached Kathmandu, which I hadn't seen since my days in the Ford Transit van in the mid-1970s. Nothing had changed, apart from the five-star hotel I was able to check into this time instead of bedding down on a foam mattress in the back of the Ford. Rooms in the just-built hotel had been booked for me and Jamie Wiseman, the *Mail* photographer who had been sent out from London, by the *Daily Mail's* travel company, which would not have been aware that it was some way out of town. We decided to move as close as we could to the Royal Palace and found rooms at the wonderfully named Yak and Yeti Hotel, just a couple of hundred yards from the palace.

We had to find a new angle and I was grateful that there were two of us to divide the inquiries. Jamie set off, not sure what he was looking for, while I went in another direction, not sure what I was looking for either. I tried to get into the palace but was told I would have to join the end of a huge queue of grieving Nepalese and even then it would be to bow towards a temporary shrine set up just inside the gates.

What was known by now was that Crown Prince Dipendra had gunned down and killed his father King Birendra, his mother Queen Aishwarya, brothers Princes Nirajan and Dhirendra, his sister Princess Shruti, King Birendra's cousin Princess Jayanti and sisters Princesses Shanti and Sharada, and Princess Sharada's husband Kumar Khadga. Phew.

Five other members of the royal family were wounded in the hail of bullets as Prince Dipendra went on the rampage through the palace. Then the Crown Prince walked to a small bridge over a stream running through the palace, turned the gun on himself. He was to die of his injuries three days later on 4 June.

It was an enormous story, but what I needed was a new angle. The obvious question was why? Why did the prince, who had been dining with his family and drinking heavily, leave the party and return an hour later armed with two powerful automatic weapons which he turned on everyone in sight?

As much as I tried, I couldn't find any answers, But the day was saved by Jamie—and his discovery is a perfect example of occasions when a reporter and a photographer on a job together each has to treat the other as an equal. There is a misconception that the reporter is 'the one in charge' but I have never followed that 'rule'. Jamie found me later in the day and said he had wandered down a lane and come across a man who knew what was behind the massacre. I had my doubts: why should a man 'living down a lane' know all about it when my own inquiries at the palace and speaking to scores of people in the queue had come up with nothing of any use?

It turned out that the man was a relative of an employee who had been in the palace on the night of the murders. Although all the workers had been warned not to discuss the events, it was inevitable they would talk about it with their families.

'It was a woman,' said the man, who did not want to be identified. 'It was all about a woman.'

He went on to tell an extraordinary story, so detailed that I had no doubt it was based on sound knowledge. Prince Dipendra, who was next in line to become king, had fallen in love with a commoner—and his mother, father and other members of the family had told him he could not marry her. The 'man down the lane' named the woman as Devyani Rana, the daughter of a clan that had been in a long dispute with the King's own clan.

Time was against me. The deadline was approaching. Should I take a chance on writing a story saying that love denied was the reason for the massacre? I weighed up the veracity or otherwise of the information from the 'man down the lane' and decided to go with it. The *Daily Mail* ran the story on its front page the next day— and I breathed a sigh of relief as the truth emerged in following days. A marriage dispute had been the trigger for the massacre and Devyani was the woman—but by then she had gone underground.

It was time to return to Australia. I was back for little more than a month when one of the country's most sensational crime stories broke. It was time to pack my bags again.

CHAPTER 23

The Peter Falconio Mystery

I'd thought that as outback Australian stories went, nothing could beat the Azaria Chamberlain affair. I'd seen Lindy over the years appearing on TV. By then she and Michael had had their convictions overturned by the Northern Territory Court of Criminal Appeals following the discovery of the matinee jacket, which meant that despite prosecution claims to the contrary, she had not been lying about its presence. It was also shown that what the prosecution had claimed was foetal haemoglobin—baby's blood—under the dashboard of the couple's Torana car was in fact sound-deadening fluid that had been sprayed on during the manufacture of the vehicle. That threw into doubt all the other scientific evidence presented against them.

A new chance to establish if a dingo took baby Azaria emerged in late December 2011, when the Northern Territory coroner, Elizabeth Morris, announced that in February 2012 she would open an inquest—the fourth—into the death of Azaria based on evidence about dingo attacks. The Chamberlains' lawyers said they would show that two dingos had been involved in a fatal attack on a nine-year-old boy in 2001. It was a modern-day mystery exclusive to the outback—at least it was until the evening of 14 July 2001.

That night an orange Volkswagen Kombi campervan headed up the Stuart Highway, a 3000-mile (4800-kilometre) road stretching from the Adelaide on the south coast to Darwin in the Northern Territory. British couple, Peter Falconio, aged 28, and his 27-year-old girlfriend Joanne Lees had climbed Uluru, spent a few days in Alice Springs and, with Peter at the wheel, were continuing on their journey northwards.

Shortly after sunset and just north of the tiny community of Barrow Creek—which had nothing more than a pub that sold food, drinks and fuel to passing travellers and offered a few basic rooms of accommodation—a 'ute' caught up with the Kombi, drew alongside, and the driver, with his interior light on, indicated to Peter that there was something wrong with the VW's exhaust.

Peter pulled over, Joanne told the police, and the ute stopped behind. After Peter had jumped out, she heard the two men talking at the rear of the Kombi. Then she heard a bang and the next minute the stranger was at the passenger door of the Kombi, pulling her out, throwing her to the ground, sitting on her as she fought and scratched, and trying to bind her wrists and ankles. He succeeded with her wrists, restraining her arms behind her, but was only partially successful with her ankles. Then he threw a bag, or a sack, over her head and dragged her towards his ute. He opened the front door and shoved her onto the front seat.

During the struggle, the bag had come off her head. Joanne found herself staring at what she said later was a brown dog that was on the ute's front seat. She didn't know where her assailant was at that moment, so in her desperation, with her hands restrained behind her, she lifted herself backwards over the seats and landed in the rear of the ute, the roof and sides of which were made of canvas. She wormed her way to the back of the vehicle, dropped to the road and scrambled into the nearby scrub. She hid behind a clump of bushes and then, to her sheer terror, saw the stranger walking around with a torch, his dog beside him.

She could not be sure when he eventually left, but she heard a vehicle start up and thought perhaps it might be the Kombi. She stayed in her hideout for several hours until she heard a huge truck coming down the highway. Assuring herself that it could not be the stranger's vehicle, she ran out into the road and managed to wave the truck down.

The surprised driver and his mate drove Joanne to the Barrow Creek pub where she poured out her story of terror to the publican Les Pilton and his partner Helen Jones. They called the police and later, as Joanne begged them to find out where Peter was, the police drove her to Alice Springs where they asked her to go over her story once again.

She gave them a description of her attacker: a medium-sized man with long dark hair that flowed down from beneath a black baseball cap. His dog was brown.

When she escaped over the back seats, she had been able to get through the rear of the vehicle without striking any obstructions that she could recall.

The next day police and forensic scientists found a pool of blood at the roadside, blood that was later confirmed to be that of Peter Falconio. But where was his body—if he had, in fact, been killed by the stranger?

Chris Malouf, an itinerant traveller with a ute who had been camped near Barrow Creek, pulled into the pub to get fuel—and was pounced upon by police because his description roughly matched that of the British couple's assailant. At the time, Joanne was preparing to leave the pub with police to travel to Alice Springs, but they wanted to establish if this was her attacker. They put a blindfold on her, because, she reminded them, she had been hooded for a short time, and asked her to get into the front of Malouf's vehicle. They told her to run her hands over the seats and the seat backs, but she shook her head. This wasn't the vehicle. She ran her hands over Malouf's head and then, when she was eventually allowed to look at Malouf, she said he wasn't the man. But as he continued on his way up the highway he was stopped and questioned at every roadblock until he was given a card from a senior officer to say he had already been checked out.

Even so, much later, two men fishing beside a river in the Northern Territory town of Katherine saw Malouf on the river bank and swore blind that he was the 'dead spit' image of the man in a police photo-fit picture compiled from Joanne's description of her attacker.

Because this had the makings of a big story, I flew to Alice Springs the day it broke. The following morning I went to Barrow Creek, where the blood was still sticky on the road. Police on motor bikes and on foot were scouring the ditches and paddocks looking for the missing Englishman, but he was nowhere to be found.

As the days went by, along with other journalists, I was surprised at Joanne's refusal to talk to the media, despite the urging of police—because it was clear that she needed all the help she could get if her boyfriend was to be found, dead or alive.

I began to wonder about other elements of the fascinating case as did—so I later learned—a number of police officers.

Why did the assailant take Peter Falconio's body away with him? He must have lugged it into his ute and driven off along the highway, but that was very risky at night when he might have had an accident with the kangaroos that bound across the road. Joanne might have raised the alarm already and police set up roadblocks as he made his get away with the body. Why, I wondered, hadn't the stranger simply rolled Falconio's body onto the roadside and made good his escape?

But equally puzzling was why the man had decided to drive away leaving behind a witness who would be able to provide a description of him, his dog and his vehicle to the police. Having failed to find Joanne during the hours of darkness, all he needed to have done was wait until the sun came up and he would have found her. No-one else knew she was there. No-one knew she was in trouble. It would have been easy enough to dispose of her as soon as daylight revealed her position.

There was also the question of his dog. Why hadn't the animal sniffed out the terrified woman hiding in the bush?

The Aboriginal trackers who had been called in—four very astute people I spoke to later—were equally baffled that they could find no clues as to what had happened to Peter. If he had been gunned down and then hauled to the back of the assailant's vehicle, where were the drag marks from his shoes or his skin? Where was the disturbance in the surface of the bloodstain to indicate that something had been lifted out of it?

Joanne eventually agreed to meet the press, but it was an interview she controlled. She would answer only a number of set questions that were to be put to her—and they concerned the way she had been treated by the media.

The days rolled by without a breakthrough. Peter Falconio's father Luciano and Peter's older brother Paul travelled out to Australia and were driven to Barrow Creek to look at the scene of the crime. The grief-stricken father walked through the bushes staring here and there as if he hoped to find his son lying there, injured and alive. There was both hope and desperation in his eyes. But of course the police and the Aboriginal trackers had covered that area more than once.

The mystery endured. There were no breakthroughs. There was no gunshot residue on the back of the Kombi. A tiny speck of blood and weeping matter that might have come from a torn fingernail was taken from the back of Joanne's T-shirt and DNA extracted from it. But there was nothing or anyone they could compare it with. There was nothing in Joanne's evidence or what they had found, or rather did not find, at the scene that could help the police. What was needed was to find Peter Falconio but he, like the stranger, had vanished.

◆

It was time for the journalists who had been covering the story to leave Alice Springs. There were other stories, none more so than the decision by Liberal prime minister John Howard to turn away a boat, the *Tampa*, full of Muslim asylum seekers—we knew their religion because a dramatic aerial photo showed dozens of them kneeling in prayer on the decks—in what was a dramatic reversal of policy. The refugees were to be sent to Nauru, a tiny speck of an island, made up mostly of hardened bird droppings, way out in the southern Pacific.

The story was of great interest to the *Daily Mail*, because Britain was having its own problems with illegal migrants. Hardly had I returned from Alice Springs with the Falconio mystery still unsolved than I was asked to fly to Nauru to write about the arrival of the asylum seekers who had been turned away from Australia.

On my first morning on the island, I wandered down the stairs from my small hotel room and was surprised to see a dozen journalists crowded around the TV. The reception was not the best and I wondered what was going on at such an early hour. I saw smoke pouring from a building and at first it looked like they were watching an action movie or an Israeli raid on a Palestinian building. Then I saw the building collapse.

'What's this?' I asked.

'Haven't you heard?' asked a photographer. 'That's the Twin Towers in New York coming down. It's been running for hours, right through our night. America is under attack!'

Not surprisingly, the arrival of asylum seekers became the last thing on everyone's mind as 9/11 was played out thousands of miles away. We spent the day glued to whatever TV screens we could find.

The worst moment—for me that is—came with a call from the *Mail*'s foreign editor, Gerry. Handling the biggest story that would ever land on his desk, he was totally calm.

'How soon can you get to Pakistan?' he asked.

I felt the frustration overwhelm me, as if someone had thrown a cloak over my head. 'Gerry, as you know, I'm in Nauru—it's just a pile of bird shit in the middle of the Pacific Ocean, there's no plane out of here for another three days and …'

He'd already hung up and who could blame him? He was despatching any reporters he could find to key places in the world because it was becoming obvious that the attackers were Muslim and reporters had to be positioned in the Middle East, Afghanistan, Pakistan and anywhere else deemed relevant. And I, along with a team from the BBC and a number of other British correspondents, were trapped on a dot of land in the Pacific, unable to go anywhere.

To make things worse, the president of Nauru, Rene Harris, had invited us all to dinner at his residence, at which he wanted to talk about asylum seekers. None of us wanted to go. We all wanted to be in on 'the action' one way or another. But we were marooned.

We were driven up the hill to the president's house that evening and sat at a long table that had been set up outdoors. He gave us all T-shirts—mine was so small it didn't fit—and talked about the great tragedy that had happened in the US. But his words fell on deaf ears. Each of us was thinking about the story in his or her own way and how we were without doubt the only bunch of journalists on the planet who were so far away from one of the biggest stories of the modern world.

◆

But three months later I was checking in to the smashed-up Intercontinental Hotel in Kabul, Afghanistan, along with *Daily Mail* photographer Mark Large. By now Osama bin Laden and his Al Qaeda devotees had been identified as the figures behind the attack and, because he had been known to have training camps in Afghanistan with the blessing of the ruling Taliban, it was he and the Taliban who were targeted by the Americans. The Northern Alliance, an army based in the north of the country, had, with US backing, swept down through Afghanistan, forcing the Taliban out of Kabul and on towards the south, towards Kandahar.

David Williams, the *Daily Mail*'s chief reporter, and photographer Jamie Wiseman had been with the Northern Alliance as it progressed south. They kept their equipment charged through car batteries, slept under the stars and maintained hydration with bottles of water sweetened with fruit juice, sugar and a touch of salt. Now that Kabul had been captured, they moved out and Mark and I moved in. Jamie was a whiz with electronics—when Mark and I took over their room we found that Jamie had 'borrowed' electricity from a nearby power line and had strung up lighting everywhere. There was even a handy plank protruding from the window on which to prop the three-panelled satellite phone receiver in order to get a good signal away from the walls of the hotel.

Mark returned to London after a few weeks, but I was asked to remain in Kabul because the Taliban were still firing rockets from desert bases. I stayed for a very long three months, where, in-between travelling out into the desert regions, I became the master chef for a group of journalists, cooking vegetable soups and rice meals over a small stove balanced on my lavatory seat (because that's where the buckets of water, which we had to pay a fortune for, were kept). Why none of us did not go down with dysentery I'll never know—although I did make sure to boil the water thoroughly!

I'd always enjoyed playing golf in unusual places—just to add to the difficulties I'd already found with the game—and I was mad enough to play a few holes at what was the most dangerous course in the world. The Kabul Golf Club had been long abandoned so there were no green fees to pay. I borrowed some clubs from a sports shop in Kabul and headed out to the course with my caddy—a Kalashnikov-carrying militiaman, accompanied by his one-legged friend, a victim of a mine.

All the fighters had gone but they had left a lot of their bombs, guns and grenades lying around so the last thing you wanted to do was try to be nearest to the 'pin'. Despite the course being unused for years, the curator Mohammad Nazir was still around and he agreed to accompany me to weigh up my chances of going into a ditch to look for a ball and coming back with both legs still intact. The hills, he said, were alive with the sound of exploding mines and the bunkers were quite a hazard because there were all kinds of nasties buried in the sand.

So why on earth did I decide to play there? I'd been in Afghanistan for nearly a month, and I simply felt the calling. As it turned out, after a few practise swings, I became the first golfer to hit off at the nine-hole country club since 1988. I'd brought my own flag along—a stick with a red cloth triangle on the end—and managed to get around the course without blowing myself up, blasting my way out of one bunker (in golfing terms, that is) and chipping onto one of the dusty 'greens' from under the barrel of a 75mm Russian Howitzer gun. But I had to abandon the game after a few holes when the only ball I had—and which hadn't been used for decades—exploded on the tee as the driver smashed into it once too often.

'Did you enjoy your game?' Mr Nazir asked.

'Very much,' I replied. 'And it was free too—didn't cost me an arm and a leg.' His laughter followed my car down the hillside.

I travelled around most of the country, talking to villagers about the war, but the biggest question on my lips (and everyone else's, of course) was 'where is Osama bin Laden?' On one occasion I went with a small team of Canadian soldiers to a village to check out a newly erected shrine to an 'important person' who had been killed in an allied bombing raid. They didn't need to exhume the body—it turned out from numerous inquiries and a weeping widow that the deceased was not bin Laden but a local chief.

Immediately after the attack on New York it seemed to me that the decision to attack Afghanistan was correct: who knew what else was being planned? The evil had to be stamped out immediately and as the Taliban had allowed bin Laden to run his military camps in the country, it was the Taliban that had to be kicked out. That was fine—I agreed with all that.

The problem was the decision to keep allied forces in the country. The Northern Alliance had forced the Taliban out of Kabul and down to Kandahar and perhaps they would have been able to maintain control. We don't know the answer to that, but the ongoing presence of the US and its allies gave the Taliban a reason for striking back. Which, as we all know, they continued to do with increasing losses to western troops.

◆

But back to golf. After my game with the apes and on the Kabul course, there was a third strange setting where I enjoyed a few strikes of an iron.

The Americans had successful set a small robot rover rumbling across the surface of Mars in July 1997. On our TVs we saw the little machine rolling across a red, dusty and occasionally rocky landscape. I knew somewhere that looked exactly like that, near Coober Pedy in South Australia, and I thought the *Mail* might get a fun story out of it. So with Townsville-based photographer Cameron Laird, I flew to the mining town. We drove out into the red desert. We brought a Union flag (it wasn't called the Union Jack any more), a pole and an A-frame ladder with us. We attached the flag to the pole, Cameron climbed the ladder and began taking pictures as I stood beside the flag and hit a few golf balls into the distance with a borrowed club. It was our idea of claiming Mars for Britain, with a game of golf thrown in. Well, the first men on the moon had struck a golf ball so why not on Mars-Earth?

The next day the *Mail* ran the picture and the story under the headline: 'Mailman on Mars!'

We were pretty chuffed with ourselves—until the first complaint came in. It was from a retired army colonel in Surrey. 'I say, you fellows,' he said in a phone call to the Foreign Desk, 'it's all very well taking our flag out into the middle of nowhere but at least you could have hung the damned thing the right way up!'

Oops. We'd attached it upside down. Not that I realized the error at the time because to me the Union flag had always looked the same whichever way it was displayed. But it has broad white stripes and thin ones and they have to be in the right order. The top white stripe nearest the pole has to be one of the broad ones.

More and more complaints poured in and the first edition of the paper had only just hit the streets at 11PM at night. What sharp-eyed people were buying newspapers and studying Union flags at that time of the night?

'Er, can't we just tell them that we're down-under and because we're upside down …' I wondered aloud.

'No,' That won't work,' said Cameron.

'How about a Photoshop job for the second edition? Can you kind of "repaint" the stripes on the computer and resend the picture?'

'Nope. Can't do that either. Unethical.'

So we let it ride. Or rather, flutter. Eventually the complaints stopped but they had put a dampener on what we thought had been a fun idea.

◆

I'd returned to Australia for only a few weeks after a three-month stint in Afghanistan when I was asked to go back to Kabul because British troops were being sent out there to support the Americans. My second assignment would add another three months. This time I set myself up at the Bagram Air Base, where I was given a camp bed in a large tent shared by other reporters. We used a second tent as our 'office' but the dust was simply terrible and I could not understand why none of our computers gave up the ghost.

From time to time I'd go out on a mission with the Brits, travelling to the 'front line' and watching them blow up caves where large caches of Taliban munitions had been stored. Rumours persisted that Osama bin Laden was now living in a fantastic cave complex large enough to hold vehicles. It was reported to be deep underground with air coming in through a series of pipes. Wherever he was, the Americans were determined to track him down and after a number of fierce battles with insurgents every corpse was checked in case the terrorist mastermind had been destroyed. But it was never to be.

The press shared shower facilities with the Americans—and their toilets. They had a lot of fun with their toilets. On one dark night, particularly dark for one unfortunate soldier that is, a helicopter took off from near a bank of portaloos and the downdraft from the rotors bowled them all over. Fortunately the one containing the lone soldier landed on its side, so he was able to open the door and scramble out. He was covered from head to toe with the loo's contents. If he'd had an M16 handy I think he would have shot the helicopter down.

Two years later, I was despatched to Iraq because the *Mail* wanted to maintain a presence in that war-ravaged country after the arrest of Saddam Hussein. I checked into the Al Hamra Hotel in Baghdad at about the time a wave of car bombings was starting—the first of what was to become a pattern that, in coming years, claimed the lives of thousands. My first experience of this came when, with Colin Freeman, a British freelancer writing for several newspapers, I heard that 80 people had been blown up in the southern city of Basra, 280 miles (450 kilometres) from Baghdad. We were already about a third of the way there, because we had travelled to the holy city of Najaf, some 90 miles (145 kilometres) south of the capital, in the hope of getting an interview with the radical Shia cleric Moqtada al-Sadr. But the bombing took precedence. Such mass killings were to become an almost regular event in Iraq but in 2003 it was an outrage that shocked the world.

It was evening when Colin and I arrived at one of the sites of what turned out to be three coordinated bombings. There was a huge hole in the road and blood and body parts were splattered on the pavement and nearby walls. We planned to move on to the other sites, even though darkness was setting in, but a police officer told us, 'If you go there, you will be killed. The people behind this are still running loose. If they see you, they will kill you. Go to your hotel and stay there.'

We took his advice and later learned than several civilians gathered around the wreckage at the other sites had been gunned down by snipers. There is no doubt that a couple of westerners turning up at dusk would have been a certain target. Even so, we had to file our stories and the only way to get a satellite phone signal on our handheld Thuryas was to walk up the narrow street outside the hotel and stand at the side of a busy road as the traffic roared by. To say I felt exposed would be an understatement. But we got away with it and eventually set out on the long trip back to Baghdad with a hired car and driver and Arab-speaking award-winnning *Sunday Times* journalist Hala Jerberfor. The journey was nerve-wracking and we were told to sit low in our seats at the rear of the car in case our white faces were noticed. The inevitable toilet breaks meant we had to stand exposed to the road peeing against the wheels of the car hoping that a bullet from a passing vehicle wasn't going to find us.

The episode in Basra was followed by an incident in Falluja that makes me shudder to this day. Falluja was the town where four American contractors had been shot and burned in March 2004, before their mutilated bodies had been towed through the streets and two of them strung up from a bridge. It was a ghastly warning to all western forces to get out of Iraq. 'Fallujah is the graveyard of Americans,' the frenzied crowd chanted.

In the wake of this atrocity, I travelled to Falluja with *Daily Telegraph* reporter Toby Hamden. Our nervous driver Mohammed, who was also our interpreter, took us around the city. We soon found out why the Americans were hated. We were taken to houses that had been blown apart by American shells. In one house a man held up his charred copy of the Koran. His bedroom had burst into flames during a shelling and his precious holy book had been damaged. We were led to a mosque where a huge hole had been blasted in a minaret by a US shell. The cleric could speak good English so, as we chatted to him, our interpreter drifted away. He stood at the back of a large crowd that had gathered—reporters interviewing people always attracted a group—and happened to be standing beside two men. It was a casual move that saved our lives.

He heard one say, 'No, I'll get the gun but you can shoot them.'

The other man said, 'I'll get it. I'm faster. It will take me five minutes. Will they still be here?'

'I'm sure of that. They've just started talking.'

Mohammed came hurrying up to us, grabbed my arm and, butting into the conversation with the cleric, said with great urgency: 'We go now, now, now!'

Toby and I smiled at the priest and made our apologies. We had, of course, no idea what this was all about and it was only as Mohammed sped us away in the car that he told us what he had heard. We'd had an incredible escape.

I filed a story about the incident to the *Daily Mail*. It was at that point that Gerry on the Foreign Desk—as well as chief reporter David Williams—agreed it was time for me to leave. Not because of the danger, for that would always be present for any journalist, as the months past and the years to come proved, but simply because my dramatic account had run well back in the paper at the bottom of a page.

'You go through all this to get a tiny piece in like that, it's just not worth it,' said Gerry. 'What's the point of you being there when the interest in Iraq has dropped to this level?'

I remained for Saddam Hussein's court appearance and sentencing to death before pulling out.

◆

Not long after I had returned to Australia, news came through from Baghdad that, along with two Americans, an English civil engineer, Ken Bigley, had been captured by terrorists in Iraq on 16 September 2004. Pictures of the three, dressed in orange suits—the type insurgents dressed their captives in if they were condemned to execution—sitting shackled in a cage as they pleaded for their lives were unforgettable. It was going to be difficult to get them out of there because not even the western forces on the ground knew where they was being kept.

Ken was married to a Thai woman, Sombat, known by her nickname of Lek. They already had a fine house in north-east Thailand and and he had planned this last trip to Baghdad to make enough money for the two of them to live on for some time into the future. The *Mail* asked me to talk to Lek about their lives together. After some difficulty I finally found the house not far from the Laos border. But Lek was staying with her sister 'somewhere south of Bangkok'. I lost a couple of days talking to neighbours and friends before someone gave me the sister's address.

Lek, a tiny woman with tear-weary eyes, was sitting with about ten family members on an outdoor porch when I approached. Despite her obvious worries, she was ready to talk about her life with Ken: how they had met when she was working as a waitress in a German restaurant in Bangkok and the kindness he had always shown her. She brought out photographs of their wedding ceremony, others of them walking arm in arm along a beach laughing. Now every night she watched with fingers in her mouth as the news came on and that terrible image of Ken, her beloved husband, stared out with absolute terror on his face. It was her husband, his face, looking straight at her and nobody else in the whole world, it seemed.

The *Daily Mail* was monitoring the Ken Bigley crisis in Iraq, receiving reports from people on the ground as well, of course, as having access to all the wire services. I promised Lek that if I received any news I would pass it on to her immediately. 'I want to know, whatever it is,' she said.

Not wanting to give her the feeling of being crowded, I stayed in a Bangkok hotel, making the 90-minute trip to her sister's house every couple of days or so, to tell her that there was no progress. She was also being kept informed of events by the British embassy, which included the two Americans being executed by their captors.

On the evening of 8 October David Williams, the *Mail's* chief reporter, called me to say the news was bad. Ken's captors had performed the very worst kind of atrocity: they had sawed off Ken's head as he screamed for mercy. The news was a few hours old and I suspected that by then the embassy people had told Lek that her husband had been put to death. I doubted whether this was a time to go calling, but I wanted to find out her reaction. Not that I wouldn't have been able to guess.

It was pitch dark as I walked in through the wide gates of her sister's home and saw the family gathered together under a lamp on the porch. I was certain they were grieving. But then Lek stood up to greet me, expectation on her face. I realized, with a sinking heart, that she hadn't heard.

'What has happened?' she asked because I had never visited the house in the evening before. I simply stared at her, hoping my expression would convey the news—no words that I could utter would suffice. She threw her hands to her face as the realisation hit her. I walked over and put my arm around her and said, 'I'm sorry.'

She and all her relatives began weeping, the night air filled with their cries. They didn't ask for details and I wasn't prepared to give them. I began to leave, but Lek said, 'Please wait. I want you to take me somewhere.'

Ten minutes later Mike, the hotel driver I had been using, drove us, on Lek's instructions, to a karaoke bar beside the main highway. We sat at a table in the empty establishment and ordered tea. I had managed to carry out an interview of sorts as we drove there and I wanted to send Lek's comments back to London. But I felt I couldn't break away from the table—until the most bizarre opportunity arose. Lek called a waitress over, asked for a particular song to be put on the screen, then stood in the middle of the empty restaurant and began singing into a microphone. The driver and I stared in amazement at one another. I seized the opportunity to step outside and file my story from my mobile phone, standing in a dark ditch as the trucks roared by. I learned from Lek later that the song she sang, over and over, had been a favourite of hers and Ken's and they'd often sung it together.

Lek travelled to Ken's funeral in the north of England. I kept in touch with her for several months afterwards and learned that she was struggling financially. She had the big house but no income. Later I lost all contact with her. Perhaps one day I'll find her again.

◆

Back in Sydney there had been dramatic developments in the Peter Falconio affair. A man had been arrested for rape on 28 August 2002. Bradley Murdoch, a former motor cycle gang member and self-confessed drug dealer, frequently made the run from South Australia to Broome, in north-west Australia, with marijuana stashed in empty fuel tanks in his four-wheel-drive ute.

Everything about Murdoch fitted the man who had attacked Joanne and Peter. His ute was similar, he was carrying weapons when police pounced on him outside a Woolworth's store north of Adelaide, and in his vehicle they found more guns and handcuffs made from cable ties as well as duct tape—although Murdoch denied to me later that there were handcuffs in his vehicle.

He had been arrested because a woman, a former prostitute, had claimed he had raped her and her daughter. That proved a dilemma for the police because before he could be interviewed and charged in Darwin, in the Northern Territory, in connection with the suspected murder of Peter Falconio, he had to face a court in Adelaide, in South Australia, on the rape charge. And if he was found guilty and sent to jail in Adelaide, it could be years before there was an end to the Falconio case.

Murdoch was found not guilty of rape in 2003 and sent to Darwin. His DNA was taken—and police declared it was a match with the smear found on Joanne Lees's T-shirt. On the face of it, police had their man.

People who had doubted Joanne's story accepted they had got it wrong. Because I was one who had written about the discrepancies in her account, I was asked to talk about my feelings on TV, in an interview with the Australian Broadcasting Corporation. If there had been discrepancies in Joanne's story, I agreed with the interviewer, it must have been because she was so traumatized she could not remember the fine details.

The following day I received a phone call from a man in Perth, Western Australia. He had seen the interview and said: 'Mate, Brad Murdoch isn't the man. Check it out more and you'll learn the truth.'

I agreed to meet him. Although he gave me his name, which checked out, I promised not to reveal his identity. He gave me the names of Murdoch's friends who would be able to support his claims of innocence. Of course, friends of someone accused of a major crime might say 'he didn't do it' and I made sure I kept an open mind.

My contact's wife, who was present at the meeting, looked at stills from CCTV footage from an Alice Springs filling station, which police said showed Murdoch buying fuel in the hours after the Barrow Creek incident. She said she believed she knew who the man in the picture was—and it wasn't Brad Murdoch. She gave me a name, but to this day the man has refused to speak to me. The police dismissed his involvement.

But as I travelled throughout Western Australia and the Northern Territory, moving from one contact to another, the discrepancies that had first worried me could not be dismissed. Putting together the entire picture from their information—which included several meetings with Murdoch's very pleasant mother and father, Colin and Nance—I identified a number of inconsistencies:

Joanne could not have clambered from the front seats of Murdoch's vehicle into the back because the cabin was sealed—there was no access to the rear from the cabin.

She could not, as she was to later claim when she spoke of confusion, have been pushed into the back from the side of the vehicle because Murdoch had erected a steel security mesh under the canvas cover.

He was not a man of medium height—he was a giant of a man, standing 6 foot 4 inches (193 centimetres).

He has never had hair down to his shoulders and at the time of the Barrow Creek incident he had a crew cut.

He had a dog, Jack, which travelled everywhere with him but it wasn't brown. It was one of the most distinguishable dogs on earth—a dalmation, a white dog with black spots.

Joanne never once mentioned the most prominent of Murdoch's features—he had no front teeth. Whenever he spoke—and he did speak to Joanne—his missing teeth were immediately noticeable.

He did change the features of his van after Falconio went missing, as police claimed—but he had ordered the work to be done before the incident. The pleasant and honest people I spoke to at a Broome workshop said he had paid for parts to have a hard roof put over the rear well in advance of the incident.

And there is one burning question. How did Murdoch, if he were the killer, have the time and ability to dig a grave in the hard desert? The ground is like concrete in the winter. How did he manage to dig so deep and so efficiently that, at the time of writing ten years after the event, the body has not been found.

Those were among the discrepancies. As I wondered where I could go from there, Murdoch's girlfriend, Jan Pitman, suggested I try to see him while he was on remand in Darwin's Berrima Jail where, years earlier, Lindy Chamberlain had been incarcerated in the women's section.

Murdoch agreed to talk to me. We sat at a table in the outdoor visiting area where, not surprisingly, he told me he couldn't help me or himself much because he wasn't at Barrow Creek that night. Yes, he travelled the route from Adelaide to Broome frequently. Although he wouldn't admit to carrying marijuana on those runs, he dropped enough hints to leave me in no doubt that was what he did. He came across as a pleasant, affable man, as perhaps anyone charged with murder might when trying to convince a reporter of their innocence. When I left I realized I was right back where I started: questioning aspects of Joanne's story but having no real answers as to what had really happened out there on the dark highway.

◆

The ongoing saga was interrupted by the terrible events that occurred on 26 December 2004, when an undersea earthquake shuddered the Indian Ocean and sent a massive tidal wave crashing onto shores all around south-east Asia and as far away as the east African coast. An estimated 220,000 people were drowned or smashed into buildings as two powerful waves swept over the coastlines. Thousands of western tourists were on holiday in the Phuket region of southern Thailand and that was where I flew to with my good friend and photographer Cameron Laird.

The scenes were unimaginable. Where luxury hotels had stood there was just debris. Everything for up to a mile inland had been smashed, although, strangely, some buildings remained standing, seemingly untouched, while others around them had been razed to the ground. But where were all the victims? The police were telling of thousands missing, but only a relatively small number of bodies had been found.

Within three days we had the answer we all feared. The ocean was silent again, as flat as a millpond, but one by one it gave up its dead—those missing thousands who had been carried away when the seawaters retreated. In the silence of the night they slowly rose up, breaking the surface with a gentle plop here, an almost inaudible pop there. Soon the sea off Khao Lak was filled with bloated bodies, bumping into one another in a peaceful breeze.

The Thais went out and brought them in and carried them to whatever empty ground they could find along the coastline. If there is one enduring scene it is of a young Thai pathologist, a white mask over her face as she knelt among the swollen dead lying on their backs, their arms stiff and reaching for the sky. She was plucking hair from the heads of the dead.

'It's for DNA,' she said. Even as she spoke, the stomach of the man she was kneeling beside burst open, spraying her, me and Cameron with its contents. 'It happens,' she said, wiping us down with a cloth.

Dear God. These are the people whose contribution at the scenes of disasters is often overlooked. She was graceful, devoted and was not deterred by the horrors that for her would continue for many days to come.

◆

When Bradley Murdoch's murder trial got under way in October 2005, a British forensic expert, Jonathan Whitaker, told the court that using a technique known as low-copy numbers he had been able to find traces of Murdoch's DNA inside the tape that made up the crude handcuffs used on Joanne and on the steering wheel and on the gearstick of the Kombi. His technique, Murdoch's defence lawyer argued, was unsafe and the FBI refused to use it.

At the end of the eight-week trial Murdoch was found guilty. He was sent to jail for life with a non-parole period of 28 years. Joanne walked from the court and said she was satisfied with the result but now wanted Bradley Murdoch to tell her and the Falconio family where the body of Peter lay. When the tenth anniversary of his disappearance came around in August 2011 there had still been no sign of him despite widespread police searches.

A book I wrote about the Peter Falconio case provoked widespread discussion and I have been constantly asked, both in person and by email, whether I thought Bradley Murdoch was the killer. My answer to this day is: I don't know. What I have said all along, and continue to say, is that the entire case is a conundrum. Based on the DNA on Joanne's T-shirt (even if we dismiss the low-copy DNA technique), Bradley Murdoch must have been there. But based on Joanne's description of the man, his van, his dog, Murdoch's movements (if that was him at the filling station in Alice Springs why did he drive all the way back there to get fuel, possibly with Falconio's body in the back?)—based on all that, he couldn't have been there.

We have a case of a man who was there but wasn't. Or a man who wasn't there but was.

One thing is certain. If Peter Falconio's body is found anywhere along the route that Murdoch would have taken to travel from the Stuart Highway to Broome it will be time for Murdoch to stop claiming his innocence. Until then, the question will remain: where is the body?

I called on Murdoch in July 2011 at the Alice Springs Correctional Facility, where he agreed to chat to me for the allotted hour. He had lost all his appeals but he held out hope that forensic evidence prepared by an expert in the UK would secure his freedom. He stared directly at me and said, 'I didn't kill Peter Falconio.'

What for me is the most puzzling aspect of all is the sworn testimony of a young man who knew Peter Falconio well in Britain. He had partied with him and Joanne in Brighton and they'd had drinks together. The man worked in the department of an insurance company that investigated false claims, mainly by people who had faked their deaths. In sworn testimony, which he passed to the *Daily Mail*, he told of a question that Falconio had nagged him about on several occasions: what methods, Falconio wanted to know, did people use to fake their deaths and how were they eventually found out?

I am not suggesting Peter Falconio faked his death or that there was any plan to make a false insurance claim, but I remain puzzled about the man's testimony. I would safely bet that of all the people who set out from England in 2000 Peter Falconio was the only one to ask how deaths were faked and later disappear under the most curious of circumstances on the other side of the world.

CHAPTER 24

The Missionary and the Cloned Dog

The craving for 'boy's own' adventures sometimes led to imaginations running wild in the *Mail*'s editorial department. In the jungles and vast oceans—the Indian to the east of Australia, the Pacific to the west and the Southern Ocean to the south—that were in my 'patch' there was always the potential for something bizarre to crop up, which would have the editor rubbing his hands with glee. But the preconceived notions were often stretched to the limit—as was the case of 'the Hobbit'.

Hobbits, are, of course, a fictional diminutive race who inhabit J.R.R. Tolkien's lands of Middle Earth, so in 2004 when a team of Australian scientists found the skeleton of a tiny woman, who would have stood just 3 feet (90 centimetres) tall, on the floor of a huge cave in the centre of the Indonesian island of Flores, they named her 'The Hobbit'.

The scientists were convinced that she belonged to a previously undiscovered branch of the human race, one of a group of people who had evolved on Flores but had failed to develop as the rest of humankind grew from *Homo erectus* to *Homo sapiens*. The controversy continues to rage today on whether The Hobbit was suffering from dwarfism or whether she really was a member of a separate species of the human race.

The discovery resulted in fanciful visions at the *Mail*. Was it at all possible, just possible, that some hobbits were still running around the jungles of Flores? I was despatched to find out. But where on earth was I to start looking? While I had very serious doubts that this assignment was going to turn up anything, I decided to head for the eastern part of Flores, which looked relatively unpopulated.

At the tiny airport I found an English-speaking guide, Rahmad, who drove me to a small beachside lodgings. Later I explained the purpose of my trip—and watched him as I did so, expecting him to burst into laughter. But a mask of seriousness swept over his face.

'Yes, there are people like that,' he said. 'They live in the jungle. They are like monkeys, but they aren't monkeys. They steal food and run off and they frighten people.'

This sounded very much like the antics of monkeys to me, but Rahmad insisted they weren't. He hadn't seen any himself but he knew a village where a man would be able to tell me a very strange story.

The following day we drove for two hours to a small coastal village. I was introduced to Kali, a fisherman in his 60s. When commissioning editor Liz Hunt at the *Mail* read my version of his story, she admitted letting out a small squeal.

One day, about ten years earlier, Kali was walking on the beach when, about 50 yards (45 metres) away, he saw a group of naked children gathered around something. Curious, he began heading towards them. He was about 10 yards away when one of them, a girl he guessed by the long hair down her back, suddenly became aware of his approach and turned—and his heart almost stopped. She had the face of a monkey (that was what made Liz squeal!). The entire group of about eight then turned towards him. They all had monkey faces, but they were not monkeys, he insisted, because they had smooth skins and when they ran away from him their movements were human.

Kali inspected the place around which the group had gathered. It was an open grave. In it lay the decomposing body of another of the strange creatures. With the help of other villagers, he wrapped it in a cloth and carried it to an unoccupied hut and there it remained, wrapped and untouched for the next few years.

In time, Kali went to inspect the corpse—and to his disbelief found that the entire skeleton had vanished.

'Who do you think took it?' I asked.

He shrugged, then suggested that 'they' had returned one night and retrieved the body.

I didn't know what to make of it but as I travelled around the district with Rahmad, I listened to story after story of 'tiny people with long hair' being seen breaking into homes to steal food. Everyone insisted they weren't monkeys. From numerous trips into remote jungle regions I was well aware that myths, rumour and black magic were all part of daily life and perhaps whispers of the mysterious hobbits who lived in the jungle had set imaginations running amok.

I was to have personal experience of the way fear of the unknown could result in things getting out of hand. Rahmad had warned me that many people in the area had never seen a white person in the flesh—in magazines and on TV, where a communal set was available, yes, but not in real life—and there was a danger that when they came face to face with me they might think I was a ninja.

I'd always thought that a ninja was a mediaeval Japanese warrior who threw metal stars at people's throats, but on this remote island that was the name given to a ghost. That spirit could be an after-life form of someone who had lived before, but whoever he (or it) might be, any suggestion of a ninja being around—and rumour had it they turned up at dusk—put the fear of God into everyone.

As Rahmad was driving me into the last village of the day a man was tending some cattle. The moment he saw me in the passenger seat his eyes literally bulged and he turned on his heels and fled.

'Did you see that?' I asked Rahmad.

'He thinks you're a ninja,' said Rahmad.

Despite a sudden feeling of dread, I was able to talk to people in the village without incident. As the light was fading, we headed back down the same road. But a group of about a dozen men armed with sticks and machetes were waiting.

'Oh, oh,' said Rahmad. I didn't like the sound of that one little bit.

He stopped the car a few yards from the group, who were smacking the sticks and the blades of their bush knives against their hands in a threatening manner. Rahmad said he'd go and talk to them. That was a very good idea, I said.

I watched as he had an animated argument with the agitated group, who glared at me with angry faces. He was shaking his head vigorously—presumably denying that I was an evil spirit. After several minutes the group of men parted and Rahmad returned to the car with the news that he'd convinced them I was a real person and meant them no harm. The moral of the story was obvious: if you're a Caucasian, don't go to remote Indonesian villages at dusk.

A year later I was back in Flores, this time with photographer Cameron Laird. Word had leaked out that a village of small people had been found about a mile from the cave where the hobbit woman had been discovered. As with my first visit, I set off filled with doubt about the veracity of the few sentences that had run on one of the Indonesian wire services, which had picked up a story from the Indonesian newspaper *Kompas*. But what we found was stunning. In the village of Rampapasa there was a colony of little people, almost all under 5 feet (152 centimetres), with tiny heads. Living so close to The Hobbit's cave, the question, which has still not been answered, is whether these people were related to The Hobbit. What was certain—they weren't suffering from dwarfism and they weren't pygmies because their bodies were equally proportioned.

Talking to some of the 75 families living there, I learned that stories had been passed through the generations of ancestors who had been even smaller. It was an extraordinary tale and, to prove to the world that I had met this curious group of people, we gathered up a few and I posed with them (I'm 6 feet 1 inch or 185 centimetres tall). Their heads reached to my chest. The *Mail* later declared that 'it' had found a whole village of hobbits!

◆

I've covered some bizarre stories over the years and, although the hobbit assignments were strange enough, few can match the amazing saga of the kidnapped Mormon and the cloned dog.

In early August 2008, a story ran on the wires about a Californian woman who had paid £25,000 to a South Korean laboratory to have her dead pit-bull terrier cloned. It was the first transaction of its kind. My immediate reaction was to think that there was some truth in this because years before I had flown to Seoul to talk to a doctor who claimed to have cloned a human—or rather, he had managed to get a human egg started on the road towards development before discarding it because of international laws preventing such experiments. As the years went by, South Korean scientists announced they had successfully cloned the world's first dog, an Afghan hound named Snuppy.

The American woman, Bernann McKinney, had brought a piece of tissue from the ear of her beloved pit-bull terrier Booger, which had been frozen after the dog died, to South Korea. The DNA source material was used to produce five pups, all of them Booger clones. The ecstatic Ms McKinney went on TV in South Korea and told the world how happy she was to have lost one dog but to have gained five.

As the happy story did the rounds, Gerry on the *Mail* Foreign Desk, in an idle moment, rang me. 'Look, this is a very, very, very long shot, but a reader has called in to say that this woman's name bears some resemblance to another woman who made headlines years ago. Her surname is the same and the face is a little bit familiar to me, I must say.'

Gerry reminded me of the events surrounding a woman called Joyce McKinney, an American ex-beauty queen who had gone on the run from British justice 30 years earlier, having been the star of one of the most bizarre, entertaining and downright saucy court cases in living memory.

In 1978 she had jumped bail in the UK and disappeared after being charged with kidnapping a 17-stone (108-kilogram) Mormon missionary, whom she had chained to a bed in a Devon cottage with mink handcuffs and forced to have sex with her. 'I loved him so much,' she said, 'that I would ski naked down Mount Everest with a carnation up my nose if he asked me to.'

Gerry repeated the 'long shot' inquiry he wanted me to make: he was intrigued to know if the two McKinneys, the blonde beauty queen and the possibly barking mad Californian, were one and the same person.

'It's too much to believe, but when you've got a spare moment have a look at it,' said Gerry.

The following day I called a South Korea newspaper and spoke to a reporter who had covered the announcement of the cloned dogs. I wanted to know if Ms McKinney was still in Seoul and whether he knew how I could contact her. He didn't have a direct phone number but he had a mobile number for the public relations woman for the cloning laboratory.

When I rang the PR's number she said she was having lunch but it would be no trouble to put me in touch with McKinney because she was sitting right beside her in the restaurant. Well, that was a stroke of luck to start with. There was much more luck to come.

The happy owner of five Boogers spoke into my ear: 'Bernann here.'

'Oh, hello there, Bernann,' I said, introducing myself. 'Congratulations on the birth, or rather the recreation, of your dear dog Booger.'

'Thank you,' she said. 'I'm so excited. This is the happiest day of my life.'

'Well, that's great, Bernann. But there's just one thing I'd like to check with you. I wonder if you're the same Miss McKinney—Joyce that is—who was involved in a rather peculiar affair in the UK many years ago.'

I heard the sharp intake of breath. Then there was silence.

'Hello?' I said. 'Are you still there?'

Then she was talking again: 'Are you going to ask me about my dogs or not? Because that's all I'm prepared to talk to you about.'

It had to be her. It wasn't a flat-out denial. But then she would not have wanted to be exposed as the Mormon kidnapper. Joyce McKinney had been born in Avery County, North Carolina, in August 1949, the daughter of two school teachers, and at the age of 23 had been crowned Miss Wyoming.

She later enrolled at Brigham Young University in Utah, the heartland of Mormon America. There she met 19-year-old Kirk Anderson, a towering fellow drama undergraduate some seven years her junior. They had a brief fling and later McKinney claimed that she had miscarried his baby. A devout Mormon, Anderson apparently sought advice from his bishop, who told him to sever ties with Joyce and get out of town—fast.

But she hired private detectives to trace Anderson, who was tracked to Ewell, in Surrey, England, where he was living as a door-to-door Mormon missionary. Hungry for love, Joyce McKinney flew to Britain in the summer of 1977 accompanied by an architect friend Keith May.

Armed with an imitation revolver, May confronted Anderson on the steps of Ewell's Church of the Latter Day Saints, and frog-marched him to a car in which Joyce McKinney was waiting. The bespectacled Mormon was rendered unconscious with chloroform, hidden under a blanket, and driven to Okehampton in Devon, where his kidnappers had hired a 17th-century 'honeymoon' cottage.

The hapless Mormon was shackled to the bed in those mink-lined handcuffs for two days as Joyce tried to persuade him to marry her and father her children. She slipped on a see-through nightie, played a cassette of sentimental music and tried her best to stimulate him. It was a bondage game played out with his full consent, she claimed later. But he told a court: 'I couldn't move. She grabbed the top of my pyjamas and tore them from my body until I was naked. I didn't wish it to happen. I was extremely depressed and upset after being forced to have sex.' Fearing he would be kept prisoner for weeks, Anderson promised to marry his captor. But once she had loosened his chains, he escaped and went straight to the police.

Joyce McKinney and her partner in grime, Keith May, decided to make good their escape but were arrested at a police roadblock three days later. They were charged with false imprisonment and possessing an imitation firearm.

At Epson Magistrate's Court there was an entertaining, if not downright titillating, comment from McKinney's lawyer, who said of Anderson: 'Me thinks the Mormon doth protest too much—you have seen the size of Mr Anderson and you have seen the size of my client.' She spent three months on remand in London's Holloway Prison, to which she had been driven, weeping for all to see through the bars of a black police car, before being released on bail.

It seemed that the case, which had already become a worldwide cause celebre, had run its course. But there was more fun to come. McKinney and May, who had also been on bail, fled to Canada using false passports and disguised as deaf mime artists so their American accents wouldn't give them away when they left Britain.

Joyce McKinney, the international fugitive, appeared at the Hilton Hotel in Atlanta, Georgia, disguised as a nun. But before long the media caught up with her and she dropped her disguise to revel in her sexual notoriety. She posed topless for a number of glamour magazines before she was arrested. She was freed on bail and by then—1979—there seemed to be no interest in the UK for forcing her extradition. In the meantime, Joyce McKinney had allegedly vanished into an increasingly desperate world of prostitution, drug abuse and psychiatric problems.

By the late 1990s, McKinney was back in North Carolina, dogged by ill health and often in a wheelchair, living on benefits in a remote farm with three ponies and a fiercely devoted pit-bull called Hamburger for company. On one occasion, she had broken into a dog pound to rescue a pit-bull terrier—possibly Hamburger—which was to be put down for mauling a jogger. 'I love those pit-bulls,' she explained. 'They're such sympathetic animals.'

Locals who knew of her controversial past treated with her suspicion. She had a reputation for litigation and was described as 'one wild woman'.

In a rare comment on the Mormon affair, in 1999 she said, 'I loved Kirk and all I really wanted was to see his blond-haired babies running round my home. Nobody can understand what it is to lose the man you love to a cult, and I believe that is what the Mormons are.'

Keith May was last heard of selling plumbing supplies in California, and Kirk Anderson was a real estate agent in Utah.

What then of the woman I spoke to in Seoul, 'Bernann McKinney', who was claiming to be a Hollywood scriptwriter and university lecturer? Before I spoke to her, she told a Korean newspaper that she was 57 and a former beauty queen. She was, she said, a grandmother and had sold her home to pay for her dog's cloning.

The cloning company said it would normally charge £75,000 for the controversial procedure, but they had given McKinney a discount in return for her participation in the publicity campaign. The company clearly had no idea of the publicity tidal wave that was to come when my story about the affair was published.

In another Korean interview Ms McKinney described herself as being the victim of an horrific attack by an enraged bull mastiff which shredded her left arm to the elbow, tore open a leg and ripped three fingers from her left hand. She survived only because her faithful Booger chased it off. Even then, she said, the injuries were so bad that she was confined to a wheelchair while surgeons reconstructed her left hand and arm. Booger remained by her side throughout her recuperation and gave her the will to go on.

The *Daily Mail* was eager to point out the similarities and any differences between the woman in Seoul and the Mormon kidnapper. Joyce would be celebrating her 59th birthday at the time of the cloning. Bernann claimed to be two years younger—although it's a fact that former beauty queens often reduce their ages later in life. Both Joyce and Bernann used wheelchairs, while the latter's late pit-bull Booger sounded very similar in name to Joyce's faithful Hamburger. There was no record of a Bernann McKinney living in Los Angeles, nor did anyone of that name belong to the Screenwriter's Guild. No university drama department had heard of any such teacher, but it is an indisputable fact that Joyce was once a drama student.

However, the most persuasive circumstantial evidence to suggest that Joyce and Bernann were the same woman was that a Joyce Bernann McKinney was registered as living in Avery County, North Carolina, the birthplace of the Mormon sex slave kidnapper. She had been on the voter's register there since 1988.

'Who started all this?' 'Bernann' McKinney demanded to know when I spoke to her in Seoul as she prepared to return to the US with one of the cloned puppies (the others were to remain under the care of the scientists who brought them into the world).

I said I believed she was the Mormon kidnapper.

'I'm only going to talk to you about the dogs and the death of Booger,' she said. 'I've got people waiting to dine with me. I'm not talking about anything else.'

And that was that. She would neither confirm nor deny the link. But, weighing up the body of evidence, it seemed that 30 years on the notorious Joyce McKinney had once again gone to astonishing lengths to get her longed-for 'babies'.

After studying every photograph I could find of the Mormon kidnapper of years earlier and of the owner of the cloned puppies, I had no doubts that the two women were the same. Her evasive answers added to my beliefs. The *Daily Mail* decided there was enough evidence to run with the story, cloning the two women into one, so to speak.

As the days went by Bernann finally confessed, telling the Associated Press that she had indeed been Joyce McKinney, although 'that woman has been gone for a long time.

'I thought people would be honest enough to see me as a person who was trying to do something good and not as a celebrity,' she said. 'My mother always taught me "Say something good or say nothing at all." I think I gave people too much credit.'

CHAPTER 25

Taming the Tiger

She was deeply tanned, with blonde streaks in her hair. When I took a photo of her as she strolled into the lobby of Melbourne's Crown Casino, I had no idea of the explosive impact that shot would have around the world.

In fact, I took two pictures and they were to lead to what was one of the big news stories of 2009: the unmasking of Tiger Woods as a philanderer. The woman was Rachel Uchitel and she had arrived at the hotel-casino on 12 November for a secret tryst with the world's greatest golfer, Tiger Woods.

I'd begun this book with a golf story, so it's appropriate that I end it with one. But this is a story and a half.

Those two photos would lead to the exposure of Tiger's many affairs. The pictures were the key that opened the door, so to speak, to years of deceit by the man lauded as a role model for young people and the sporting world. With two clicks of a camera button over a period of less than a minute, the process of exposing Tiger's deception of his wife Elin had begun.

In a roundabout way, Tiger can blame the internet's impact on journalism for my presence in Melbourne. As the foreign budget on the *Daily Mail* shrank and attention turned to the web pages—although the newspaper itself was still doing exceptionally well, with its constant two million readership—my own income began to fall. So, when the US magazine *National Enquirer* began looking for a journalist to cover a story for them in Australia I put my hand up. They had first asked my friend, freelancer Frank Thorne to do the job but he was in Queensland covering a new episode of the British TV reality show *I'm a Celebrity—Get Me Out of Here!* So Frank asked if I could do the *Enquirer* job.

I had not taken any assignments for any other publication over the many years I'd worked for the *Mail*, but as this was an urgent plea from the *Enquirer* and with no-one else available for the job, I agreed to do it. But first I rang Gerry on the *Mail*'s Foreign Desk and checked if he minded whether I took on the assignment, details of which at that stage were still unknown to me.

'Go for it,' he said. He was well aware that foreign-based reporters around the world were beginning to feel the impact of newspapers clicking a few computer keys to find out what was going on in the world rather than having to pay a man on the spot. But the story I took on for the *National Enquirer* was a prime example of why 'the man on the spot' remains, and will always remain, irreplaceable, no matter whether we all end up reading the news on our smartphones or iPads or any other digital device.

'There's a woman we believe might be arriving in Australia to attend the golf,' the man at the *Enquirer* told me. 'She might be visiting Tiger Woods. We simply want you to find her and tell us that she's there. Don't approach her. Just identify her and let us know.'

They gave me Rachel's name. I was told that when she was seen at a US airport, apparently preparing to fly to Melbourne, she was wearing a black top with a gold motif of dragons, black pants and grey cowgirl-style calf-length boots with tassels hanging from the backs. The *Enquirer* had no idea where she might be staying, but they gave me the number of a flight that would be arriving in Melbourne, where the Australian Open golf championship was getting under way. Who was this woman, I wondered. A groupie …?

There was no sign of the person they had described among the disembarking passengers. I waited for two hours after the plane had landed and then decided she had either slipped past me or hadn't been on the flight.

Where to next? How do you find a woman whose description you had when she left the US, but who, by now, might have changed her clothes? I rang the major hotels but no-one by the name of Rachel Uchitel had booked in. The only place to head for was the Crown Casino, where I knew Tiger and many golf officials were staying. Tiger and his mother were in a huge suite on the top floor, passing in and out through a private lift that ran from the underground carpark. I'd already telephoned the Crown and had received a negative response when I gave Rachel's name. But I felt I had nothing to lose by wandering around the reception area and an adjoining lobby where staff were putting up a Christmas tree. For an hour I strolled about, watching tourists snap pictures of the tree going up—photos were banned in the neighbouring casino, of course, but this was an area where nobody minded camera flashes.

I lost count of the number of times I completed a circuit of the lobby, the main corridors and even the riverside path running beside the casino. Before I saw her. At first it was just the long hair running down over her shoulders that caught my attention as she walked to a white pillar to stand in the check-in line. Then I saw the black top with the gold dragon motif. But the most prominent feature were those cowgirl boots with the tassels.

I had been instructed not to approach her, nor to let on that I knew who she was—just confirm that she was in Melbourne and then the *Enquirer* would work out what to do from there. I had to be absolutely sure this was the right woman so, having checked with a security man that it was 'all right' to take pictures in the lobby and been given a nod of approval, I moved as close as I dared to Rachel and took a picture, shooting blindly from the hip so as not to draw attention to myself. By coincidence, just two days before the *Enquirer* had contacted me I had bought a small Sony camera, a WX1, specifically designed to take pictures in low light unassisted by a flash. Rachel was standing side-on but enough of her was recognisable to confirm that this was the woman the *Enquirer* wanted to find.

She was suddenly called over to another part of the lobby by a man who, I later found out, had travelled with her. He was talking to a security official. As Rachel joined them I saw this as the chance of taking another picture, perhaps this time catching her more face-on. But because they were standing as a group of three, facing each other, no matter what angle I chose there was always someone looking my way. And other guests were passing to and fro in front of me. It seemed impossible to get another picture. Then, for a split second, there was a gap and the eyes of Rachel's companion were on her, not me, so I took one more picture—again from the hip. Then the woman was on her way to her suite, accompanied by the security guard.

Shortly afterwards I received a call from the man at the *Enquirer*. He was in a panic. First, he spilled the beans. Rachel, he said, had been having an affair with Tiger and she had flown to Australia to be with him. Tiger would be playing golf during the day and playing with Rachel during the night, was the way he put it to me. But a problem had arisen. An opposition magazine was onto the story too, and had, the *Enquirer* man learned, put a call in to Rachel to ask her why she was in Melbourne. She had denied emphatically she was there, claiming she was in Los Vegas.

'Well, that's not true,' I said, 'because, based on the description you've given me, I've seen her here at the Crown Casino, which I'm currently sitting outside.'

'But she's adamant she's in Vegas,' said the *Enquirer* man. 'How can you confirm it's her?'

'How about a couple of pictures?' I said.

He couldn't believe what I'd said. I emailed the photos. One was the side-on shot. The second, grabbed in that very brief opportunity, suffered, not surprisingly, from camera shake, but Rachel's features were clear.

The *Enquirer* man rang right back. 'It's her, it's definitely her! Now we can run with our story. And stick around because you might see her fleeing to the airport. Tiger will want her out of there in a flash.'

I didn't see Rachel again and I suspect Tiger and the man who had accompanied her had made her vanish from Melbourne, just as the *Enquirer* had suspected.

The story of Tiger Woods having an affair was huge. But neither I nor the *Enquirer* could have guessed the chain of events that would follow the publication of the story. My pictures were run alongside claims by a close friend of Rachel's who told of the golfer's affair with her.

But that was just the thin end of the wedge (no golfing pun intended). Night-club hostesses, models, you name it, all came forward to tell of their flings with Tiger. It transpired that Rachel's companion in Melbourne, whose face I had captured in that second, blurry photo, was Tiger's trusted boyhood friend Bryan Bell. He knew about many of Tiger's trysts and had arranged Rachel's flight across the Pacific.

In that famous incident shortly after publication of the *Enquirer*'s story, Tiger drove from his Florida mansion in the early hours of the morning and crashed his car. There were claims Elin had chased him and hit him with a golf club, but later, after they had gone to the divorce court, she denied any blows had been struck.

◆

We all followed his humble apology on TV and the not-surprising decision of his wife to divorce him. I feel no remorse, neither do I take any pride, in starting this whole thing off—it was a job and I did it to the best of my ability.

But I know that in persevering as I had in Melbourne I had struck a positive blow for journalism. Publishing newspapers and books online is here to stay but without journalists being able to investigate the big stories, file despatches from troublespots and humour readers with fun observations, the online world will be a very sad and repetitive place as the same stories from just one source and with little investigation are bounced around the world from newsroom to newsroom.

The speed at which information is beamed around the globe is a threat to good old-fashioned journalism, because getting it right takes time and patience.

I live in fear of the day when a journalist and photographer team which has sped to a troublespot is told: 'Don't bother sending anything, boys, we've got it all from Twitter and Facebook.' In fact, it has already begun. My photographer friend Cameron Laird was on his way to the Christchurch earthquake in 2011 when the newspaper pulled him back during a flight change-over in Sydney. Smartphone pictures had beaten him.

The danger with the internet is that it also threatens the written word. TV networks are available online and newspaper online editions are introducing more videos. Perhaps one day no-one will be reading anything on their smartphones or pads, just watching pictures.

If you enjoy reading books in their paperback form and are reading one on a flight, just look around you and see how many others are doing the same. Most eyes, I guarantee, will be glued to the movie. A few might, just might, be using an e-book reader. But I wonder if the time will come when even on those, animations will start to replace words.

Many years ago, I sat on the lawns in front of the New South Wales Parliament in Sydney interviewing film star Jacqueline Bissett. She said the same thing: 'People will always take the easy way out.'

I hoped then that she might be wrong.

But I think she might have been right.

About the Author

Richard Shears, a foreign correspondent with London's *Daily Mail*, has covered stories all over the world, from Yellowknife in Canada to the African continent, the tiny island of Mog Mog in the Pacific and the Antarctic Circle. Working at the *Mail*, first as a staffer in London and as foreign correspondent in New York and then in Australia, the most extraordinary stories have come his way.

His assignments, one of which has resulted in him being awarded a prestigious UK Press award for foreign reporting, have included wars all over the world, among them the conflicts in Iraq, Afghanistan and East Timor.

Richard Shears has written over 30 books, including fiction, true crime and general non-fiction. Recent books include *Bloodstain: The Vanishing of Peter Falconio* and *Wildlife Warrior: The Life of Steve Irwin*.

£14.99